Lean Sustainability

While Lean principles have been around for decades, the practices have yet to keep current with the growing area of Sustainability. This book provides an implementation approach to integrating Lean and Sustainability principles toward a circular economy.

Lean Sustainability: A Pathway to a Circular Economy illustrates an integrated Lean and Sustainability approach that is applicable to manufacturing, healthcare, service, and other industries. This comprehensive approach will guide organizations toward a circular economy to drive competitive business practices further while being environmentally, socially, and economically responsible. The eBook version includes full color images.

This book will help any industry practitioner interested in helping their business improve flow, reduce waste, and become more environmentally conscious.

Lean Sustainability
A Pathway to a Circular Economy

Elizabeth A. Cudney
Sandra L. Furterer
Chad M. Laux
Gaganpreet S. Hundal

CRC Press
Taylor & Francis Group
Boca Raton London New York

CRC Press is an imprint of the
Taylor & Francis Group, an **informa** business

Designed cover image: © shutterstock

First edition published 2024
by CRC Press
6000 Broken Sound Parkway NW, Suite 300, Boca Raton, FL 33487-2742

and by CRC Press
4 Park Square, Milton Park, Abingdon, Oxon, OX14 4RN

CRC Press is an imprint of Taylor & Francis Group, LLC

ISBN: 978-1-138-58411-2 (hbk)
ISBN: 978-1-138-58410-5 (pbk)
ISBN: 978-0-429-50619-2 (ebk)

DOI: 10.1201/9780429506192

Typeset in Times
by SPi Technologies India Pvt Ltd (Straive)

Dedication

I would like to dedicate this book to my amazing husband, Brian, and our two wonderful children, Caroline and Josh.

Elizabeth A. Cudney

I would like to dedicate this book to my wonderful husband Dan, and three awesome children, Kelly, Erik, and Zach from whom I continually derive the meaning of life.

Sandra L. Furterer

I dedicate this book to my wonderful wife, Dawn Laux, and our three great kids, Lauren, Emily, and Luke.

Chad M. Laux

I would like to dedicate this book to my amazing parents, Harpreet Hundal and Rupinderjeet Hundal, my lovely wife Jasmine, and my great mentor Dr. Chad Laux.

Gaganpreet S. Hundal

Contents

Foreword

There may be no better application of quality management methods to Sustainability than Lean. After all, Lean is about eliminating waste. In *Lean Sustainability: A Pathway to a Circular Economy*, Drs. Elizabeth (Beth) Cudney, Sandra Furterer, Chad Laux, and Gaganpreet Hundal take a comprehensive view of Lean principles and carefully illustrate how each of these principles can be applied to making meaningful improvements in Sustainability. The authors include the application of the most basic ideas in Lean, 5S, and the underutilized, but incredibly powerful, ideas of mistake proofing, as well as more advanced and even less used quality management tools such as total productive maintenance and visual management.

Almost every organization today is involved in Sustainability initiatives. For some, it is only talk and future plans, but the majority are engaged in well-meaning initiatives that, if successful, will have significant results for both the organization's bottom line and the environment. What is causing many less-than-successful or only partial results is the hope that just by putting a priority on Sustainability and having many memos, meetings, and posters about Sustainability something will be done. Unfortunately, as we all know, that never works. We need to make Sustainability part of our strategic planning, we need clear goals and measurements, and we need specific plans and actions to reach our goals. These actions need to be based on tools and methods that have been proven to work and are well known in our organization.

Fortunately, these tools and methods exist. For more than 30 years leading companies around the world have been applying, improving, and extending a set of tools and methods that collectively are called Lean. *Lean Sustainability* not only explains the tools and methods of Lean; it adds more advanced quality methods such as Hoshin Kanri and shows clearly how they apply to Sustainability initiatives. There are numerous books and articles explaining Lean and other quality management methods, but this book is the first to show clearly how well they fit in creating meaningful results in Sustainability and provides examples of how these tools and methods can be used.

If anyone needs a place to start, open Chapter 11. Here, the authors show how the most basic method of Lean, the 5S approach, can have quick results. Some of the figures in this chapter should be blown up and posted on many walls in all organizations. These five tools can truly make a difference on the shop floor, in the operating room, or in any office.

A particular value of this book is the rich examples for each tool and method and then the four chapters at the end with in-depth case studies of applications ranging from agriculture and healthcare to an airport and, perhaps, the toughest environment of all – a university. These chapters reinforce the strength of this book, a comprehensive introduction to Sustainability, systems thinking, the circular economy, and how to integrate Lean into a Sustainability framework. The book also includes suggestions on how to select Lean Green projects and how to use value-stream maps for eco-friendly flows of materials and information.

There is no challenge more important now than developing the means for increased global prosperity while protecting the only world we have. New thinking in designing products and services is severely needed. The authors are providing a wonderful basis for this thinking – and providing many of the tools we need to achieve breakthroughs in Sustainability by showing us how to use tools and methods we already know in new ways. These tools and methods will help us improve our business performance and our environment. This book should be on many leaders' bookshelves and shared with everyone in an organization wanting to make a difference in how they do business.

A. Blanton Godfrey

Preface

Lean is a way of thinking, a methodology, and a set of tools that removes waste to enhance flow and standardize and streamline business processes. Manufacturing, service, and healthcare organizations have implemented Lean to reduce waste and improve flow. The most competitive organizations integrate Lean throughout their supply chain. While Lean principles have been around for decades, the practices have yet to keep current with the growing area of Sustainability. Sustainability is an increasingly important business strategy for competitive and environmental reasons. Sustainable practices also help businesses become more resilient and recover from a crisis. Companies have become competitive with Lean practices; however, companies need to consider Sustainability practices when implementing Lean. Lean and Sustainability pursue similar goals within an organization and are inherently interconnected. To fully embrace these principles, Lean organizations should integrate Sustainability principles with their Lean practices, which eventually results in achieving a circular economy. Therefore, it is necessary to integrate Lean and Sustainability practices to drive competitive business practices further while being environmentally, socially, and economically responsible.

This book aims to provide a comprehensive approach to integrating Lean and Sustainability principles toward a circular economy to enhance business operations further. We want to help industry practitioners implement an integrated Lean and Sustainability strategy toward a circular economy to improve flow, reduce waste, and become more environmentally conscious.

Author Biographies

Elizabeth Cudney, PhD, is President of Cudney Consulting Group, LLC. She is Professor of Data Analytics in the John E. Simon School of Business at Maryville University. She received her BS in Industrial Engineering from North Carolina State University, Master of Engineering in Mechanical Engineering and MBA from the University of Hartford, and doctorate in Engineering Management from the University of Missouri – Rolla. Dr. Cudney received the 2022 Crosby Medal from ASQ for her book on Lean Six Sigma. She also received the 2021 Bernard R. Sarchet Award from ASEE EMD for "lifetime achievement in engineering management education." She received the 2021 Walter E. Masing Book Prize from the International Academy for Quality for her book on Lean Six Sigma. In 2018, Dr. Cudney received the ASQ Crosby Medal for her book on Design for Six Sigma. Dr. Cudney received the 2018 IISE Fellow Award. She also received the 2017 Yoshio Kondo Academic Research Prize from the International Academy for Quality for sustained performance in exceptional published works. In 2014, Dr. Cudney was elected as an ASEM Fellow. In 2013, Dr. Cudney was elected as an ASQ Fellow. In 2010, Dr. Cudney was inducted into the International Academy for Quality. She received the 2008 ASQ A.V. Feigenbaum Medal and the 2006 SME Outstanding Young Manufacturing Engineering Award. She has published 11 books, 14 book chapters, and over 200 peer-reviewed publications. In addition, she has presented numerous keynote presentations internationally. Dr. Cudney is a certified Lean Six Sigma Master Black Belt. She holds eight ASQ certifications, which include ASQ Certified Quality Engineer, Manager of Quality/Operational Excellence, and Certified Six Sigma Black Belt, among others.

Sandra L. Furterer, PhD, MBA, is a Professor of Practice at The Ohio State University, in the Department of Integrated Systems Engineering. She is the Lead Faculty for the Bachelor of Science in Engineering Technology program at Ohio State. She has applied Lean Six Sigma, Systems Engineering, and Engineering Management tools in healthcare and other service industries. She previously managed the Enterprise Performance Excellence Center in a healthcare system, and was a VP leading Lean Six Sigma change efforts in banking. Dr. Furterer received her PhD in Industrial Engineering with a specialization in Quality Engineering from the University of Central Florida in 2004. She received an MBA from Xavier University, and a Bachelor and Master of Science in Industrial and Systems Engineering from The Ohio State University. She is an ASQ Certified Six Sigma Black Belt, Certified Manager of Quality/Organizational Excellence, Certified Quality Engineer, an ASQ fellow, and a certified Six Sigma Master Black Belt.

Dr. Furterer received the 2022 Bernard R. Sarchet Award from ASEE EMD for "lifetime achievement in engineering management education." Dr. Furterer is an author or co-author of several academic journal articles, conference proceedings, and eight reference textbooks on Lean Six Sigma, Design for Six Sigma, Lean Systems, and Systems Engineering, including being the co-editor for the *ASQ CQIA Handbook* and the *ASQ CMQ/OE Handbook*, and the editor of the *ASQ CQPA Handbook*. Her latest book is *Systems Engineering: Holistic Life Cycle Architecture, Modeling and Design with Real-World Application* (2022). She also wrote the Lean Systems chapter in *Maynard's Industrial and Systems Engineering Handbook*, Sixth Edition, 2022.

Chad Laux, PhD, is an Associate Professor in the Department of Computer and Information Technology at Purdue University. Dr. Laux teaches and conducts research and is an internationally recognized expert and leader in Lean and Six Sigma. He received his PhD in Industrial and Agriculture Technology from Iowa State University, where he received the Silvius-Wolansky Fellowship for outstanding research. He co-leads the Purdue Polytechnic Holistic Safety and Security Research Impact Area, serves as Associate Editor of the International Journal of Lean Six Sigma, serves as Education Chair for the American Society for Quality, and serves on numerous committees at Purdue. He has over 200 published works and has chaired or advised over 100 graduate students. Chad is a Senior Member of the American Society for Quality (ASQ), a member of the American Society for Engineering Education (ASEE), the Institute of Electrical and Electronics Engineers (IEEE), and the Association of Technology, Management, and Applied Engineering (ATMAE). Dr. Laux also serves as Associate Editor for the *International Journal of Lean Six Sigma* (IJLSS). He is an award-winning author as a recipient of the ASQ Crosby Medal, and the Walter E. Masing Book Prize from the International Academy for Quality for the book *The Ten Commandments of Lean Six Sigma: A Guide for Practitioners*.

Gaganpreet S. Hundal, PhD, is a systems researcher with three years of professional experience working in the roles of research manager, postdoctoral research associate, and graduate research assistant. He received his PhD in Technology from Purdue University and Masters in Industrial Engineering from PEC University of Technology. Dr. Hundal's research experiences and interests are in Lean-sustainable systems, user experience research, Industry 5.0, and sustainable IoT design for cyber-physical systems. He has worked as a Postdoctoral Research Associate with Sociotechnical Systems Research Center at the Massachusetts Institute of Technology. Dr. Hundal has seven peer-reviewed publications and one of his publications titled "Lean Six

Sigma as an Organizational Resilience Mechanism in Health Care during the Era of COVID-19" has been selected by the WHO to include in their research database. He is a certified Lean Six Sigma Master Black Belt from Purdue University. Dr. Hundal has four years of teaching experience and has been awarded an exceptional graduate teaching award from Purdue Polytechnic for promoting active and experiential learning teaching methodologies. He envisions integration of Lean and Green practices to design sustainable systems.

1 Introduction

OVERVIEW

To remain profitable, organizations must focus on lowering costs while maintaining quality and increasing productivity. Organizations have turned to the Lean philosophy to help achieve this goal. Lean is a well-known approach for continuous improvement utilized in many industries. Lean improves business processes by improving flow and reducing waste. Manufacturing, service, and healthcare organizations are industries that have had success implementing Lean (Cudney, Furterer, & Dietrich, 2013). Lean is a collection of ideas, tools, techniques, and initiatives such as value stream mapping (VSM), kanban, kaizen, pull systems, 5S, one-piece flow, poke yoke, just-in-time, and others.

Lean tools such as value stream mapping, 5S, single-minute exchange of dies (SMED), mistake proofing, flow, and Hoshin Kanri also lend themselves to incorporating Sustainability principles. Processes include value-added (VA) and non-value-added (NVA) activities required to convert raw materials into a finished product or service while consuming energy. Lean tools map material and information flow and simplify processes to identify and eliminate waste. Even with these shared principles, Lean techniques neglect environmental performance and impact. The most competitive organizations integrate Lean throughout their supply chain. To fully embrace these principles, Lean organizations should integrate Sustainability principles with their Lean practices to reach the benefits of a circular economy. While Lean principles have been around for decades, Lean practices have yet to keep current with the growing area of Sustainability (Swarnakar et al., 2020).

Companies are competitive with Lean practices; however, companies need to consider Sustainability practices when implementing Lean (Swarnakar et al., 2022). The three pillars of Sustainability include environmental, economic, and social. From an environmental aspect, there is a connection between Lean tools and Sustainability by focusing on reducing waste (minimizing waste disposal) and raw material consumption (improving resource efficiency), reducing defects and improving energy efficiency by reducing the space required for the operation (Swarnakar et al., 2021). Organizations can reap economic savings from reducing energy, raw materials, and water consumption and recovery of waste materials. From the social perspective, Lean and Sustainability are connected through work safety, hygiene, and ergonomic aspects such as safer operational conditions, improving employee morale and commitment, improving the working environment, and improving employee awareness about environmental, health, and safety issues.

Lean and Sustainability pursue similar goals within an organization and are inherently interconnected. Therefore, it is necessary to integrate Lean and Sustainability

DOI: 10.1201/9780429506192-1

practices to drive competitive business practices further while being environmentally, socially, and economically responsible. Consequently, it is natural to incorporate Sustainability principles into existing Lean tools.

Integrating Lean and Sustainability accelerates and streamlines processes within and between companies, increasing value. The integration leads to a circular economy, a restorative and regenerative system, with economic and Sustainability benefits. Current industry practices focus on improving a linear take, make, and dispose of model. However, a circular economy reduces resource dependencies and increases product, component, and material utility and value. Organizations must break down structural barriers between production and consumption/use to develop more sustainable value creation. This system reduces resource input and waste, emission, and energy leakage by closing material and energy loops. Integrating Lean and Sustainability through long-lasting design, maintenance, repair, reuse, remanufacturing, refurbishing, and recycling organizations can achieve a circular economy. Reusing and sharing unnecessary and unwanted materials, components, and products eventually help these items have an extended life.

This book aims to provide a detailed implementation approach to integrating Lean and Sustainability principles toward a circular economy to enhance business operations in any industry. An integrated Lean and Sustainability approach can guide organizations toward a circular economy to improve flow, reduce waste, and be environmentally conscious.

CONCLUSION

With the growing global focus on Sustainability, the industry must also consider environmentally friendly ways to integrate with their Lean efforts. The next chapter provides an overview of Lean and highlights current best practices, followed by an overview of Sustainability. The chapters on Lean and Sustainability provide a foundation for their integration through the various Lean tools.

REFERENCES

Cudney, E., Furterer, S., & Dietrich, D. (2013). *Lean systems: Applications and case studies in manufacturing, service, and healthcare*. New York, NY: CRC Press.

Swarnakar, V., Singh, A. R., Antony, J., Tiwari, A. K., & Cudney, E. (2021). Development of a conceptual method for sustainability assessment in manufacturing. *Computers & Industrial Engineering*, *158*, 107403.

Swarnakar, V., Singh, A. R., Antony, J., Tiwari, A. K., & Cudney, E. (2022). Prioritizing indicators for sustainability assessment in manufacturing. *Sustainability*, *14*(6), 3264.

Swarnakar, V., Singh, A. R., Antony, J., Tiwari, A. K., Cudney, E., & Furterer, S. (2020). A multiple integrated approach for modelling critical success factors in sustainable Lean Six Sigma implementation. *Computers & Industrial Engineering*, *150*. DOI: 10.1010/j.cie.2020.106865.

2 Lean Overview

OVERVIEW

In today's world of highly increased demand for modern tools, equipment, and a wide variety of products, cost-effectiveness, quality, and timely delivery are the critical factors for success in the industry. To meet the ever-increasing rise in global competition and customer demands, companies must reduce prices and, therefore, find a means of reducing costs to sustain a profit. Organizations must focus on quality, efficiency, and customer value to compete globally. The pressing need for increased productivity while reducing costs has driven an increased awareness of Lean principles. Lean is a powerful philosophy backed by several tools and techniques for improving quality, productivity, profitability, and market competitiveness for any corporation (Alexander et al., 2021).

As a continuous process improvement methodology, Lean eliminates waste, reduces cycle time, and improves process flow. Lean uses various proven methods initially pioneered by the Toyota Manufacturing Company under the Toyota Production System (TPS) banner. From its beginnings at the Toyota Corporation, Lean manufacturing has aimed to reduce production costs by eliminating waste in operations (Cudney & Elrod, 2011).

The foundation of today's Lean philosophy is the Toyota Production System (TPS), which leaders developed at Toyota, including Taiichi Ohno, Shigeo Shingo, and Eiji Toyoda, during Toyota's formative years as an automobile company. TPS was initially called just-in-time production. Toyota practiced and perfected a production system that involved manufacturing the right thing at the right time and quantity, also known as just-in-time (JIT). This production system helped Toyota achieve high productivity levels and become one of the most profitable automobile companies. The Ford Production System was used to assemble cars, which was the basis for the TPS. Just-in-time (JIT) production philosophies joined with TPS, which evolved into Lean. James P. Womack and Daniel T. Jones coined the term "Lean Thinking" in their book *Lean Thinking* (Womack & Jones, 1996). The term "Lean Enterprise" broadens the scope of a Lean program from manufacturing to embracing the enterprise or entire organization (Alukal, 2003). While Lean started in the automotive industry, other industries, such as manufacturing, healthcare, and service, have shifted to improving processes to address these issues, thereby improving productivity (Cudney et al., 2011).

Lean aims to improve quality, productivity, profitability, and market competitiveness by identifying and reducing waste and improving flow throughout an enterprise. Lean focuses on the customer by addressing what is value-added and non-value-added. Just-in-time (JIT) means delivering the right amount of products or services

DOI: 10.1201/9780429506192-2

at the right time and in the right condition. Organizations should only produce products and services when a signal is received from the customer, enabling their efficient pull through the system. A Lean system efficiently responds to fluctuating customer demands and requirements. Customers' needs and expectations are ever-changing. To remain competitive, all organizations must become more responsive to customers. Lean emphasizes the elimination of waste and the creation of flow within an enterprise.

LEAN PRINCIPLES

The primary focus of Lean is satisfying or exceeding customers' expectations by addressing value-added and non-value-added tasks. Value-added tasks are the only operations the customer is willing to pay for in a product or service. Typically, these processes transform the product or service based on customer requirements. The idea for creating flow is to deliver products and services just-in-time. JIT necessitates producing and delivering products and services only when the customer exerts a pull through a signal, typically a purchase. Lean systems enable an immediate and effective response to fluctuating customer demands and requirements. Womack and Jones (1996) defined five principles as a base for Lean (Figure 2.1). They are:

1. **Specify Value** – This reflects the *value* derived by the end customer of the product or service. The greater the value, the higher the satisfaction and customer loyalty levels.
2. **Identify the value stream** – The organization must identify the *value stream* steps and know what the customer values to maintain what brings value and eliminate waste to reduce costs and maximize profit.
3. **Create Flow** – Products *flow* through the remaining value-added steps in an integrated sequence.
4. **Pull** – This system enables the company to only produce based on an actual *pull* from the customer.
5. **Continuous improvement** – This principle seeks *perfection*.

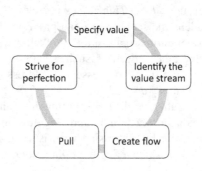

FIGURE 2.1   Five Lean principles.

TPS PILLARS

The Toyota Motor Corporation (1998) described TPS as a framework for efficiently using resources by eliminating waste. The TPS empowers employees to identify activities that do not generate customer value. However, TPS is not a "how-to" approach. TPS contains concepts that form the foundation for management and employees to work together for positive change.

In 2001, Toyota formalized "The Toyota Way." TPS contains two conceptual pillars: just-in-time and jidoka, as illustrated in Figure 2.2. The two pillars of Lean focus on increasing production efficiency by consistently and thoroughly eliminating waste. Toyota also focuses on respecting humanity. Organizations are often successful with waste reduction and elimination. However, Lean practitioners and leaders often misunderstand the interpretation of respect for people (or humanity). The Lean culture enables employees to perform consistently (reducing inconsistency or mura) without overburdening (muri). To strive for the pursuit of perfection, there is also trust throughout all levels of the organization.

JIT is the production of only the required number of products or services when needed by the customer. There are three basic types of pull systems: replenishment pull, sequential pull, and mixed pull system, with combined elements of the previous two (see Chapter 17). In all three cases, the essential technical elements for systems to succeed are (1) flowing product in small batches (approaching one-piece

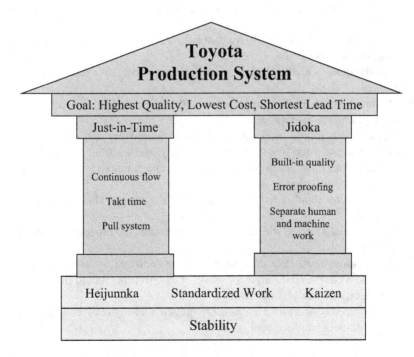

FIGURE 2.2   The Toyota Production System.

flow where possible); (2) pacing the processes to takt time (to stop overproduction); (3) signaling replenishment via a kanban signal; (4) leveling of product mix and quantity over time. A continuous flow process moves one product at a time through each process step rather than batching multiple units together for each step. Takt time is the rate at which work must be performed to meet customer demand on time.

Jidoka is often referred to as autonomation or automation with a human touch. Jidoka enables quality at the source. Poka-yokes eliminate defects from happening in the first place. Andons are signals to signal a defect or problem. Autonomation empowers employees to build quality into products and services every day. We must ask five why's to understand the root cause. We must stop the line when we have a problem to fix it immediately. Built-in quality will help us finalize the pillar.

Liker (2004) summarized the Toyota System into 14 principles:

1. Management decisions should focus on the organization's long-term goals, which often means sacrificing short-term financial goals.
2. Process improvement should focus on creating a continuous flow to bring problems to the surface.
3. Processes should focus on using pull systems, which reduce or eliminate overproduction.
4. The workload should be leveled to a constant rate using heijunka to provide consistency (eliminate mura) and eliminate stress or overburden (muri).
5. Leadership must create a culture that enables employees to stop and fix problems.
6. Process improvement must strive to standardize processes through empowering employees.
7. Organizations should employ visual management to make problems apparent.
8. Organizations should use appropriate and reliable technology to improve processes and help employees.
9. Organizations should invest in growing their employees to be leaders who understand the work, live the Lean philosophy, and teach it to others.
10. Organizations must develop their employees and teams to follow the organization's philosophy.
11. Organizations should challenge and help their supply chain network to improve.
12. It is essential to go to the Gemba and understand the process to improve (Genchi Genbutsu).
13. Organizations must take their time to make decisions by considering all options and deciding through consensus. Organizations should then implement decisions quickly (nemawashi).
14. Leadership should create a learning organization through reflection (hansei) and continuous improvement (kaizen).

Lean principles enable significant economic benefits for organizations while improving quality, costs, and cycle time. The Lean approach focuses on the identification and elimination of waste. Many organizations waste vast amounts of time and money. Therefore, organizations must focus on making processes more efficient. The Lean methodology seeks to increase efficiency and improve the services and products. Lean attempts to reduce complications, eliminate wasteful practices, and simplify the business process. Lean can eliminate the wasted overhead that increases operating costs for manufacturers and, in turn, increases prices for their customers.

WASTE

The central premise of Lean is to identify wastes, also known as non-value-adding (NVA) activities, and then eliminate or reduce them. Waste includes activities that consume time, money, and resources and does not add value to the final product or service. In other words, any activity that consumes resources such as time, labor, or money but does not add to the product's value is considered waste. Careful planning and implementation of Lean methods are effective in controlling waste. Organizations must examine the value procession and identify and eliminate the waste or value leaks to create a Lean system. Any wasted resource in creating a product means the product provides less value to the customer. With increasingly global competition, providing a product or service customers can afford to take precedence over simply setting prices as "costs plus profit." Maintaining profits and providing affordable service means the organization must reduce costs. Lean can reduce costs while maintaining or even improving quality levels. The focus of Lean is to remove overburden (muri), inconsistency (mura), and waste (muda), as shown in Figure 2.3. Customers receive the required results by designing inconsistencies (mura) out of products, processes, and services. Creating flexible processes eliminates stress or overburden (muri), which leads to waste (muda).

FIGURE 2.3 Comparison of muda, mura, and muri.

Shigeo Shingo, one of the developers of the Toyota Production System (TPS), identified seven major wastes in a system (Liker, 2004). The Western world later added the eighth waste: unused employee creativity or non-utilized talent. The eight wastes are considered non-value-added activities and should be reduced or eliminated. Waste is anything that adds cost to the product without adding value. The acronym DOWNTIME often denotes the eight wastes, which include:

- Defects: Defects are errors in not making the product or delivering the service correctly the first time resulting in rework or scrap.
- Over-Production: Producing more finished or WIP products or materials than necessary to satisfy customers' orders or faster than is needed. Overproduction leads to the waste of transportation and inventory.
- Waiting: Wait or delay for equipment or people. The waste of waiting is the time WIP spends waiting in queue for or in front of a machine. Waiting waste also includes idle time for operators and machines.
- Non-utilized talent: Not using people's skills, mental, creative, and physical abilities.
- Transportation: Transportation waste is the transport or unnecessary movement of raw material, work-in-process (WIP) inventory, and finished goods throughout the manufacturing life cycle. WIP includes all the unfinished products in the production process that are waiting in queue for processing or stored in the warehouse. Storage leads to inventory waste and requires additional transportation to retrieve the product for further processing.
- Inventory: Storing and accumulating raw materials, semi-finished WIP, and finished goods.
- Motion: Unnecessary motion or activities, usually at a micro or workplace level, by operators and movements of machines before, during, and after the process. Unnecessary motion is often due to poor or improper workplace layout.
- Extra processing: Effort that adds no value to a product or service, which results in unnecessary use of tools and equipment. Extra processing often stems from incorporating requirements not requested by the customer.

LEAN TOOLS

Lean manufacturing aims to achieve low inventories, cellular manufacturing, quick setup, and process flexibility (Klier, 1993). Lean tools improve the company's operations. Lean principles that incorporate efficiency and effectiveness include value, value-stream mapping, flow, pull, and perfection (Womack & Jones, 2005).

Lean utilizes significantly fewer resources to produce a wider variety of products at higher levels of product quality and service. Value stream mapping (VSM) displays the existing process. Flexible work systems and 5S help organize the factory. Standard work, SMED, total productive maintenance (TPM), and jidoka assist in the design and implementation of improved processes. JIT and heijunka connect the company to its suppliers and customers. Lean tools to reduce waiting time include group technology, cellular manufacturing, synchronous manufacturing, focused factories, 5S, visual control systems, kanban, rapid replenishment, JIT supply, and JIT shipping. While common Lean tools used to reduce the amount of activity duration and cost include visual control systems, 5S, standard work, SMED, jidoka, and TPM. Jidoka and TPM reduce the amount of material used. SMED, 5S, visibility in layout, and the ability to perform multiple functions result in substantial flexibility in production. Poka-yoke eliminates waste due to defects and process unreliability (Mukhopadhyay & Shanker, 2005; Pavnaskar et al., 2003; Rivera & Chen, 2007). JIT aims to synchronize the pace of the entire production system and produce at takt time (Deif, 2010).

Pavnaskar et al. (2003) classify Lean manufacturing tools, provide guidance for using these tools, and establish a connection among problems, wastes, and Lean tools through various examples. Wang et al. (2009) surveyed Lean tool implementation by various companies. They concluded that companies typically start with implementing standardized work, 5S, kaizen, and kanban, as these tools could take less than five years to implement. The second stage is to implement 5S, poka-yoke, kaizen, JIT, and standardized work, which typically takes five to ten years. It is necessary to demonstrate proof of the success of a new system to gain the acceptance of management and operators (Mukhopadhyay & Shanker, 2005). Therefore, while applying Lean tools in a company, it is necessary to go step-by-step, work on various projects, and integrate them into a plant-wide Lean system.

The following chapters discuss the most commonly used Lean tools to eliminate waste and achieve flow in more detail:

* value stream mapping (Chapter 8),
* business process mapping (Chapter 9),
* 5S (Chapter 11),
* visual management (Chapter 12),
* single-minute exchange of dies (SMED, Chapter 13),
* total productive maintenance (TPM, Chapter 14),
* mistake proofing (Chapter 15),
* standard work (Chapter 16),
* flow, pull, and kanban (discussed in detail in Chapter 17)
* green supply chain management (Chapter 18), and
* Hoshin Kanri (Chapter 19).

The Lean philosophy applies to any area of a business process – manufacturing, design, marketing, and human resources, among others. Implementing Lean depends on the motivation and creativity of the instigating leadership. The organization must look for new opportunities to make the best of Lean principles. Lean as a philosophy is about more than just surpassing competitors. Lean is about being best-in-class for every process and product.

Lean requires transforming processes, organizational culture or behavior, and the management system. Implementing the Lean philosophy is a continuing and long-term goal that can deliver some results quickly. However, it may take years before the approach becomes a core aspect of an organization's culture.

Kaizen is the philosophy in which one seeks to improve continuously. Kaizen is a state of mind never to accept the status quo. *Kai* means change. *Zen* means for the good. Therefore, kaizen is a constant, small, incremental change to improve a process. Changes today to improve should be second nature tomorrow. It drives us to improve. Kaizen should also focus on using one's imagination before turning to costly improvements.

The improvement cycle begins with exposing and quantifying problems. The next step is determining the root cause. After uncovering the root cause, organizations should implement poke-yoke or mistake-proofing solutions. After implementation, the focus is standardization and adherence. Because this is a cycle, the process continues for further improvements.

CONCLUSION

Lean is a continuous improvement methodology used across industries to identify and eliminate waste. The Lean methodology focuses on small, incremental improvements to reduce costs and improve quality. While the Lean philosophy is well documented, existing Lean tools do not focus on Sustainability. The next chapter provides an overview of Sustainability and common Sustainability metrics that organizations can incorporate into Lean tools.

REFERENCES

Alexander, P., Antony, J., & Cudney, E. (2021). A novel and practical conceptual framework to support Lean Six Sigma deployment in SMEs. *Total Quality Management & Business Excellence*, *33*(11–12), 1233–1263.

Alukal, G. (2003). Create a lean, mean machine. *Quality Progress*, *36*(4), 29–35.

Cudney, E., Corns, S., Grasman, S., Gent, S., & Farris, J. (2011). Enhancing undergraduate engineering education of lean methods using simulation learning modules within a virtual environment. *Proceedings of the 2011 ASEE Annual Conference & Exposition*.

Cudney, E., & Elrod, C. (2011). A comparative analysis of integrating lean concepts into supply chain management in manufacturing and service industries. *International Journal of Lean Six Sigma*, *2*(1), 5–22.

Deif, A. (2010). Computer simulation to manage lean manufacturing systems. *2nd International Conference on Computer Engineering and Technology* (Vol. 6, pp. 677–681).

Klier, T. (1993). Lean manufacturing: Understanding a new manufacturing system, *Chicago Field Letter*, March, Vol. 67, pp. 1–4, ABI/INFORM Global.

Liker, J. (2004). *The Toyota way: 14 management principles from the world's greatest manufacturer*. New York: McGraw-Hill, New York.

Mukhopadhyay, S., & Shanker, S. (2005). Kanban implementation at a tyre manufacturing plant: A case study. *Production Planning & Control*, *16*(5), 488–499.

Pavnaskar, S., Gershenson, J., & Jambekar, A. (2003). Classification scheme for lean manufacturing tools, *International Journal of Production Research*, *41*(13), 3075–3090.

Rivera, F., & Chen, F. (2007). Measuring the impact of lean tools on the cost-time investment of a product using cost-time profiles. *Robotics and Computer Integrated Manufacturing*, *23*(6), 684–689.

Toyota Motor Corporation (1998). *The Toyota production system – Leaner manufacturing for a greener planet*. Tokyo, Japan: TMC, Public Affairs Division.

Wang, P., Mohamed, Y., Abourizk, S., Asce, S., & Rawa, A. (2009). Flow production of pipe spool fabrication: Simulation to support implementation of lean technique. *Journal of Construction Engineering and Management, 135*(10), October 1027–1038.

Womack, J. P., & Jones, D. T. (1996). *Lean thinking: Banish waste and create wealth in your corporation.* London: Simon & Schuster.

Womack, J. P., & Jones, D. T. (2005). *Lean solutions: How companies and customers can create value and wealth together.* Brookline, MA: Lean Enterprise Institute.

3 Sustainability Overview

OVERVIEW

Global organizations are increasingly focusing on understanding and measuring the impact of their operations on Sustainability. In line with these efforts, organizations are turning to quality management approaches to improve their processes and reduce environmental impact. The focus of organizations has shifted to safeguarding our ecosystem.

Our actions and activities as individuals and organizations have led us to five significant phenomena: extinction, global warming, lifestyle diseases, pollution, and resource scarcity. The Intergovernmental Science-Policy Platform on Biodiversity and Ecosystem Services (IPBES) Global Assessment Report of Biodiversity and Ecosystem Services (2019) stated, "around 1 million animal and plant species are now threatened with extinction, many within decades, more than ever before in human history." Furthermore, since 1980 greenhouse gas emissions have doubled, and the average global temperatures have increased by at least 1.8 degrees Fahrenheit (0.7 degrees Celsius). The UN (2019) summarizes the impact through the following statistics:

GENERAL

- 75%: terrestrial environment "severely altered" to date by human actions (marine environments 66%)
- 47%: reduction in global indicators of ecosystem extent and condition against their estimated natural baselines, with many continuing to decline by at least 4% per decade
- 28%: global land area held and/or managed by Indigenous peoples, including >40% of formally protected areas and 37% of all remaining terrestrial areas with very low human intervention
- ±60 billion: tons of renewable and non-renewable resources extracted globally each year, up nearly 100% since 1980
- 15%: increase in global per capita consumption of materials since 1980
- >85%: of wetlands present in 1700 had been lost by 2000 – loss of wetlands is currently three times faster, in percentage terms, than forest loss

---

DOI: 10.1201/9780429506192-3

Species, Populations, and Varieties of Plants and Animals

- 8 million: total estimated number of animal and plant species on Earth (including 5.5 million insect species)
- Tens to hundreds of times: the extent to which the current rate of global species extinction is higher compared to the average over the last 10 million years, and the rate is accelerating
- Up to 1 million: species threatened with extinction, many within decades
- >500,000 (±9%): share of the world's estimated 5.9 million terrestrial species with insufficient habitat for long-term survival without habitat restoration
- >40%: amphibian species threatened with extinction
- Almost 33%: reef-forming corals, sharks, and shark relatives, and >33% of marine mammals are threatened with extinction
- 25%: average proportion of species threatened with extinction across terrestrial, freshwater, and marine vertebrate, invertebrate, and plant groups that have been studied in sufficient detail
- At least 680: vertebrate species have been driven to extinction by human actions since the 16th century
- ±10%: tentative estimate of the proportion of insect species threatened with extinction
- >20%: decline in average abundance of native species in most major terrestrial biomes, mostly since 1900
- ±560 (±10%): domesticated breeds of mammals were extinct by 2016, with at least 1,000 more threatened
- 3.5%: domesticated breed of birds extinct by 2016
- 70%: increase since 1970 in numbers of invasive alien species across 21 countries with detailed records
- 30%: reduction in global terrestrial habitat integrity caused by habitat loss and deterioration
- 47%: proportion of terrestrial flightless mammals and 23% of threatened birds whose distributions may have been negatively impacted by climate change already
- >6: species of ungulate (hoofed mammals) would likely be extinct or surviving only in captivity today without conservation measures

Food and Agriculture

- 300%: increase in food crop production since 1970
- 23%: land areas that have seen a reduction in productivity due to land degradation

- \>75%: global food crop types that rely on animal pollination
- US\$235 to US\$577 billion: annual value of global crop output at risk due to pollinator loss
- 5.6 gigatons: annual CO_2 emissions sequestered in marine and terrestrial ecosystems – equivalent to 60% of global fossil fuel emission
- ±11%: world population that is undernourished
- 100 million: hectares of agricultural expansion in the tropics from 1980 to 2000, mainly cattle ranching in Latin America (±42 million ha) and plantations in Southeast Asia (±7.5 million hectares, of which 80% is oil palm), half of it at the expense of intact forests
- 3%: increase in land transformation to agriculture between 1992 and 2015, mostly at the expense of forests
- \>33%: world's land surface (and ±75% of freshwater resources) devoted to crop or livestock production
- 12%: world's ice-free land used for crop production
- 25%: world's ice-free land used for grazing (±70% of drylands)
- ±25%: greenhouse gas emissions caused by land clearing, crop production, and fertilization, with animal-based food contributing 75% to that figure
- ±30%: global crop production and global food supply provided by small land holdings (<2 ha), using ±25% of agricultural land, usually maintaining rich agrobiodiversity
- \$100 billion: estimated level of financial support in Organisation for Economic Co-operation and Development (OECD) countries (2015) to agriculture that is potentially harmful to the environment

Oceans and Fishing
- 33%: marine fish stocks in 2015 being harvested at unsustainable levels; 60% are maximally sustainably fished; 7% are underfished
- \>55%: ocean area covered by industrial fishing
- 3–10%: projected decrease in ocean net primary production due to climate change alone by the end of the century
- 3–25%: projected decrease in fish biomass by the end of the century in low and high climate warming scenarios, respectively
- \>90%: proportion of the global commercial fishers accounted for by small-scale fisheries (over 30 million people) – representing nearly 50% of global fish catch
- Up to 33%: estimated share in 2011 of the world's reported fish catch that is illegal, unreported, or unregulated

- >10%: decrease per decade in the extent of seagrass meadows from 1970 to 2000
- ±50%: live coral cover of reefs lost since the 1870s
- 100–300 million: people in coastal areas are at increased risk due to the loss of coastal habitat protection
- 400: low oxygen (hypoxic) coastal ecosystem "dead zones" caused by fertilizers, affecting >245,000 square kilometers
- 29%: average reduction in the extinction risk for mammals and birds in 109 countries thanks to conservation investments from 1996 to 2008; the extinction risk of birds, mammals, and amphibians would have been at least 20% greater without conservation action in the recent decade
- >107: highly threatened birds, mammals, and reptiles estimated to have benefitted from the eradication of invasive mammals on islands

Forests
- 45%: increase in raw timber production since 1970 (4 billion cubic meters in 2017)
- ±13 million: forestry industry jobs
- 50%: agricultural expansion that occurred at the expense of forests
- 50%: decrease in the net rate of forest loss since the 1990s (excluding those managed for timber or agricultural extraction)
- 68%: global forest area today compared with the estimated pre-industrial level
- 7%: reduction of intact forests (>500 square kilometers with no human pressure) from 2000 to 2013 in developed and developing countries
- 290 million hectares (±6%): native forest cover lost from 1990 to 2015 due to clearing and wood harvesting
- 110 million ha: rise in the area of planted forests from 1990 to 2015
- 10–15%: global timber supplies provided by illegal forestry (up to 50% in some areas)
- >2 billion: people who rely on wood fuel to meet their primary energy needs

Mining and Energy
- <1%: total land used for mining, but the industry has significant negative impacts on biodiversity, emissions, water quality, and human health

- ±17,000: large-scale mining sites (in 171 countries), mostly managed by 616 international corporations
- ±6,500: offshore oil and gas ocean mining installations (in 53 countries)
- US$345 billion: global subsidies for fossil fuels resulting in US$5 trillion in overall costs, including nature deterioration externalities, coal accounts for 52% of post-tax subsidies, petroleum for ±33%, and natural gas for ±10%

Urbanization, Development, and Socioeconomic Issues

- >100%: growth of urban areas since 1992
- 25 million square kilometers: length of new paved roads foreseen by 2050, with 90% of construction in the least developed and developing countries
- ±50,000: number of large dams (>15m height); ±17 million reservoirs (>0.01 hectares)
- 105%: increase in the global human population (from 3.7 to 7.6 billion) since 1970 unevenly across countries and regions
- 50 times higher: per capita GDP in developed vs. least developed countries
- >2,500: conflicts over fossil fuels, water, food, and land currently occurring worldwide
- >1,000: environmental activists and journalists were killed between 2002 and 2013

Health

- 70%: proportion of cancer drugs that are natural or synthetic products inspired by nature
- ±4 billion: people who rely primarily on natural medicines
- 17%: infectious diseases spread by animal vectors, causing >700,000 annual deaths
- ±821 million: people face food insecurity in Asia and Africa
- 40%: of the global population lacks access to clean and safe drinking water
- >80%: global wastewater discharged untreated into the environment
- 300–400 million tons: heavy metals, solvents, toxic sludge, and other wastes from industrial facilities are dumped annually into the world's waters
- 10 times: increase in plastic pollution since 1980

Climate Change

- 1 degree Celsius: average global temperature difference in 2017 compared to pre-industrial levels, rising ±0.2 (±0.1) degrees Celsius per decade
- >3 mm: annual average global sea level rise over the past two decades
- 16–21 cm: rise in global average sea level since 1900
- 100% increase since 1980 in greenhouse gas emissions, raising the average global temperature by at least 0.7 degree
- 40%: rise in the carbon footprint of tourism (to 4.5Gt of carbon dioxide) from 2009 to 2013
- 8%: of total greenhouse gas emissions are from transport and food consumption related to tourism
- 5%: estimated fraction of species at risk of extinction from 2°C warming alone, rising to 16% at 4.3°C warming
- Even for global warming of 1.5 to 2 degrees, the majority of terrestrial species ranges are projected to shrink profoundly

The Brundtland Commission (United Nations Commission on Sustainable Development, 1987) defined Sustainability as "meeting the needs of the present without compromising the ability of future generations to meet their own needs." According to David Suzuki,

> There are some things in the world we can't change – gravity, entropy, the speed of light, and our biological nature that require clean air, clean water, clean soil, clean energy, and biodiversity for our health and wellbeing. Protecting the biosphere should be our highest priority or else we sicken and die. Other things, like capitalism, free enterprise, the economy, currency, the market, are not forces of nature, we invented them. They are not immutable, and we can change them. It makes no sense to elevate economics above the biosphere.

SUSTAINABILITY PRINCIPLES

Sustainability has three "pillars" or "components." According to Elkington (1994), the three dimensions are environmental (or ecological), economic, and social factors. Barbier (1987) presented the first visual representation of these pillars, as shown in Figure 3.1. From the decisional paradigm perspective, Chofreh and Goni (2017) identified numerous dimensions pertinent to decision-making in system implementation, with the critical dimension cited at the strategic level. Organizations employ Sustainability metrics for economic, environmental, and social pillars to strategize and benchmark Sustainability initiatives across different industries.

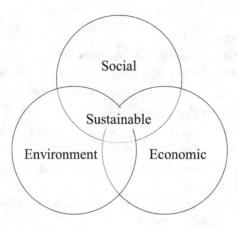

FIGURE 3.1   Sustainability components.

The United Nations (2012) used the three pillars of Sustainability during the development of 17 Sustainable Development Goals (SDGs). SDGs aim to promote sustained economic growth, ensure access to affordable and sustainable energy, build resilient infrastructure, and provide a productive workplace environment (UN, 2012). The 17 goals encompass 169 associated targets with a goal of achievement by 2030. Figure 3.2 illustrates the 17 UN SDGs.

The targets associated with UN SDGs are encouraging. However, organizations need more detail regarding theoretical foundations and metrics for driving Sustainability initiatives (Purvis, Mao, & Robinson, 2019). As noted by Vandenbrande (2020), large, global organizations are more actively engaged in Sustainability efforts than small- and mid-sized enterprises (SMEs). Further, Vandenbrande (2020) states that SMEs understand Sustainability as an environmental issue; they focus mainly on avoiding environmental violations and their costs. For example, Ford Motor Company began using sustainable fabrics in their vehicles in 2008 (Bain, 2013). In addition, Walt Disney World Resort has a corporate focus on reducing single-use plastics and using plastic-free packaging for their princess dolls (Zahn, 2021).

For an organization to truly focus on Sustainability, there must be a concerted effort with adequate resources. Organizations must dedicate time for their employees to become familiar with Sustainability and work on Sustainability projects. Dedicating employee time is difficult since most organizations focus efforts on ensuring current operations meet customer demand (Antony et al., 2022). In addition, Sustainability resources focus on the macro level rather than the process level. Dew (2022) noted that Sustainability efforts benefit from a project approach using a cross-functional team. Therefore, this chapter highlights the Sustainability frameworks and metrics cited in the literature. The following section describes these metrics.

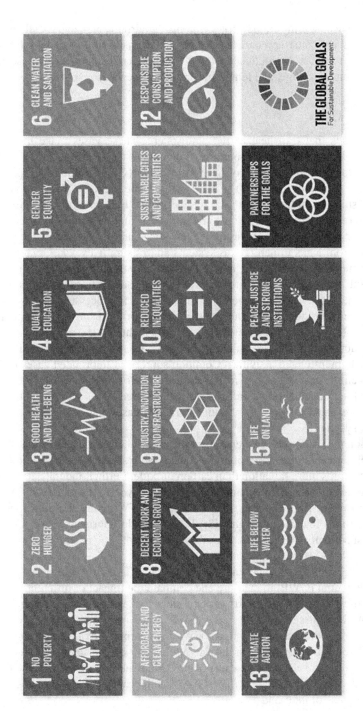

FIGURE 3.2 United Nations Sustainable Development Goals (UN, 2012).

Sustainability Metrics

Three pillar Sustainability framework (economic, environmental, and social) and life cycle analysis are some approaches used to define Sustainability metrics (Thanki, Govindan, & Thakkar, 2016). Sustainability efforts often focus on greenhouse gases (GHG), effluent discharge, and renewable and non-renewable resources.

Greenhouse Gases

GHG are gases that trap heat in the atmosphere. These gases make the planet warmer. According to the Environmental Protection Agency (EPA, 2022), 79% of GHG emissions in 2020 were from carbon dioxide (CO_2), followed by methane (CH_4) at 11%, nitrous oxide (N_2O) at 7%, and fluorinated gases at 3%. Carbon dioxide mainly stems from fossil fuels used for energy and transportation; therefore, the best way to reduce carbon dioxide is to reduce fossil fuel consumption by conserving energy or producing energy through renewable sources. Whereas methane typically stems from leaks in natural gas systems and raising livestock. Organizations can reduce methane emissions by upgrading equipment used to produce, store, and transport oil and natural gas. Nitrous oxide stems mainly from agriculture, fuel consumption, wastewater management, and industrial processes. Nitrous oxide emissions can be reduced by reducing fuel consumption, using pollution control technologies (e.g., catalytic converters), upgrading technologies, and switching fuel sources. Fluorinated gases are unlike other gases because they are caused almost entirely by human-related activities. Common sources of fluorinated gases include ozone-depleting substances (e.g., refrigerants) and industrial processes such as aluminum and semiconductor manufacturing. Fluorinated gases can be reduced by adopting fluorinated gas recycling, using alternative gases, and eliminating leaks in refrigerant systems.

The amount of time each gas remains in the atmosphere varies. For example, the lifetime of methane in the atmosphere is considerably shorter than carbon dioxide, but methane traps more radiation than carbon dioxide. Further, the impact of methane is 25 times greater than carbon dioxide over 100 years. Nitrous oxide can stay in the atmosphere for 114 years, and its impact on warming the atmosphere is almost 300 times that of carbon dioxide. Finally, while fluorinated gases make up the smallest percent of GHG emissions, they are the most potent and longest-lasting type.

The Intergovernmental Panel on Climate Change (IPCC) developed the Global Warming Potential (GWP) to measure and compare the impact of different gases on global warming. The GWP converts gas emissions to a carbon dioxide equivalent by multiplying the emission with the gas's GWP. Since most gases warm the planet more than carbon dioxide per unit mass, GWP uses carbon dioxide as the equivalent for comparison. Therefore, carbon dioxide has a GWP of 1 since it is the reference unit. GWP presents values for gases as ranges. Methane has a GWP of 27–30, and nitrous oxide has a GWP of 273. The GWP for fluorinated gases can range from thousands to tens of thousands.

EFFLUENT DISCHARGE

Effluent discharge is often referred to as wastewater. Effluent discharge is any form of treated or untreated liquid waste from industrial or commercial businesses that flows into surface waters. Effluent discharge does not include waste from kitchens, toilets, surface water, or domestic sewage. There are national regulatory standards and guidelines for handling wastewater, such as those from the EPA in the United States (Long & Cudney, 2012). More specifically, the Clean Water Act in the United States requires the regulation (with permits) of direct effluent discharges under the National Pollutant Discharge Elimination System (NPDES). Effluent discharge is water pollution. The contaminated liquids migrate through the soil and water, impacting our ecosystem. Accessible, clean water is a global issue, as noted in SDG 6 Clean Water and Sanitation. While pretreating effluent and adhering to stringent standards is expensive, organizations can reduce the impact of effluent discharge through improved technology (e.g., transforming organic matter into electricity or fuel) and treatment methods (e.g., removing elements from the effluent) that enable the reuse of water.

RENEWABLE AND NON-RENEWABLE RESOURCES

Renewal resources can be grown again or renewed during a person's lifespan. Examples of renewable resources include trees, air, and water. However, organizations must be careful to conserve natural resources because they can still run out. For example, only 2.5% of the Earth's water is fresh. Organizations must also protect natural resources from pollution. As Meadows et al. (2004) noted, renewable resources are sustainable when used slower or equal to their regeneration rate. Organizations must focus on reducing, reusing, and recycling to protect renewable resources.

Non-renewable resources include mineral and metal ores and fossil fuels. Organizations often use ores and minerals to make metals. Fossil fuels include oil, natural gas, and coal, which we typically burn for energy. Once used, non-renewable resources cannot be replaced or take longer than a person's lifespan to replace. There is a fixed amount of non-renewable resources. Many non-renewable resources could be exhausted in the near future. To reduce reliance on non-renewable resources, particularly for energy, many organizations are investing in wind, solar, and hydrogen power.

It is important to note that these phenomena are interconnected. For example, while water is a renewable resource, if organizations do not adequately handle their effluent discharge, then fresh water will cease to exist (SDG 6 Clean Water and Sanitation), which directly impacts SDG 3 Good Health and Well-Being, SDG 14 Life Below Water, and SDG 15 Life on Land.

The use of Sustainability metrics in Lean initiatives is still relatively new. Figure 3.3 highlights the Sustainability metrics used and cited in the literature.

Sustainability metrics are essential to identifying and benchmarking improvement initiatives for practitioners. The significance of the metrics is to develop a robust Sustainability roadmap considering Lean bottom-line benefits as well.

Economic metrics	Findings	Reference
Cost reduction, profitability, process improvement	The application of the Lean-green-Six Sigma integrated framework minimized the cost of energy and mass stream by 7-12%.	Cherries, Elfezazi, Govindan et al., 2017
Electric power consumption, water consumption, harmful gases release, and waste segregation	Integrating Lean and green identified several scopes for improving environmental performance, such as those needed to implement a measurement system.	Hellenic et al., 2017
Employee's air pollution, health safety, and energy use	Lean-green performance has trade-offs.	Sawhney et al., 2007
Employee satisfaction and human factors (e.g., dissatisfaction, conflicts, and cohesiveness among employees)	Lean-green integration can support human integration.	Wong and Wong, 2009
Employee training, employee satisfaction, and information sharing	Strategic alignment is crucial in driving Lean Sustainability. Alignment is when an organization links its structures and resources with its strategy and business environment.	Pearce et al., 2018
Material costs, production costs, general costs, and selling price	Organizations can improve costs and incomes with innovative environmental approaches to Lean systems.	Aguado et al., 2013
Material flow, energy consumption flow, transportation flow, and carbon emission flow	Lean Green value stream map application lead to total carbon emission reduction by 39%; carbon efficiency increase by 107%.	Zhu et al., 2020
Material use, energy consumption, non-product output, and pollutant releases	Implementing four Lean methods, which include JIT, TPM, VSM, and kaizen/CI, improves environmental performance.	Garza-Reyes et al., 2018
Operational costs	Lean and Sustainable production techniques report 2-3% potential cost savings at each stage of the supply chain.	Zokaei and Simons, 2006
Operational, environmental, and inventory costs	The impact of Lean-green integration on the economy is positive by reducing inventory and scrap levels.	Azevedo et al., 2012
Quality, cost, productivity, lead time, profitability, product, design, brand value, market position, and customer satisfaction	Integrating Lean green requires a combination of practices from both paradigms.	Thanki et al., 2016
Reduction of air emissions, effluent waste, and solid wastes, and the ability to decrease consumption of hazardous materials	The indirect effect of Lean practices on environmental performance through green practices and the integration foster both.	Inman and Green, 2018
Resource efficiency, greenhouse gas (GHG) emissions, fuel consumption, feed spillage, labor productivity, and employee satisfaction	The study reduced the use of diesel by 50% and improved fuel efficiency due to improvements in the feed storage of silos. GHG emissions decreased due to a reduction in the first calving age. Due to a more structured workplace, employees spent less time searching for tools.	Barth and Melin, 2018
Safer working conditions, improved skills sets/employability, and customer satisfaction	Lean-green integration can benefit production by creating a healthy work environment.	Ng et al., 2015
Total costs of energy and mass	Lean-Green integration can mitigate average resource use from 30-50% and costs by 5-10%.	Pampanelli et al., 2014
Volatile organic compound (VOC) emissions and hazardous waste	The simultaneous implementation of Lean and green practices was more efficient than the sequential implementation. The study also noted that collaborations between operations managers and environmental managers are essential.	Galeazzo et al., 2014
Water efficiency and energy	Lean Six Sigma was an enabler of greater environmental Sustainability in the dairy processing industry.	Powell et al., 2017

FIGURE 3.3 Sustainability metrics.

CONCLUSION

Sustainability is a growing area of focus across the globe and industries. However, most organizations continue to need help with implementing Sustainability metrics. The most used Sustainability metrics include resource use, water and energy consumption, non-product output (e.g., hazardous waste), and pollutant releases. The next chapter will extend the concept of Sustainability by addressing systems thinking and the circular economy.

REFERENCES

Antony, J., Swarnakar, V., Cudney, E., & Pepper, M. (2022). A meta-analytic investigation of lean practices and their impact on organizational performance. *Total Quality Management & Business Excellence, 33*(15–16), 1799–1825.

Bain, D. (2013). How Ford is helping to bring sustainable auto fabrics to the globe. Torque News, May 28, 2013, https://www.torquenews.com/397/how-ford-helping-bring-sustainable-auto-fabrics-globe

Barbier, E. B. (1987). The concept of sustainable economic development. *Environmental conservation, 14*(2), 101–110.

Chofreh, A. G., & Goni, F. A. (2017). Review of frameworks for Sustainability implementation. *Sustainable Development, 25*(3), 180–188.

Dew, J. R. (2022). Sustained effort. *Quality Progress*, January, 22–26.

Elkington, J. (1994). Towards the sustainable corporation: Win-win-win business strategies for sustainable development. *California Management Review, 36*(2), 90–100.

EPA (2022). Overview of greenhouse gases. https://www.epa.gov/ghgemissions/overview-greenhouse-gases

Long, S., & Cudney, E. (2012). Strategic process integration of energy and environmental systems in wastewater treatment plants. *International Journal of Energy and Environment, 3*(4), 521–530.

Meadows, D., Randers, J., & Meadows, D. (2004). *Limits to growth: The 30-year update.* Chelsea Green Publishing.

Purvis, B., Mao, Y., & Robinson, D. (2019). Three pillars of Sustainability: In search of conceptual origins. *Sustainability Science, 14*(3), 681–695.

Thanki, S., Govindan, K., & Thakkar, J. (2016). An investigation on lean-green implementation practices in Indian SMEs using analytical hierarchy process (AHP) approach. *Journal of Cleaner Production, 135*(1), 284–298.

UN (2012). The future we want. Resolution adopted by the general assembly on 27 July 2012 (A/RES/66/288). United Nations, New York.

UN Report (2019). UN Report: Nature's dangerous decline 'unprecedented'; species extinction rates 'accelerating'. https://www.un.org/sustainabledevelopment/blog/2019/05/nature-decline-unprecedented-report/

United Nations Commission on Sustainable Development (1987). Framing sustainable Development: The Brundtland Report – 20 years on. https://www.un.org/esa/sustdev/csd/csd15/media/backgrounder_brundtland.pdf

Vandenbrande, W. W. (2020). The role of quality management in ensuring a sustainable planet. *The Journal for Quality and Participation, 42*(12), 8–12.

Zahn, J. (2021). Disney goes plastic-free for Disney princess dolls packaging. https://toybook.com/disney-goes-plastic-free-for-disney-princess-dolls-packaging/

4 Systems Thinking and the Circular Economy

OVERVIEW

Organizations embarking on a Lean journey must understand systems and Systems Thinking and why it is critical to have a systems view when implementing Lean principles and tools. It is necessary to understand systems, the types of systems, and the principles of Systems Thinking. These concepts are essential for organizations to drive their continuous improvement initiatives, particularly with the integration of Sustainability toward a circular economy. This chapter aims to encourage organizations and teams to think about the entire business as interconnected processes to select improvement activities with the most significant impact on the organization.

DEFINING A SYSTEM

During Lean implementation, it is critical to consider the organization as a system of integrated processes. What is a system? There are many different definitions of a system. The first definition is one of the more recent and fundamental definitions from the biology discipline. According to Bertalanffy (1968), "A system is a set of elements in interaction." From a quality perspective, Evans and Lindsay (2011) define a system as "A set of functions or activities within an organization that work together for the aim of the organization." From a systems engineering perspective, INCOSE (2015) defines a system as "any set of related parts for which there is sufficient coherence between the parts to make viewing them as a whole useful."

Further, INCOSE (2015) defines an engineered system as "A context containing both technology and social or natural elements, developed for a defined purpose by an engineering life cycle." An engineered system can consist of hardware, software, facilities, policies, documents, processes, and people. Finally, Deming and Orsini (2013) defined a system as follows:

> A system is an interconnected complex of functionally related components, divisions, teams, platforms, whatever you call them, that work together to try to accomplish the aim of the system. A system must have an aim. Without an aim, there is no system. The aim of the system must be clear to everyone in the system. The aim includes plans for the future.

There are several types of systems: product, service, enterprise, and system of systems. Product systems consist of a product and its elements. An example is an airplane, made up of fuselage, wings, empennage, cargo, engines, vertical and horizontal stabilizers, and electrical and hydraulic components. Service and service systems

DOI: 10.1201/9780429506192-4

provide outcomes or services through the performance of processes, people, and, most times, technology. An example of a service system is a banking center which provides a myriad of financial services, including bank account openings, providing loans, and investment opportunities.

Enterprises and enterprise systems are when one or more organizations or individuals work together to provide a product or service. In an enterprise system, there is a shared purpose or mission, coordination, communication, and interaction between the organization and parts of the system. A hospital or medical system is an example of an enterprise system, where many providers provide multiple healthcare services, such as emergency, inpatient, outpatient, laboratory testing, and women's health.

A system of systems includes several enterprises and service, and product systems brought together to achieve a common purpose. A system of systems is usually interconnected systems of a broader scale, such as an airport that contains product systems (e.g., airplanes, equipment, facilities), service systems (e.g., airport security, ticketing, gate services), and enterprises (e.g., airline companies, contractors). Another example could be a transportation system for a geographic area, including a highway system, rail system, air travel system, and waterway system. However, it is essential to note that one person's system may be another person's system of systems. Some may call the product system airplane example above a system of systems (Furterer, 2022).

A Lean system provides an enterprise-wide view of the organization (Cudney, Furterer, & Dietrich, 2014). In many cases, organizations need to consider the enterprise system starting from the big picture, or the value stream, to the details of the processes and procedures when implementing Lean. The concept of systems aligns with Deming's view of a production system by connecting customers and suppliers to the organization's inner workings (processes) (Deming, 1982). Figure 4.1 provides an example of a hospital system in Deming's view of a production system.

A very early view of a system is from the Tomb of Paheri, constructed around 1500 BC. Paheri was a property owner and governor. One of the figures on the west wall shows Paheri's role of supervising farm work, which consisted of harvesting, hunting, fishing, and loading boats. Figure 4.2 illustrates a systems model, a functional decomposition of the activities critical to life in ancient Egypt, and the cyclical and year-round nature of these agricultural functions.

Between 385 and 323 BC, the philosopher Aristotle stated, "The whole is more than the sum of its parts" (Bertalanffy, 1972, p. 407), which addresses the principle of holism from the systems thinking principles.

SYSTEMS THINKING PRINCIPLES

Systems thinking considers patterns of behavior and the connectivity of system elements, as well as the impact of the interactions of systems elements impacting other parts of the system. Systems thinking considers the boundaries or scope of the system, the dependencies of the elements, their relationships to each other, and the behaviors of the system. The goal of systems thinking is to simplify the understanding of a system so that systems can be engineered and improved (Furterer, 2022).

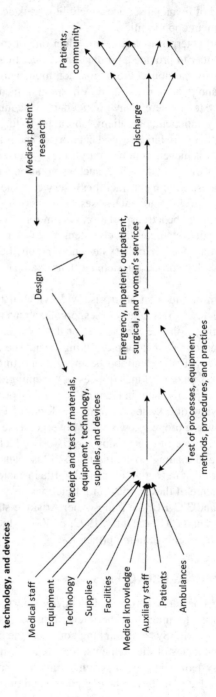

FIGURE 4.1 A hospital system through Deming's lens of a production system.

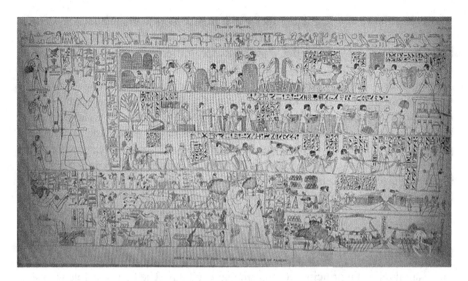

FIGURE 4.2 West Wall Tomb of Paheri. (*Source:* Zachary Furterer, Photo from the Ancient Egypt exhibit at the Cincinnati Museum Center, July 2019)

Teams must understand the system's components and the relationship of the components to each other and the environment regarding Lean Sustainability. The team should first identify, understand, and document the value streams of the enterprise (Cudney, 2009). The system and value streams connect the organization to its external customers and suppliers, as well as the processes and the internal customers (employees). It incorporates processes identified as workflows and events. Through value stream mapping, Lean tools help continuous improvement teams understand the activities performed to achieve value for the customer. By mapping the value streams, a team can begin to understand where the constraining activities, bottlenecks, delays, and wastes exist in their processes.

Once an organization identifies the value streams through value stream mapping, they must understand how to identify and manage bottlenecks in the processes, how to relate the capacity and performance measures of one process to another, and how to use that information to determine the organization's best service or product mix (Cudney, 2013). Some improvement efforts will only impact small portions of the business, while others can affect the entire organization (Tucker & Cudney, 2009).

The Theory of Constraints (TOC) is a management philosophy proposed by Goldratt (1984) to identify and leverage the constraints of a system. The basis of TOC is that every organization has at least one constraint that limits it from getting more of whatever the goal – typically, profit (Cudney, Furterer, & Dietrich, 2014). The TOC defines a set of tools organizations can use to manage constraints. Most organizations are linked processes that transform inputs into saleable outputs. The TOC models this chain of linked processes. The foundation of the system is the theory that a chain is only as strong as its weakest link.

A constraint is any restricting factor that limits the performance of a system in terms of output (Krajewski et al., 2010). Capacity is the maximum rate of output of a system. Teams may categorize constraints into different types. The first type of categorization is known as physical. This constraint may include physical space, product quality, machine performance, work area capacity, or material shortages. A second constraint is categorized as market quantity demanded. In this scenario, market demand for a product is less than process capacity, leading to underutilization. Finally, the third constraint includes managerial constraints, which tend to inhibit the performance of a system through inappropriately issued metrics, strict worker policies, and inflexible cultural mindsets that stymie optimized system utilization (Cudney, Furterer, & Dietrich, 2014). A bottleneck is a specific type of constraint that inhibits the performance of a complete system by slowing down an entire system at a single resource point, thereby governing the performance of a complete system.

CIRCULAR ECONOMY

There are three main principles of the circular economy. The first principle is to stop waste from being produced initially by designing systems to eliminate waste and pollution. The next principle focuses on circulating products and materials by keeping products in use or converting an unusable product to raw materials. The third principle is to regenerate nature by supporting natural processes. In today's economy, organizations generally take materials from the planet, make a product, and then throw them away as waste, resulting in a linear process where the products are not reused or recycled. In the concept of a circular economy, viewing the design, production, reuse, and recycling as a system is critical to Sustainability and sustaining the environment. The circular economy tackles global challenges such as climate change, biodiversity loss, waste, and pollution as an interconnected system. The principle of a circular economy follows a closed-loop system (Ellen Macarthur Foundation, 2023).

CONCLUSION

Systems thinking is critical to making process improvements that impact the overall organization rather than just a disconnected subset of a system. Lean practitioners must consider the big picture and holism that is characteristic of systems thinking to achieve a circular economic approach. In addition, practitioners should focus on improvements tied to the organization's strategic objectives through the systems' connectivity and the value their value systems provide to their customers. The next chapter presents the Lean Green Culture, which describes a culture that supports Lean and Sustainability practices.

REFERENCES

Bertalanffy von, L. (1968). *General system theory: Foundations, development, applications* (rev. Edition). New York: Braziller.
Bertalanffy von, L. (1972). The history and status of general systems theory. *Academy of Management Journal, 15*(4), 407–426.

Cudney, E. (2009). *Using Hoshin Kanri to improve the value stream.* New York, NY: CRC Press.

Cudney, E. (2013). Value stream mapping: Hoshin planning at Carjo manufacturing. In D. Kudernatsch (Ed.), *Hoshin Kanri: Enterprise strategy implementation of lean management tools* (pp. 197–210). Stuttgart, Germany: Schäffer-Poeschl.

Cudney, E., Furterer, S., & Dietrich, D. (2014). *Lean systems: Applications and case studies in manufacturing, service, and healthcare.* Boca Raton, FL: CRC Press.

Deming, W. E., (1982). *Out of the crisis.* MA: MIT Press.

Deming, W. E., & Orsini, J. N. (2013). *The essential Deming. [electronic resource]: Leadership principles from the father of total quality management.* New York, NY: McGraw-Hill.

Ellen Macarthur Foundation, Circular economy introduction, https://ellenmacarthurfoundation.org/topics/circular-economy-introduction/overview#:~:text=It%20is%20based%20on%20three,business%2C%20people%20and%20the%20environment. Accessed: 2/4/2023, Ellen Macarthur Foundation.

Evans, J. R., & Lindsay, W. M. (2011). *Managing for quality and performance excellence* (8th Edition). Austell, GA: South-Western Cengage Learning.

Furterer, S. (2022). *Systems engineering holistic life cycle architecture modeling and design with real-world applications.* Boca Raton, FL: CRC Press.

Goldratt, E. M. (1984). *The goal: A process of ongoing improvement.* Great Barrington, MA: North River Press.

INCOSE (2015). Systems engineering handbook: A guide for system life cycle processes and activities, version 4.0. San Diego, CA, USA: International Council on Systems Engineering (INCOSE), INCOSE-TP-2003-002-03.2.2.

Krajewski, L., Ritzman, L., & Malhotra, M. (2010). *Operations management: Processes & supply chains* (9th Edition). Hoboken, NJ: Prentice Hall.

Tucker, E., & Cudney, E. (2009). Using value stream mapping for financial analysis. *Proceedings of the American Society of Engineering Management Conference*, Springfield, MO.

5 Cultivating a Lean Sustainability Culture

CREATING CULTURE

To enact a strategy for Lean and Sustainability success does not simply happen. As Peter Drucker notes, "culture eats strategy for breakfast." This chapter discusses the culture and approaches for Lean and sustainable adoption. The need to improve Lean Sustainability requires a culture where a Lean and Sustainability strategic approach integrates process improvement techniques and environmental Sustainability strategies (Garza-Reyes, 2015). Powerful process improvement strategies such as Lean are needed to drive both operational and environmental success strategies to meet Sustainability goals (Garza-Reyes, 2015). Thus, an implementation team tasked with creating a Lean culture can also create a culture of Sustainability. The other primary idea is learning. Taichi Ohno stated that the most critical element in Toyota's Production System, the foundation for Lean, is the human condition and how humans learn Lean (Ohno, 1987). The traits of learning Lean are synthesized and summarized in Figure 5.1 (Laux et al., 2011).

Through this perspective, Lean is more organic and evolutionary than revolutionary regarding successful adoption. Lean is organic with respect to how individuals learn and engage across the enterprise, which adds to systemwide change. Lean involves cooperation among individuals through a collection of tasks managed by a teacher (Sensei), reinforced through consistent reflection (Ohno, 1987; Suzaki, 1987).

Among the most well-known philosophies incorporating these traits comes from David Mann (2015), who proposes that creating a successful Lean culture can be based upon creating a Lean management system where learning and applying Lean principles can result in a culture change.

CULTIVATING LEAN

Lean assumes the presence of standardized work, where operations use visual management principles. However, this presents a conundrum, where knowledge work that powers service and other non-manufacturing enterprises often need more visibility. Visualizing the work through techniques such as Gemba, 5S, and value stream mapping requires visibility (Agustiady & Cudney, 2022). In addition, without visibility, it can be challenging to create accountability in Lean management, which was also present in the Toyota Production System. However, organizations do not have the luxury of implementing Lean in the Toyota culture. How can an organization create a culture where Lean management can succeed? Mann (2015) developed a philosophy of culture change based upon a Lean management system consisting of leader standardized work, accountability, and visual controls. These elements focus on process

 DOI: 10.1201/9780429506192-5

Lean Learning Trait	Definition	Source
Cooperative	Lean focuses on groups of individuals learning for the collective achievement of organizational goals.	Mann (2015)
Evolutionary	Lean is based upon moderate change in the workplace and exhibited by kaizen improvement.	Womack & Jones (1996)
Learning organization	Lean focuses on all personnel learning through accumulated experience through relentless reflection.	Liker (2004); Ohno (1987); Suzaki (1987)
Organic	Lean focuses on a systematic organization around a set of ideas.	Suzaki (1987)
People-centered	Lean focused on developing people where technology serves the human condition.	Ohno (1987); Liker (2004)

FIGURE 5.1   Learning Lean traits.

improvement. The underlying premise of Mann's cultural philosophy focuses on the individual and how individual changes add to a change in the organization. This premise begins with a manual and conscious effort to develop the right routines. Through consistency, these routines become habits and more automatic as the person develops expertise through conscious learning, as shown in Figure 5.2. Routines become behavior, where individuals learn to respond to changes via feedback in their work. Finally, over time learning occurs where culture arises (Mann, 2015).

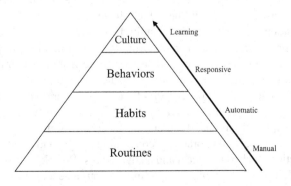

FIGURE 5.2   Learning Lean culture.

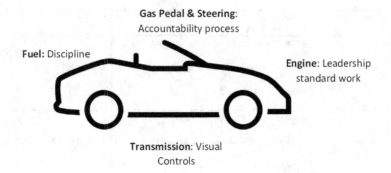

FIGURE 5.3   Mann's (2015) principles of Lean culture implementation.

Mann (2015) recognized that while Lean efforts focused on production, considerably fewer efforts focused on management's role in Lean adoption. Cultural change requires resources, which come from management. Therefore, leader standard work, like production standard work, is a primary principle that powers the rest of a Lean system. Leader standard work makes daily tasks routine (daily accountability process) and focuses attention (via visual controls) on process improvement through disciplined use of Lean techniques (Mann, 2015). Mann uses a vehicle metaphor to help implementers illustrate Lean culture, as shown in Figure 5.3.

This philosophy also accounts for another successful trait of Lean: collective effort. An organization that implements Lean in select areas (production) where much less, if any, emphasis is put upon management to adopt Lean work is likely to result in a less successful implementation. Management work needs to be more transparent with respect to Lean, whereas standardized work is more knowledge-based. Organizations should create a Lean culture where everyone has a part to play, which can result in a more collective organizational approach. Leader standard work powers the rest of Lean, provides structure and routine, and helps management work toward coaching. Adopting a Lean culture results in personal transformation, and coaching is an essential element. People learn best by doing and participating actively with persistent reflection on understanding. A Lean culture requires a teacher (or Sensei) to guide the way. An effective Sensei will question, probe, and be insistent in learning. This approach requires discipline, which the teacher can provide, but the discipline to truly adopt Lean is up to the individual (Mann, 2015). Gemba, or daily accountability processes, provides an opportunity for learning how to work in a culture of Lean. Gemba is where management can move from managing to coaching; teaching by asking instead of telling. Teams should use questions to understand process performance and provide opportunities for team members to continually improve and foster creativity, which is critical for sustaining Lean efforts.

Mann's principles align with the literature where the ability to adopt Lean successfully stems from soft Lean practices concerning people and relations rather than hard Lean practices such as technical and analytic tools (Bortolotti et al., 2015). Ohno (1987) states that technology plays a role in Lean but a secondary one. A management system is much more critical, where the elements give tools to change and sustain a Lean culture built around a process focus. Sustainability, regarding becoming Green, can also be based on systemic progress.

CULTIVATING SUSTAINABILITY

To integrate Sustainability, a management system, much like Mann's (2015) Lean culture approach focused on the environment, can guide Lean and sustainable integration. Here, an enterprise management system (EMS) approach could support cultural efforts since an EMS is a systematic and holistic effort: an organized way to manage a company based upon environmental principles. An EMS is a structured approach to managing and understanding an enterprise's environmental aspects and impacts (Chintalapudi et al., 2016). Many organizations have adopted an EMS framework to meet environmental requirements. Therefore, EMS serves as a guide for an organization to internally and externally evaluate environmental performance. Growing environmental concerns have forced organizations to face the challenges of reducing their carbon footprint and assessing environmental impacts to improve Sustainability (Chintalapudi et al., 2016). In addition, an increasing number of industries face growing environmental regulations with which organizations must comply, primarily through regulatory compliance, forcing companies to adopt environmentally sustainable policies and strategies. That motivation to improve Lean can concurrently improve environmental performance and compliance. In its Environmental Professional's Guide, the US Environmental Protection Agency (EPA) contends that Lean should connect to environmental Sustainability because of its emphasis on a culture of continuous process improvement (EPA, 2009). Therefore, the implementation team should understand how environmental concerns impact their organizational and regulatory framework. This pressure to improve may be a way to leverage regulatory concerns in building a Lean sustainable culture (Ping-Kuo et al., 2020). In terms of acceptance and implementation of the EMS standards, the International Organization for Standards (ISO) 14001 is the recognized standard for an EMS approach to Lean and Sustainability (Chintalapudi et al., 2016). The popularity of the ISO 14001 EMS approach may be due to ISO's effort to provide an EMS approach, regardless of industry sector, demographics, or size, to facilitate the reduction or prevention of environmental impacts as a result of an organization's processes, products or services (ISO, 2015). The EMS management systems approach is top-down.

As a first stage, an organization must develop a sustainable/environmental policy developed by senior management. An EMS approach contains three main elements: prevent pollutants, comply with regulations, and aim for continuous improvement (ISO, 2015). The second stage of ISO 14001:2004 implementation is planning. Every organization is different, but the planning element will include identifying environmental aspects and impacts, resulting in an environmental management program. The third stage is the implementation and control phase, or the "action" element of the EMS framework: communication channels, documentation methods, and measurement responsibilities are defined and prioritized by the team in order of importance (Chintalapudi et al., 2016). The fourth stage is the corrective action phase, where the organization monitors previously defined metrics and identifies and resolves non-conformances. The last stage of the ISO 14001:2004 EMS framework is a management review, where the organization creates a detailed schedule of metrics for evaluation and demonstrates the overall effectiveness. An essential aspect of the ISO 14001 standard to note is that it is a framework consisting of process standards, not performance standards. This aspect means that ISO 14001 stimulates management systems concentrating on prevention instead of remedial action. ISO standards are continually reviewed and updated periodically. In 2015, ISO applied revisions to the ISO 14001:2004 standard to incorporate the latest trends and ensure its compatibility with other management system standards (ISO, 2015). Today, there is a family of ISO 14000 standards to support the implementation team: ISO 14001:2016 guidelines on implementation and ISO 14001:2019 offering flexibility in implementation. As a generic standard, ISO14001 may be applied in any organization, regardless of size, type, or scope of activity (ISO, 2023).

A few examples offer an integrated framework of an EMS with compliance-focused process improvement for Sustainability. Puvanasvaran, Tian, Suresh, and Muhamad (2014) demonstrate how to integrate Lean principles into an EMS approach based upon ISO 14001 as a practical guide for continual improvement. Other ISO 14001 integrated approaches suggest the need for quantitative assessment methods for improvement and further needed for Lean and sustainable adoption (Fura, 2013; Singh et al., 2015). An EMS and Lean example from manufacturing demonstrated that Lean management positively impacted sustainable practices, where ISO 14001 adoption added synergy to Lean sustainable integration (Ping-Kuo et al., 2020). The same study also found that significant employee involvement and management attitudes were important to a spirit of cultural improvement in Lean and Sustainability (Ping-Kuo et al., 2020). The importance of people is evident; however, the right attitude is equally important.

An implementation team should be on the lookout for a lack of real improvements in Lean and sustainable performance. A strategy for culture change based upon measurable assessment helps mitigate this problem (what gets measured gets improved), but what is not measured or easily measured can sink a team's drive for real culture change.

The Iceberg theory, also known as the "theory of omission," is a term used to describe a technique of writing coined by American writer Ernest Hemingway. Hemingway believed that the deeper meaning of a story should not be immediately evident but should shy through implicitly. Edward Mall developed the Iceberg Model of Culture, illustrating how the Iceberg theory might apply to cultural aspects (Li, 2020; Mall, 1976). The visible aspects of culture are only "the tip of the iceberg," but most of what drives the cultural transformation is below the surface, unseen and subconscious (Li, 2020; Mall, 1976). Cultural renewal involves the observable workplace, but below the waterline lies the great mass of beliefs, attitudes, values, and philosophies that organizations often take for granted (Li, 2020). Braithwaite (2011) points out that culture change involves concerted efforts, usually over lengthy periods, to influence and shape behaviors and practices on the one hand and attitudes and values on the other. Hines et al. (2011) applied the iceberg culture model to Lean transformation, where they found five significant variables that drive Lean transformation, including (1) behavior and engagement, (2) leadership, (3) process management, (4) strategy and alignment, and (5) technology, tools, and techniques. The two visible variables above the waterline are technology, tools, techniques, and process management. However, strategy and alignment, leadership, and behavior and engagement are below the waterline (Hines et al., 2011). Cultural elements of strategy and alignment, leadership, behavior, and engagement are critical in enabling a Lean Sustainability effort. While hidden, processes, tools, and techniques are visible and present in both Mann's and the EMS approach to Lean Sustainability. To revisit Garza-Reyes (2015), Lean will enable Sustainability principles through an explicit approach of both soft and hard practices.

CONCLUSIONS

This chapter introduced how to create a Lean and Green culture by focusing on individual learning Lean and extending a Lean culture to Sustainability principles in a managed systematic way. Learning Lean through daily work is all-encompassing, both production and management, where all individuals engage in Lean, focused on process improvement and reinforced by evaluation and reflection. Once in place, extending these same principles to Sustainability may be done through similar "soft" practices, such as those laid out in a managed system, focused on the environments to guide the implementation team, even if certification of such a system is not a goal. To help guide an organization to a culture of Lean and Sustainability, learning how to do, manage, and sustain the actual work may occur through a management system. An organization's culture is its DNA and fundamental to engaging in any endeavor. In the next chapter, applying a framework for Lean and Sustainability are steps that the organization should take in its Lean and Green journey.

REFERENCES

Agustiady, T., & Cudney, E. (2022). *Building a sustainable lean culture: An implementation guide*. New York, NY: CRC Press.
Bortolotti, T., Boscari, S., & Danese, P. (2015). Successful lean implementation: Organizational culture and soft lean practices. *International Journal of Production Economics, 160,* 182–201.
Braithwaite, J. (2011). A lasting legacy from Tony Blair? NHS culture change. *Journal of the Royal Society of Medicine, 104*(2), 87–89.
Chintalapudi, K., Hewetson, B., & Laux, C. (2016). A Conceptual Framework for Lean Six Sigma and Environmental Sustainability Integration: ISO 14001:2015. The Sixth International Conference on Lean Six Sigma. Edinburgh, UK.
Environmental Protection Agency. (2009). The environmental professional's guide to Lean Six Sigma. http://www.epa.gov/lean/environment/toolkits/professional/resources/Enviro-Prof-Guide-Six-Sigma.pdf
Fura, B. (2013). Improving ISO 14001 environmental management systems. *Polish Journal of Environmental Studies, 22*(6), 1711–1722.
Garza-Reyes, J. (2015). Green Lean and the need for Six Sigma. *International Journal of Lean Six Sigma, 6*(3), 226–248.
Hines, P., Found, P., Griffiths, G., & Harrison, R. (2011). *Staying lean thriving, not just surviving* (2nd Edition). New York, NY: Productivity Press.
ISO. (2015). ISO 14001 Revision. http://www.iso.org/iso/iso14001_revision
ISO. (2023). ISO 14001 and related standards: Environmental management. https://www.iso.org/iso-14001-environmental-management.html

Laux, C., McFall, K., & Newton, K. (2011). Creating authentic laboratory experiences for Lean manufacturing. *Proceedings of the ASEE Conference for Industry and Education Collaboration*. San Antonio, TX.

Li, N. (2020). How to implement Lean Six Sigma in China: A case study of three manufacturing companies [Doctoral dissertation, Purdue University].

Liker, J. K. (2004). *The Toyota way: 14 management principles from the world's greatest manufacturer*. NY: McGraw-Hill.

Mall, E. (1976). *Beyond culture*. New York, NY: Random House.

Mann, D. (2015). *Creating a lean culture* (3rd Edition). NY: Productivity Press.

Ohno, T. (1987). *Toyota production system*. NY: Productivity Press.

Ping-Kuo, C., Lujan-Blanco, I., Fortuny-Santos, J., & Ruiz-de-Arbulo-López, P. (2020). Lean manufacturing and environmental Sustainability: The effects of employee involvement, stakeholder pressure and ISO 14001. *Sustainability*, *12*(18), 7258.

Puvanasvaran, P., Tian, R. K. S., Suresh, V., & Muhamad, M. R. (2014). Lean environmental management integration system for Sustainability of ISO 14001:2004 standard implementation. *Journal of Industrial Engineering and Management*, *7*(5), 1124–1144.

Singh, B., Brueckner, M., & Padhy, P. (2015). Environmental management system ISO 14001: Effective waste minimization in small and medium enterprises in India. *Journal of Cleaner Production*, *102*, 285–301.

Suzaki, K. (1987). *The new manufacturing challenge: Techniques for continuous improvement*. New York, NY: Simon and Schuster.

Womack, J. P., & Jones, D. T. (1996). *Lean thinking: Banish waste and create wealth in your corporation*. New York, NY: Simon and Schuster.

6 Integrated Lean and Sustainability Framework

INTRODUCTION

While organizations may desire to improve their impact on the environment; however, they lack a methodology for integrating Sustainability into their continuous improvement efforts. This chapter presents an integrated Lean Green Sustainability framework. This framework includes Lean and Green Sustainability principles, tools, and methodologies from the quality improvement Plan-Do-Check-Act phases integrated with the circular economy five Rs of refuse, reflect, reduce, reuse, and recycle. The framework provides a simple yet powerful way to navigate Lean improvements that support Sustainability.

SUSTAINABILITY FRAMEWORKS

A framework should be generic and inclusive of common information needs for a broad spectrum of practitioners (Heemskerk et al., 2002). Multiple studies propose a framework for the implementation of Sustainability (Chofreh et al., 2017). According to Chofreh et al. (2017), Sustainability frameworks include various dimensions. These dimensions consider Sustainability and decisional paradigms. The Sustainability paradigm consists of several dimensions pertinent to Sustainability.

LEAN AND SUSTAINABILITY FRAMEWORKS

Lean is a concept to generate a continuous improvement system and eliminate waste throughout the organization from production to the supply chain, which improves quality, reduces costs, and adds value for customers (Duarte & Cruz-Machado, 2013; Cudney & Elrod, 2011; Simpson & Power, 2005). Lean management is a system that improves productivity based on finite resources (Hartman, 2015). Lean focuses on increasing output with optimized usage of input resources by reducing waste and increasing process efficiency. Sustainable Green strategies focus on eliminating environmental wastes related to water, energy, air, and solid and hazardous waste (Duarte & Cruz-Machado, 2013). Lean and Green paradigms have a commonality in the context of waste reduction, continuous improvement, efficiency-driven improvement, and emphasis on cleaner production (Vinodh et al., 2011; Bhattacharya et al., 2019). Verrier et al. (2016) note the potential impact of Lean tools, such as the Gemba walk, value stream mapping, visual management, 5S, and total productive maintenance, have resulted in the improved environmental performance of several companies. King and Lenox (2001) demonstrate the adoption of Lean management practices in

DOI: 10.1201/9780429506192-6

the form of ISO 9001 standards which results in lower inventory levels and reduces waste generation and emissions.

The benefits of implementing total productive maintenance as a Lean and Green strategy mean proactive maintenance fostering environmental Sustainability due to the ability of practitioners to increase machine life and mitigate potentially adverse effects of non-optimized functioning through emissions (Farias et al., 2019). Chiarini (2014) underlines the impact of 5S implementation in reducing mistakes during a rubbish sorting process, leading to less repetitive strain injuries, fostering social aspects of Sustainability performance, and fostering recycling. Sustainable VSM, a term coined by Brown et al. (2014), integrates both Lean and Green concepts to track waste in the process and foster optimized use of resources. Pampanelli, Found, and Bernardes (2014) demonstrate that continuous process improvement tools may reduce resource use from 30% to 50% on average. For example, close supplier relationships foster information sharing on a real-time basis, which helps reduce a bullwhip effect that leads to excess production, transportation, and stock holding that ultimately impacts the environment (Leon & Calvo-Amodio, 2017). Relationships with suppliers and key stakeholders are an important way of ensuring strong social Sustainability leading to competitive advantages (Herrera, 2015). A Lean and Green House developed by Hines (2009) highlights essential practices in delivery, environment, and quality pillars. The strategic house also highlights the strategic tools that support the mitigation of Lean and Green waste (muda) (Hines, 2009).

The waste of non-utilized talent/resources is not part of the seven classical wastes in the original Japanese wastes; however, recognizing that people are the most crucial part of Lean led to the addition of this waste (Cudney, 2012). The Environmental Protection Agency (EPA) published *The Lean and Environmental Toolkit* in December 2006 (Kidwell, 2006) to describe how organizations can apply conventional Lean tools to environmental waste. *The Toolkit* discusses using Lean manufacturing tools to improve material flow that impacts the environment, such as energy, chemicals, and other kinds of waste (EPA, 2006). Biggs (2009) published an in-depth study on integrating Lean thinking and environmental improvement, concluding that organizations can provide environmental benefits through Lean thinking. However, there was no direct intention to reduce environmental impact. Moreira, Alves, and Sousa (2010) conducted a study to integrate the concepts of Lean thinking and eco-efficiency that identified the three leading causes of production waste due to weak environmental performance, such as energy consumption, material consumption, and pollutant emissions. The study also highlighted that organizations could embed the environmental impacts of energy use, material consumption, and emissions into the seven classic Lean wastes of overproduction, inventory, transportation, motion, defects, waiting, and over-processing.

The Lean and Green Model by Pampnelli et al. (2014) takes a systems approach with mass and energy flow analysis within system boundaries. The model highlights the input, operational, and output metrics for Lean and Green system analysis (Pampanelli et al., 2014). This model is important to understand applications of the Lean and Green model for systems analysis and developing key performance indicators to evaluate processes.

The Lean and Green matrix by Fercoq et al. (2016) integrates the seven types of Lean waste with the hierarchy of the 3Rs (reduce, reuse, recycle) of a Green system and the maturity model proposed by Verrier et al. (2016). A study by Inman and Green (2018) classified Lean and Green performance evaluation criteria based on productivity, inventory, and profitability as operational performance criteria and energy consumption as environmental performance criteria. Waste reduction, cost reduction, and quality were criteria common to both the Lean and Green paradigms (Leong et al. 2018). From the environmental perspective, the term "waste" includes water consumption, raw material waste, and energy waste, or, from the operational perspective, defects, scrap, and overproduction (Nahmens & Ikuma, 2012). Therefore, waste reduction is associated with cost reduction from both operational and environmental perspectives (Farias et al., 2019). The approach of total quality environmental management (TQEM) expands the narrow definition of quality by demonstrating that quality management and environmental management systems have synergistic effects (Garza-Reyes et al., 2018). The Lean and Green models highlighted in this section identify the common key concepts such as waste reduction, lead time reduction, monitoring process indicators, value stream mapping, employee satisfaction, visual management, and supply chain relationships (Strzelczak, 2017). Manufacturing, supply chain, and service operations are the most common industrial types where organizations have adopted Lean and Green models, as highlighted in a review study by Hundal (2022).

LEAN GREEN SUSTAINABILITY FRAMEWORK

Lean and Sustainability frameworks highlighted in the prior section provide the basis for the Lean Green Sustainability framework. This framework, shown in Figures 6.1 and 6.2, includes the Lean and Green Sustainability principles and tools integrated with the quality improvement Plan-Do-Check-Act methodology along with the Sustainability 5Rs of refuse, reflect, reduce, reuse, and recycle (Fernandes, 2020).

THE 5RS (REFUSE, REFLECT, REDUCE, REUSE, AND RECYCLE)

Refuse: Plan not to use materials, processes, energy, or equipment that are not sustainable or environmentally friendly.
Reflect: Reflect to identify sustainable and environmentally friendly processes, products, and service delivery.
Reduce: Reduce the amount of materials, equipment, and overproduction by focusing on efficiency and productivity practices.
Reuse: Reuse materials, equipment, facilities, and energy sources.
Recycle: Recycle materials internally or externally to keep them out of landfills.

Organizations should use the five Rs in a cyclical and circular fashion aligned to PDCA. Organizations should use the refuse and reflect elements while planning the improvement effort, scoping the project, and designing products, processes, equipment, and facilities. Additionally, planning raw materials to be purchased as part of the refuse and reflecting Sustainability activities.

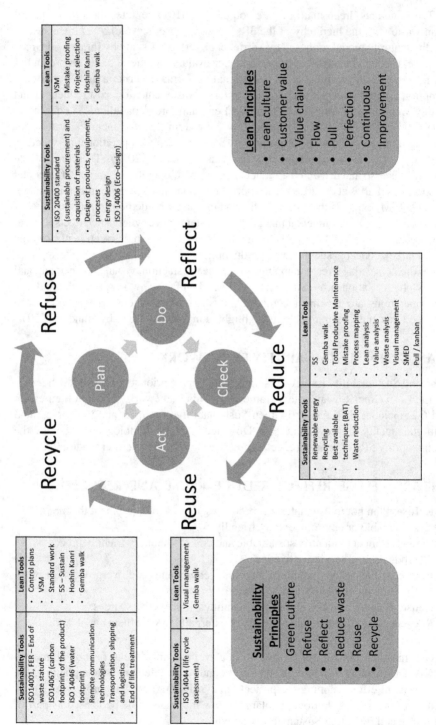

FIGURE 6.1 Lean Green Sustainability framework (LGSF).

PDCA Phase	Sustainability Principles – 5Rs	Lean Principles	Sustainability Tools	Lean Tools
Plan	• Green culture • Refuse • Reflect	• Lean culture • Customer value	• ISO 20400 standard (sustainable procurement) and acquisition of materials • Design of products, equipment, and processes • Energy design • ISO 14006 (eco-design)	• VSM • Mistake proofing • Project selection • Hoshin Kanri • Gemba walk
Do	• Reduce waste	• Value chain • Flow • Pull	• Renewable energy • Recycling • Best available techniques (BAT) • Waste reduction	• 5S • Gemba walk • Total productive maintenance • Mistake proofing • Process mapping • Lean analysis • Value analysis • Waste analysis • Visual management • SMED • Pull / kanban
Check	• Reuse	• Perfection	• ISO 14044 (life cycle assessment)	• Visual management • Gemba walk
Act	• Recycle	• Perfection • Continuous improvement	• ISO14001, FER – end of waste statute • ISO14067 (carbon footprint of the product) • ISO 14046 (water footprint) • Remote communication technologies • Transportation, shipping, and logistics • End-of-life treatment	• Control plans • VSM • Standard work • 5S – Sustain • Hoshin Kanri • Gemba walk

FIGURE 6.2 Lean Green Sustainability framework.

Lean tools and principles align nicely with reducing waste by supporting more efficiency and productivity and eliminating rework and scrap in processes. Organizations commonly perform this step in the Do phase of the PDCA. Reuse is the "R" of focus in the Check phase, verifying that as waste is eliminated and reduced in the "Do" phase, verification of the reuse, which organizations should perform in

Check. Organizations address recycling in the Act phase, where teams roll out improvements more permanently, and materials, equipment, and facility components can be recycled to be kind to the environment.

The Lean and Sustainability principles also align and support each other well. The Sustainability Principles include:

- Green culture: Incorporating a culture that supports both Lean and Green Sustainability, as discussed in Chapter 5.
- Refuse: Refusing to use or purchase materials, products, equipment, supplies, facilities, and energy sources that are not sustainable.
- Reflect: Reflect and plan to incorporate sustainable practices and tools.
- Reduce waste: Reduce waste that harms the environment and adds to landfills.
- Reuse: Plan for the reuse of resources.
- Recycle: Recycle resources either internally or externally for the organization. Organizations should partner with other organizations to enhance recycling.

Lean Principles include:

- Lean culture: Incorporating a culture focused on waste elimination, identifying, and focusing on customer value, continuous improvement, flow, and perfection.
- Customer value: Identifying and defining requirements that focus on customer value, identifying activities that add value to the customer, and eliminating those that do not add value from a customer's perspective.
- Value chain: Identifying and improving the chain of activities that add value to the customer.
- Flow: Incorporating techniques that remove delays and barriers to flowing the product or delivering the service seamlessly and without interruption, based on what the customers want to buy.
- Pull: Pulling the product or service based on what the customer wants to buy instead of building to forecasts.
- Perfection: Striving for perfection in all that the organization does.
- Continuous improvement: Continually improving to make small yet powerful changes happen.

The Sustainability and Lean tools aligned to the phases of the PDCA, as shown in Figure 6.1. Figure 6.2 aligns the tools to the PDCA phase, where an organization uses them most frequently. However, organizations could use each tool during all phases of PDCA and the 5Rs throughout the life cycle of products and services.

The following is a discussion of the elements of the framework. The framework starts by integrating the Sustainability and Lean methodologies. The quality improvement Plan-Do-Check-Act methodology is used frequently in Lean improvement efforts to guide how to develop and implement improvement. Organizations use kaizen events to incorporate PDCA activities and engage the improvement team to collaborate on improvement.

PLAN-DO-CHECK-ACT (PDCA) CYCLE

Kaizen events follow the Plan-Do-Check-Act cycle, including the following steps (Cudney, Furterer, & Dietrich, 2014).

PLAN
1. *Identify the need.* Leadership must determine the purpose of the kaizen event.
2. *Form the kaizen team.* Kaizen teams typically consist of six to eight team members.
3. *Develop the kaizen objectives.* Leadership should document the scope of the project. The objectives should be specific, measurable, attainable, realistic, and time-based (SMART).
4. *Collect baseline data on the current state.* The team should gather baseline data from the Lean Six Sigma Measure phase or collect data as needed.
5. *Develop a schedule and kaizen event agenda.* A kaizen event typically lasts one week or less.

DO
6. *Hold the kaizen event.* A sample kaizen event agenda is as follows:
   - Review the kaizen event agenda.
   - Review the kaizen objectives and approach.
   - Develop kaizen event ground rules with the team.
   - Present baseline measure and background info.
   - Hold event.
     - Define: Problem (derived from objectives) and agree on the scope of the event.
     - Measure: Review measure baseline collected.
     - Analyze: Identify root causes, wastes, and inefficiencies.
     - Improve: Create an action item list and improvement recommendations.
     - Control: Create standard operating procedures to document and sustain improvements. Prepare summary report and present to sponsor.
   - Identify and assign action items.
   - Document findings and results.
   - Discuss the following steps and close the meeting.
7. *Implement improvements.* The kaizen team should implement recommendations, fine-tune, and train employees on the new process.

CHECK/ACT
8. *Summarize accomplishments.* The kaizen team should summarize the key findings, actions taken and results achieved. The following is a list of the kaizen summary report items:
   - Team members
   - Project scope
   - Project goals

- Before kaizen description
- Pictures (with captions)
- Key kaizen breakthroughs
- After kaizen description
- Results
- Summary
- Lessons learned
- Kaizen report card with a follow-up date

9. *Control the process*. The final step is to standardize the process if the event meets the targets or re-start the kaizen event PDCA cycle if the event does not meet the targets or stabilize the process.

CONCLUSION

The Lean Green Sustainability framework guides practitioners in incorporating both Lean and Sustainable principles, practices, and tools in their organizations. The following chapters provide detailed discussions of these tools and techniques.

REFERENCES

Bhattacharya, A., Nand, A., & Castka, P. (2019). Lean-green integration and its impact on Sustainability performance: A critical review. *Journal of Cleaner Production, 236*, 117697.

Biggs, C. (2009). Exploration of the integration of Lean and environmental improvement. https://files.core.ac.uk/pdf/23/139666.pdf

Brown, V. A., Grootjans, J., Ritchie, J., Townsend, M., & Verrinder, G. (2014). *Sustainability and health: Supporting global ecological integrity in public health.* Abingdon, Oxfordshire: Routledge.

Chiarini, A. (2014). Sustainable manufacturing-greening processes using specific Lean production tools: An empirical observation from European motorcycle component manufacturers. *Journal of Cleaner Production, 85*, 226–233.

Chofreh, A. G., Goni, F. A., & Klemes, J. J. (2017). Development of a framework for the implementation of sustainable enterprise resource planning. *Chemical Engineering Transactions, 61*, 1543–1548.

Cudney, E. (2012). A comparative analysis of lean techniques. In J. C. Spohrer, & L. E. Freund (Eds.), *Advances in the human side of service engineering* (pp. 410–419). New York, NY: CRC Press.

Cudney, E., & Elrod, C. (2011). A comparative analysis of integrating lean concepts into supply chain management in manufacturing and service industries. *International Journal of Lean Six Sigma, 2*(1), 5–22.

Cudney, E., Furterer, S. L., & Dietrich, D. (2014). *Lean systems applications and case studies in manufacturing, service, and healthcare.* Boca Raton, Florida: CRC Press.

Duarte, S., & Cruz-Machado, V. (2013). Modeling Lean and Green: A review from business models. *International Journal of Lean Six Sigma, 4*(3), 228–250.

EPA (2006). https://www.epa.gov/sites/default/files/2013-10/documents/leanenvirotoolkit.pdf

Farias, L. M. S., Santos, L. C., Gohr, C. F., de Oliveira, L. C., & da Silva Amorim, M. H. (2019). Criteria and practices for Lean and Green performance assessment: Systematic review and conceptual framework. *Journal of Cleaner Production, 218*, 746–762.

Fercoq, A., Lamouri, S., & Carbone, V. (2016). Lean/Green integration focused on waste reduction techniques. *Journal of Cleaner Production, 137*, 567–578.

Fernandes, P. (2020). Circular economy as a way of increasing efficiency in organizations, Circular Economy, Climate Change, Global Warming, PORTO PROTOCOL 28 Janeiro, 2020. https://www.portoprotocol.com/circular-economy-as-a-way-of-increasing-efficiency-in-organizations/ Accessed: 2/1/2023

Gandhi, N. S., Thanki, S. J., & Thakkar, J. J. (2018). Ranking of drivers for integrated Lean-Green manufacturing for Indian manufacturing SMEs. *Journal of Cleaner Production*, *171*, 675–689.

Goni, F. A., Chofreh, A. G., Mukhtar, M., Sahran, S., Shukor, S. A., & Klemeš, J. J. (2017). Strategic alignment between Sustainability and information systems: A case analysis in Malaysian public higher education institutions. *Journal of Cleaner Production*, *168*, 263–270.

Hartman, B. (2015). *The lean farm: How to minimize waste, increase efficiency, and maximize value and profits with less work*. Chelsea, Vermont: Chelsea Green.

Heemskerk, B, Pistorio, P, & Scicluna, M. (2002). *Sustainable development reporting: Striking the balance*. Geneva: World Business Council for Sustainable Development. http://www.cecodes.org.co/descargas/publicaciones/publicaciones_wbcsd/SustainableDevReporting-Striking-thebalance.pdf

Herrera, M. E. B. (2015). Creating competitive advantage by institutionalizing corporate social innovation. *Journal of Business Research*, *68*(7), 1468–1474.

Hines, P. (2009). Lean and Green. *Source Magazine: The Home of Lean Thinking*. 3rd ed.; Caerphilly, UK: SA Partners.

Hundal, G. S. (2022). Exploring Lean & green internet of things (IoT) wireless sensors framework for the adoption of precision agriculture practices among Indiana row-crop producers (Doctoral dissertation, Purdue University Graduate School).

Inman, R. A., & Green, K. W. (2018). Lean and Green combine to impact environmental and operational performance. *International Journal of Production Research*, *56*(14), 4802–4818.

Kidwell, M. (2006). Lean manufacturing and the environment. *Target*, *22*(6), 13–18.

King, A. A., & Lenox, M. J. (2001). Lean and Green? An empirical examination of the relationship between lean production and environmental performance. *Production and Operations Management*, *10*(3), 244–256.

Leon, H. C. M., & Calvo-Amodio, J. (2017). Towards Lean for Sustainability: Understanding the interrelationships between Lean and Sustainability from a systems thinking perspective. *Journal of Cleaner Production*, *142*, 4384–4402.

Leong, W. D., Lam, H. L., Tan, C. P., & Ponnambalam, S. G. (2018). Development of multivariate framework for Lean and Green process. *Chemical Engineering Transactions*, *70*, 2191–2196.

Moreira, F., Alves, A. C., & Sousa, R. M. (2010, July). Towards eco-efficient lean production systems. In *International Conference on Information Technology for Balanced Automation Systems* (pp. 100–108). Berlin, Heidelberg: Springer Berlin Heidelberg.

Nahmens, I., & Ikuma, L. H. (2012). Effects of Lean construction on Sustainability of modular homebuilding. *Journal of Architectural Engineering*, *18*(2), 155–163.

Pampanelli, A. B., Found, P., & Bernardes, A. M. (2014). A Lean & Green Model for a production cell. *Journal of Cleaner Production*, *85*, 19–30.

Simpson, D. F., & Power, D. J. (2005). Use the supply relationship to develop Lean and Green suppliers. *Supply Chain Management: An International Journal*, *10*(1), 60–68.

Strzelczak, S. (2017). Integrated assessment of Green-Lean production. *International Journal of Automation Technology*, *11*(5), 815–828.

Verrier, B., Rose, B., & Caillaud, E. (2016). Lean and Green strategy: The Lean and Green house and maturity deployment model. *Journal of Cleaner Production*, *116*, 150–156.

Vinodh, S., Arvind, K. R., & Somanaathan, M. (2011). Tools and techniques for enabling Sustainability through lean initiatives. *Clean Technologies and Environmental Policy*, *13*(3), 469–479.

7 Selecting and Prioritizing Lean Green Projects

OVERVIEW

Selecting appropriate projects for Lean Sustainability initiatives is essential to integrating Sustainability into an organization. Project selection is also critical for successfully implementing a continuous improvement program. Identifying high-impact projects at the onset of a continuous improvement program typically results in significant breakthroughs (Cudney et al., 2022). This chapter discusses how to select and prioritize projects.

When organizations pursue a Lean Sustainability journey, it is essential to note that there often needs to be more clarity among senior managers regarding when and if a team should execute Lean projects. Organizations should initiate Lean projects when solutions to problems are unknown at the beginning. Nevertheless, this does not imply that when the solutions are known, the projects are easy to execute in organizations. For example, implementing a new software system does not require the application of Lean Sustainability methodologies since the organization knows the solution at the outset. Examples of solution-unknown projects include reducing the errors in an invoicing process, decreasing the number of defects in a manufacturing assembly operation, increasing the throughput yield of a process, increasing the yield of a process, and reducing the variation and turnaround times. In these cases, the root causes of the problem are either unknown or vaguely known to the problem-solving team. For these problems, collecting data and performing statistical analyses are necessary to understand the root causes and decide what actions to take. Many practitioners of Lean Sustainability argue that the solutions are known for these projects because they typically involve applying known proven principles instead of discovering an unknown solution (Snee & Hoerl, 2018). These Lean Sustainability projects are not necessarily more straightforward to execute because teams must apply tools, principles, and basic concepts to processes where the problems lie. This chapter focuses on solution-unknown projects using Lean Sustainability and how to select and prioritize such projects in organizations.

PROJECT CHARACTERISTICS

Executing a Lean Sustainability project requires a significant investment of time and resources. Understanding the characteristics of good projects to be executed by either Green or Black Belts in many organizations is essential. Senior management must create an appropriate environment for results-oriented teamwork (see Chapter 5). Senior management should also support and encourage the project leaders and team from project selection to completion (Antony et al., 2022).

DOI: 10.1201/9780429506192-7

There are several characteristics of good projects that organizations can use as general guidelines for project selection. The problem must align with the business's strategic objectives, hence a business priority to senior managers (see Chapter 19 on Hoshin Kanri). The solution to the problem should clearly demonstrate a significant improvement in business process performance (e.g., a defect reduction of 95%). The solution to the problem should demonstrate a significant financial improvement in hard cash savings to support the continued Lean Sustainability efforts (e.g., a minimum of $100K). In addition, the time to complete the project should be between four and six months. The baseline metrics associated with the problem should be well-defined (see Chapter 9). The problem under investigation should have the support of senior management (see Chapter 5 on Green Lean culture).

One should also understand the characteristics of bad projects associated with a given problem under investigation. If the project under consideration falls under any of the following classifications, leadership should avoid or revisit the problem area. The objectives of the project are fuzzy. No or poor metrics are associated with the problem. The project does not have potential hard cash savings. The scope is too narrow or broad. The project does not align with the organization's strategic objectives. Data is unavailable, or it is not possible to collect data to support the problem. There is no dedicated project champion for the project. There need to be more resources or adequate resources. The project is a pet project of someone in management.

CRITICAL SUCCESS FACTORS

There are several critical success factors for a Lean Sustainable improvement program, including:

- Basing the project selection on key business priorities (Furterer, 2008)
- Focusing on key business areas (Furterer, 2008)
- Aligning the program with strategic initiatives (Furterer, 2008)
- Prioritizing projects based on business strategy (Furterer, 2008)
- Defining a vision of what the organization will look like after implementing Lean and embracing the change (Sureshchandar, Chandrasekharan, & Anantharaman, 2001)
- Top management support through leadership. This factor includes management's setting goals and providing leadership and direction. (Hoffman and Mehra, 1999; Barclay et al., 2022; Antony et al., 2022)
- A strategy that is complementary and integrated with existing policies and strategies (Dale, 1994)
- Clear links between strategic goals and change strategies (Newman, 1994)

These critical success factors point to the need to align an organization's Lean program with the organization's strategic plan and to the vital business processes that enable the enterprise to meet the customers' needs and expectations (Barclay et al., 2022). It also includes the need to understand the Lean program's vision. Often, organizations identify Lean Sustainable projects from a bottom-up approach, not one that is top-down and aligned with the enterprise goals and strategic plans. Although these projects often achieve improvement and financial savings, there must be direct visibility or traceability to the organization's strategic goals.

PROJECT SELECTION RESPONSIBILITY

Before selecting projects, it is a good idea to work out a strategy for Lean Sustainability project selection. Projects should address two critical questions: (1) who will be involved in the project selection and (2) how the projects will be selected. Instead of an individual selecting a project, it is better to form a team to finalize projects. This team should consist of top management members and project champions or sponsors. Project selection may also include process owners of the respective processes in the team. The presence of top management is essential as they understand the organization's priorities better than anyone else. It is beneficial to include a representative of the finance or accounting department in this team. Their involvement will be helpful with the estimation of financial benefits from the projects as they understand the language of money (Kumar, Antony, & Cho, 2009).

When the projects are selected, generally, two approaches can be followed. Top management can select a project and assign it to the project team for execution, or the project teams can identify a project and approach top management for approval. In either case, the ultimate authority for approval of the project is with top management.

When organizations launch a Lean initiative, selecting the first or second wave of a project is a non-delegable role for the senior management team. The senior management team should select projects that link to the business's strategic objectives. Moreover, the projects should link to both the voice of the customer and the voice of the business. Some organizations involve their Black Belts in selecting projects. However, Black Belts do not always have a strong enough understanding of the business's strategic priorities. Hence, the project should be discussed with the senior management team to determine which are worthy of available resources.

Many mid-level managers, who are qualified Black Belts, may allocate resources to their pet projects. Therefore, project selection should involve several people, including the senior management team, Lean project champion, subject matter experts, and project stakeholders (Swarnakar et al., 2022). Many Lean practitioners need more exposure to high-level business issues. Therefore, they may have a somewhat myopic perspective of the project selection process (Bertels, 2003).

SELECTING AND PRIORITIZING PROJECTS

There are four main approaches to prioritizing the organization's Lean initiatives. The four methods increase in complexity and time to apply the prioritization technique. The first is a simple priority impact and effort matrix. The next is applying the Pugh initiative selection matrix. The third is applying a Quality Function Deployment House of Quality tool. The last, most complex approach is applying a systems engineering approach from the business architecture body of knowledge.

Method 1: Priority Impact Matrix

The first method is a simple impact-effort matrix. Organizations can use the priority impact matrix to prioritize their Lean Sustainability initiatives based on their potential impact and effort. In an effort impact matrix approach, the organization attempts to estimate the effort in completing a project and its impact measured in terms of benefits for the organization. A simple, typical impact is cost reduction, cost avoidance, increased customer satisfaction, improved on-time delivery, or increased process yield. In addition, typical sustainable impacts can relate to the 5Rs: refuse, reduce, repurpose, and recycle, or triple bottom line (TBL). On the other axis, the effort involves resources (e.g., workforce, budgetary support, and the support needed from senior management) for successful project completion.

Figure 7.1 presents a typical impact-effort matrix. Due to the high and low values for effort and impact, several combinations are possible. The project's initial focus should be low on effort but high on impact.

There are three main steps to applying this approach. The first step is to brainstorm the potential Lean or Sustainability initiatives. Figure 7.2 shows an example of a hospital's Lean initiatives. Organizations can use an affinity diagram to organize the potential Lean initiatives into logical Lean themes or project types, such as in Figure 7.3. The themes or project types would be generated based on the logical groupings of the brainstormed initiatives. Additionally, the team can first generate several Lean themes and brainstorm potential project initiatives within each theme. Potential Lean Sustainability themes include improving value stream throughput improvement, performing waste reduction and process analysis, standardizing work activities, reducing turnaround or changeover time, improving organization using 5S, improving flow, incorporating mistake proofing, or redesigning a process.

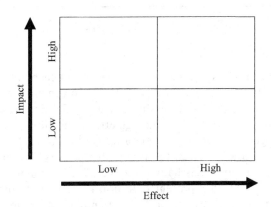

FIGURE 7.1 Effort impact matrix.

5S nursing stations
5S operating room
5S pathology lab
Improve emergency department throughput
Improve inpatient bed assignment
Improve lab turnaround
Improve operating room turnaround
Improve outpatient imaging diagnostic time
Improve women's center intake processes
Improve women's center value stream throughput
Pre-op patient readiness
Reduce bottlenecks in the orthopedic center
Reduce outpatient registration wait time
Standardize congestive heart failure treatment protocols
Standardize emergency department sepsis protocols
Standardize medical practice coding process
Standardize stroke treatment protocols
Streamline endoscopy throughput
Streamline operating instrument tracking
Streamline outpatient rehabilitation processes

FIGURE 7.2   Potential Lean initiatives for a hospital (Cudney, Furterer, & Dietrich, 2014).

The second step is to assess the impact and effort of each initiative. Use a 1 to 5 rating scale for the impact, with 1 representing a low impact and 5 representing a high impact if the project is successful. Use a 1 to 5 rating scale for the effort, with 1 being a low effort and 5 being a high effort. Then multiply the impact and effort ratings to get a priority level. Senior leadership should then rank the projects based on their priority level. Projects with a priority level between 1 and 8 are low priority. Priority levels between 9 and 17 are medium priority. Priority levels between 18 and 25 represent high-priority projects. This step provides leadership with relative priorities for the Lean initiatives. Figure 7.4 provides an example.

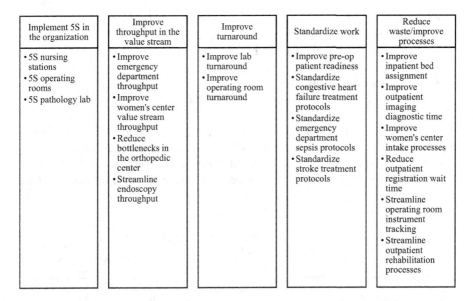

Implement 5S in the organization	Improve throughput in the value stream	Improve turnaround	Standardize work	Reduce waste/improve processes
• 5S nursing stations • 5S operating rooms • 5S pathology lab	• Improve emergency department throughput • Improve women's center value stream throughput • Reduce bottlenecks in the orthopedic center • Streamline endoscopy throughput	• Improve lab turnaround • Improve operating room turnaround	• Improve pre-op patient readiness • Standardize congestive heart failure treatment protocols • Standardize emergency department sepsis protocols • Standardize stroke treatment protocols	• Improve inpatient bed assignment • Improve outpatient imaging diagnostic time • Improve women's center intake processes • Reduce outpatient registration wait time • Streamline operating room instrument tracking • Streamline outpatient rehabilitation processes

FIGURE 7.3   Lean initiatives affinity diagram (Cudney, Furterer, & Dietrich, 2014).

The third and final step is to gain consensus from the Lean steering committee on priorities. This method is relatively simple to apply. Teams can complete the process typically in a two-hour session with the Lean planning committee.

The project's initial focus should be low on effort but high on impact. This ranking selection is to gain the attention of senior managers and demonstrate the power of Lean as a problem-solving methodology.

METHOD 2: PUGH INITIATIVE SELECTION MATRIX

The Pugh initiative selection technique evaluates and selects design concepts in new product development and Design for Six Sigma (Cudney & Furterer, 2012). Organizations use Pugh's selection technique to select concepts based on set criteria. This technique can also be applied to prioritize project initiatives here. There are three steps to determining the priorities.

Organizations should determine these criteria as a prerequisite exercise with input from various team members involved in process improvement activities across the organization. Therefore, the first step is to brainstorm the potential Lean Sustainability initiatives and create an affinity diagram by grouping them by the type of Lean Sustainability project (see the first step for the impact and effort matrix). Next, leadership should generate the criteria to compare the initiatives. Some potential criteria include the following (Cudney & Agustiady, 2016):

- Strategic alignment of the project to the organization's strategic objectives
- Contribution to measurable and quantifiable financial savings
- Impact on customer satisfaction

- Impact on quality
- Estimated completion time
- Risks associated with the project
- Environmental and waste impact
- Impact on productivity
- Impact on employee satisfaction or social impacts

The next step is to select one of the Lean initiatives as the "candidate" initiative. A candidate initiative could be one already implemented in the past or one already known as a high-priority initiative. Leadership would then compare each of the other initiatives (new) to the candidate for each comparison criterion. If the new initiative

Potential Lean Initiatives	Impact 5 = High 1 = Low	Effort 5 = High 1 = Low	Impact x Effort	Priority High = 18 – 25 Medium = 9 – 17 Low = 1 - 8
5S				
5S nursing stations	5	2	10	Medium
5S operating rooms	5	2	10	Medium
5S pathology lab	3	3	9	Medium
Throughput				
Improve emergency department throughput	5	1	5	Low
Improve women's center value stream throughput	4	3	12	Medium
Reduce bottlenecks in the orthopedic center	2	5	10	Medium
Streamline endoscopy throughput	1	5	5	Low
Turnaround				
Improve lab turnaround	3	3	9	Medium
Improve operating room turnaround	5	1	5	Low
Standard Work				
Improve pre-op patient readiness	3	3	9	Medium
Standardize congestive heart failure treatment protocols	5	2	10	Medium
Standardize emergency department sepsis protocols	5	4	20	High
Standardize stroke treatment protocols	5	3	15	Medium
Waste Elimination/Process Analysis				
Improve inpatient bed assignment	5	3	15	Medium
Improve outpatient imaging diagnostic time	3	4	12	Medium
Improve women's center intake processes	2	5	10	Medium
Reduce outpatient registration wait time	3	5	15	Medium
Streamline operating room instrument tracking	3	2	6	Low
Streamline outpatient rehabilitation processes	4	4	16	Medium

FIGURE 7.4 Priority impact and effect matrix (Cudney, Furterer, & Dietrich, 2014).

Potential Lean Initiatives							
Criteria	1	2	3	4	5	6	7
A	-	-	-	0		0	-
B	-	0	-	-		0	-
C	+	+	-	-		-	-
D	+	-	-	+	Candidate	-	+
E	+	+	-	-	Initiative	-	-
Pluses	3	2	0	1		0	1
Minuses	2	2	5	3		3	4
Zeros	0	1	0	1		2	0
Priority	1	2	6	3		5	4

FIGURE 7.5 Pugh's selection matrix (Cudney, Furterer, & Dietrich, 2014).

is better than the candidate for those criteria, they will place a plus sign (+) in the cell where the new initiative intersects the criteria. If the new initiative is worse than the candidate initiative for that criterion, the team places a minus sign (−) in the cell. However, if the new initiative is equivalent, the team places a zero (0) or (S) for the same in the cell. Figure 7.5 shows a generic Pugh's initiative selection matrix.

The highest priority initiative is the one with the most pluses and the fewest minuses. The next priority initiative is the one with the next highest pluses and fewest minuses. Figure 7.6 illustrates a sample Pugh initiatives selection matrix for a hospital's Lean initiatives.

Some organizations choose to weigh each criterion for their selection process because some criteria may be more important than others. For example, the team could weigh each criterion between 1 and 10, with 1 being the least important and 10 the most important (see Figure 7.7). Then each project is mapped against the chosen criteria, and each participant determines if the selected project has any link with the set criteria and rates this on a scale of 1 (no link) to 9 (very strong link).

Once the team identifies the weightings for each criterion, the project selection team reviews each project against the criteria. The team ranks each project against each criterion and writes their values in the corresponding cell. Finally, the total weight of scores is calculated for each project, as shown in Figure 7.8. For example, the first project is not strongly linked to completion time, employee satisfaction, productivity, or quality; therefore, the team assigns it a 5, 3, 5, and 4, respectively. There is a moderate link between customer satisfaction and risk; therefore, the team

Category	Initiative	Resource effort	Quality impact	Productivity impact	Cost impact	Risk impact	Pluses (+)	Minuses (−)	Same (S)	Priority
Waste Elimination	Streamline outpatient rehabilitation processes	+	−	−	−	−	1	4	0	Low
	Streamline operating room instrument tracking	S	+	+	−	+	3	1	1	Low
	Reduce outpatient registration wait time	+	−	−	−	−	1	4	0	Low
	Improve women's center intake processes	S	−	−	−	−	0	4	1	Low
	Improve outpatient imaging diagnostic time	+	−	−	−	−	1	4	0	Low
	Improve inpatient bed assignment	−	−	+	−	−	1	4	0	Low
Standard Work	Standardize stroke treatment protocols	+	+	−	+	+	4	1	0	High
	Standardize emergency department sepsis	+	+	−	+	+	4	1	0	High
	Standardize congestive heart failure treatment protocols	+	+	−	+	+	4	1	0	High
	Improve pre-op patient readiness	+	−	+	−	−	2	3	0	Med
Turnaround	Improve operating room turnaround	−	+	S	+	+	3	1	1	High
	Improve lab turnaround	S	+	S	−	+	2	1	2	Med
Throughput	Streamline endoscopy throughput	+	S	−	−	−	1	3	1	Med
	Reduce bottlenecks in the orthopedic center	+	S	−	−	−	1	3	1	Med
	Improve women's center value stream throughput	S	S	S	−	S	0	1	3	Low
	Improve emergency department throughput	C	A	N	D	I	D	A	T	E
5S	5S pathology lab	+	+	−	−	−	2	3	0	Med
	5S operating rooms	+	+	−	−	+	3	2	0	High
	5S nursing stations	+	+	−	−	−	2	3	0	Med

FIGURE 7.6   Sample Pugh's selection matrix for a hospital's Lean initiatives (Cudney, Furterer, Dietrich, & 2014).

Criteria	Weighting
Completion time	7
Customer satisfaction	9
Employee satisfaction	6
Environmental impact	9
Financial savings	8
Productivity	6
Quality	8
Risk	5
Strategic alignment	10

FIGURE 7.7   Weighted project selection criteria.

assigns a 7 to each of these. There is a strong relationship between environmental impact, financial savings, and strategic alignment; therefore, the team assigns an 8 to each of these.

The team calculates the total score for this project as

$(5 \times 7) + (7 \times 9) + (3 \times 6) + (8 \times 9) + (8 \times 8) + (5 \times 6) + (4 \times 8) + (7 \times 5) + (8 \times 10)$,

which equals 429. The last column of Figure 7.8 provides the total weighted score for each project. Project 4 has the highest score. Therefore, the project selection team should select Project 4 as the highest-priority project.

METHOD 3: QUALITY FUNCTION DEPLOYMENT HOUSE OF QUALITY

Quality Function Deployment (QFD) and the House of Quality matrix are excellent tools to help prioritize the project initiatives with the prioritization criteria. Figure 7.9 shows the format for the House of Quality. The prioritization criteria replace the customer requirements in the typical House of Quality, and the potential Lean initiatives replace the technical requirements.

There are five steps for creating a House of Quality (Evans & Lindsay, 2007). The first step is to brainstorm the prioritization criteria. The example uses the same criteria generated in Pugh's initiative selection technique. The team will then provide an importance rating for each prioritization criterion on a scale of 1 to 10, with one being of low importance and 10 being high importance.

The next step is brainstorming the potential Lean initiatives with the organization's Lean committee. The team uses the same list from the prior two prioritization techniques for the QFD House of Quality example.

The team should then develop the relationship correlation matrix by identifying the relationship strength between each prioritization criterion and each potential Lean initiative (Cudney & Elrod, 2011). Typically, a numerical scale of 9 (high strength of relationship), 3 (medium strength of relationship), 1 (low strength of relationship), and blank (no relationship). For example, if a prioritization criterion is reducing cost and the potential Lean initiative has a high impact on reducing cost, then a rating of 9 would be used. If it has a medium impact, the team member will assign a rating of 3. Moreover, if there is a low impact on reducing cost, a 1 would be used, and if the initiative does nothing to reduce cost, then no rating is given.

Projects	Completion time 7	Customer satisfaction 9	Employee satisfaction 6	Environmental impact 9	Financial savings 8	Productivity 6	Quality 8	Risk 5	Strategic alignment 10	Total score
Project 1	5	7	3	8	8	5	4	7	8	429
Project 2	7	8	9	4	6	8	7	4	7	453
Project 3	2	3	5	7	8	7	6	5	7	383
Project 4	8	8	6	6	7	7	7	8	8	492
Project 5	10	4	4	8	8	8	7	6	8	480

FIGURE 7.8 Weighted project selection example.

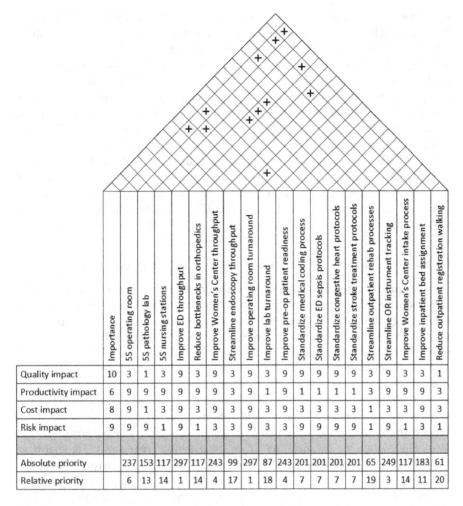

	Importance	5S operating room	5S pathology lab	5S nursing stations	Improve ED throughput	Reduce bottlenecks in orthopedics	Improve Women's Center throughput	Streamline endoscopy throughput	Improve operating room turnaround	Improve lab turnaround	Improve pre-op patient readiness	Standardize medical coding process	Standardize ED sepsis protocols	Standardize congestive heart protocols	Standardize stroke treatment protocols	Streamline outpatient rehab processes	Streamline OR instrument tracking	Improve Women's Center intake process	Improve inpatient bed assignment	Reduce outpatient registration walking
Quality impact	10	3	1	3	9	3	9	3	9	3	9	9	9	9	9	3	9	3	3	1
Productivity impact	6	9	9	9	9	9	9	3	9	1	9	1	1	1	1	3	9	9	9	3
Cost impact	8	9	1	3	9	3	9	3	9	3	9	3	3	3	3	1	3	3	9	3
Risk impact	9	9	9	1	9	1	3	3	9	3	3	9	9	9	9	1	9	1	3	1
Absolute priority		237	153	117	297	117	243	99	297	87	243	201	201	201	201	65	249	117	183	61
Relative priority		6	13	14	1	14	4	17	1	18	4	7	7	7	7	19	3	14	11	20

FIGURE 7.9 Quality Function Deployment House of Quality matrix for a hospital's Lean program (Cudney, Furterer, & Dietrich, 2014).

Next, the team should develop the trade-offs or relationships between the potential Lean Sustainable initiatives on the roof of the House of Quality (Gillis & Cudney, 2014). The team can identify a positive (+) relationship between pairs of initiatives. As a team implements an initiative and achieves its goals, it will have a positive impact or relationship with another initiative. The intersecting diamond is left blank if there is no relationship between a pair of initiatives. Suppose a negative relationship exists between two initiatives, such as when one project is worked on or implemented. A minus sign is placed in the intersecting diamond if one project negatively impacts another (Jach et al., 2022). An example of a positive relationship is a 5S project in the operating room would complement and further enhance the operating room turnaround project since a more organized environment will reduce the time searching for supplies, equipment, and instruments. A negative relationship could be implementing congestive heart standard protocols at the same time as sepsis protocols in the emergency department. Implementing both simultaneously could overtax the staff and be less productive than if the hospital implemented only one project at a time. The cell is left blank when there is no relationship between two projects that do not impact each other. For example, improving the operating room instrument tracking may have no relationship to improving the Women's Center intake processes.

Finally, teams can summarize the priorities of the Lean Sustainable initiatives by multiplying the importance weightings of the prioritization criteria by the strength of the relationships in the correlation matrix. These values help identify which Lean initiatives the organization should start first. Figure 7.9 provides a QFD House of Quality matrix for a hospital's Lean program.

METHOD 4: STRATEGIC BUSINESS PROCESS ARCHITECTURE PRIORITIZATION

The systems engineering business architecture-based approach (Furterer, 2022) can prioritize Lean Sustainable initiatives and ensure alignment with the organization's key business processes and strategies. Organizations can apply resources from a central governing steering committee to these projects. These resources will ensure alignment between the strategic business initiatives and the projects to help assess the improvement projects' success and financial savings. An enterprise view can help an organization elevate its Lean and Sustainable program to an enterprise level. The higher view enables organizations to prioritize their improvement efforts to align with the business strategy and provide more significant cross-functional process improvement for greater cost reduction. Providing an enterprise view can also help to align the organization's Lean Sustainable program with crucial business strategies and core processes. From a cross-functional enterprise view, this approach helps the organization understand if the Lean program aligns with the strategic and operational plans and focuses on crucial organizational bottleneck processes.

The strategic business process architecture (SBPA) models from the Systems Engineering business architecture body of knowledge (Furterer, 2022) provide an enterprise-wide understanding of the business. The business processes enable the extraction of key business elements that support the required capabilities of the business to meet customers' needs.

Organizations can use the strategic business process architecture modeling techniques and methods to provide prioritized alignment with the Lean program goals and the enterprise's Lean projects and improvement initiatives. This model aligns the business strategies and goals and the organization's improvement plans.

Business architecture provides models describing business entities (e.g., business processes and relevant business information), their relationships, dynamics, and rules governing their interaction to achieve enterprise-wide objectives.

Strategic Business Process Architecture Definition and Elements

The definition of SBPA focuses on modeling the key concepts and elements of the enterprise by aligning the business strategies and enabling processes to optimize the critical groups of activities (components) that enable optimized information technology (IT) and business process improvement initiatives.

Figure 7.10 provides a simplified view of the critical elements of the SBPA. The elements of the SBPA describe the business system enterprise. The SBPA includes understanding the customers and their expectations. Another essential element is documenting the business strategies and goals and the external and internal influencers of the business. The goals should relate to the business's capabilities to meet its goals. The value chain is a chain of related activities that provide value to the customer (Porter, 1985). Teams should use the value chains to decompose into business functions. The functional decomposition diagram does not depict process flows but the hierarchical organization of functions and the processes they include. The team will use each value chain and the subsequent business functions to decompose the processes further. This decomposition ensures traceability to value chains that provide customer value.

The business capabilities enable the business functions. While how a business implements its processes is likely to change frequently, the basic capabilities of a business remain constant. The advantage of a model based on the most stable elements of the business is its longevity. The business processes and their activities

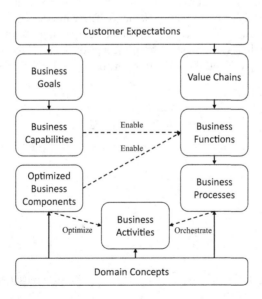

FIGURE 7.10 Key elements of the strategic business process architecture (Cudney, Furterer, & Dietrich, 2014).

describe the sequence of activities that enable the business to meet the customer's expectations and provide value through the value chains.

The optimized business components consist of the optimized activities that support the business. These components consist of activities that require similar people, processes, and technology. They allow the standardization of the business processes by componentizing the activities used in multiple business areas across many business units and markets (IBM Corporation, 2005). The enterprise information and knowledge describe the information and roles that exist in the business that is part of the business processes.

The complete SBPA models are more expansive than the simplified view shown in this chapter. However, teams can use the simplified elements to illustrate how they can be used to prioritize Lean and Sustainable initiatives that align with core business processes and business strategies.

Figure 7.11 shows the enterprise prioritization elements that teams can use to prioritize process improvements.

There are three levels to align when prioritizing enterprise initiatives, including enterprise, operational, and performance levels. The enterprise level links the organization's strategic goals, improvement initiatives, and core processes. The operational level describes and decomposes the key value chains, business functions, processes, and activities that provide customer value. The performance level provides an understanding of the critical to satisfaction (CTS) criteria most important to satisfying customers' needs, processes, and metrics that measure performance improvement.

The matrices shown in Figure 7.12 illustrate the interconnectivity between the enterprise and operational and performance elements. These matrices help ensure alignment between the organization's strategic goals, processes, and improvement projects.

The method includes several steps for project prioritization based on the respective level. At the strategic level, the steps to prioritizing the Lean Sustainable initiatives

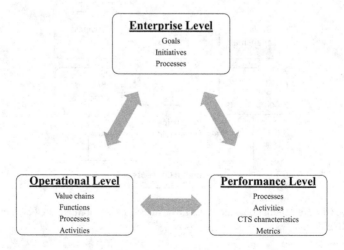

FIGURE 7.11 Enterprise prioritization elements (Cudney, Furterer, & Dietrich, 2014).

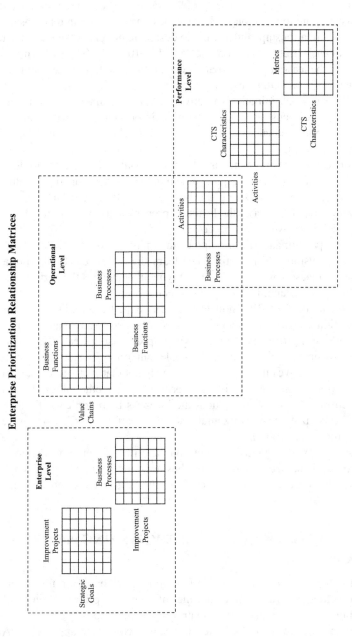

FIGURE 7.12   Enterprise prioritization relationship matrices (Cudney, Furterer, & Dietrich, 2014).

begin with listing the critical strategic goals down the left side of the Enterprise level goals and improvement projects matrix and then listing the proposed Lean Sustainable initiatives across the top of the matrix. Strength is the relationship between each goal and initiative. Teams should use a scale of 9 to designate a high relationship between the initiative helping to meet the goal, a 3 to designate a medium relationship, a 1 to designate a low relationship, and a blank to designate no relationship. Teams rate the importance of each strategic goal on a scale of 1 to 10, with 10 being the most important to 1 being the least important goal. The team then multiplies the strength of each relationship (goals and initiatives) by the importance to calculate the absolute ranking of each initiative. Each initiative's relative ranking is defined to identify the most critical initiative to focus on meeting the most important goals based on the points values (highest points equals priority 1). Figure 7.13 shows a goal and improvement project mapping example.

At the operational level, teams use the operational level matrices to decompose the value chains that provide customer value into the business functions (value chains and business functions matrix and the business functions and business processes matrix). Once a team generates the business processes at the operational level, they can map project initiatives to the processes.

Finally, the performance level helps teams map the work activities to the CTS criteria from a customer perspective. The team then maps the CTS criteria to the metrics used to measure the CTS. The team typically develops the performance level matrices during the Lean initiative's deployment phase.

Teams should use the SBPA models to prioritize the Lean initiatives aligned with the organization's business strategies. Teams then use the operational models to derive the business processes the team will improve using Lean initiatives. These process improvement initiatives help enable enterprise performance excellence because the team derives them from the value chains that relate to the key business processes across the entire enterprise. This prioritization methodology allows organizations to ensure alignment throughout the business both vertically throughout all levels of the organization and horizontally across departmental silos to provide cross-functional process integration.

The SBPA helps the organization focus on the critical Lean improvement projects and the processes that truly matter to the business and its customers. It enables the organization to meet customer expectations through streamlined and optimized processes.

COMPARISON OF METHODS FOR PRIORITIZING PROJECT SELECTION

Figure 7.14 shows the priorities of the Lean initiatives based on the different prioritization techniques. Teams calculate the difference in prioritization levels (low, medium, high) for the Impact-effort matrix and Pugh approaches and the relative priority number between the QFD and business architecture approaches. All four approaches provided different priorities. The organization's technique depends on

Category	Initiative	Reduce operating room costs (6)	Increase operating room capacity (7)	Increase emergency department capacity (3)	Improve customer satisfaction by reducing wait times (9)	Streamline processes to improve productivity (8)	Improve patient safety (10)	Improve quality of processes (9)	Reduce operational costs (4)	Absolute priority	Relative priority
Waste Elimination	Streamline outpatient rehabilitation processes				9	9	3	1	9	228	9
Waste Elimination	Streamline operating room instrument tracking	9	9		3	9	3	9	3	339	2
Waste Elimination	Reduce outpatient registration wait time				9	9	3	3	9	246	7
Waste Elimination	Improve women's center intake processes				9	9	3	9	9	300	6
Waste Elimination	Improve outpatient imaging diagnostic time	3	3	9	9	9	3	3	9	312	5
Waste Elimination	Improve inpatient bed assignment	3	3		9	9	3	9	9	339	2
Standard Work	Standardize stroke treatment protocols		9		3	9	9			222	13
Standard Work	Standardize emergency department sepsis			9	3	9	9			222	13
Standard Work	Standardize congestive heart failure treatment protocols			9	3	9	9			222	13
Standard Work	Improve pre-op patient readiness	9	9		9	9	3		9	336	4
Turnaround	Improve operating room turnaround	9	9		9	9	9	1	9	405	1
Turnaround	Improve lab turnaround				3	9	3	1	9	174	17
Throughput	Streamline endoscopy throughput				9	9	3	1	9	228	9
Throughput	Reduce bottlenecks in the orthopedic center				9	9	3	1	9	228	9
Throughput	Improve women's center value stream throughput				9	9	3	1	9	228	9
Throughput	Improve emergency department throughput			9	9	9	1		9	234	8
5S	5S pathology lab				1	3	3	1		69	19
5S	5S operating rooms	9	9		3	1	3	3	1	213	16
5S	5S nursing stations				1	3	3	1		69	19

Strategic Goals — Importance values: Reduce operating room costs = 6; Increase operating room capacity = 7; Increase emergency department capacity = 3; Improve customer satisfaction by reducing wait times = 9; Streamline processes to improve productivity = 8; Improve patient safety = 10; Improve quality of processes = 9; Reduce operational costs = 4.

FIGURE 7.13 Strategic business process architecture: Goals and initiatives prioritization (Cudney, Furterer, & Dietrich, 2014).

Potential Lean Initiatives	Impact-Effort	Pugh Initiative Selection Matrix	Difference in Impact Levels	QFD House of Quality	Strategic Business Process Architecture	Difference in Impact Levels
5S						
5S nursing stations	Med	Med	0	14	19	5
5S operating rooms	Med	High	1	6	16	10
5S pathology lab	Low	Med	1	13	19	6
Throughput						
Improve emergency department throughput	Low	High	2	1	8	7
Improve women's center value stream throughput	Med	Low	1	4	9	5
Reduce bottlenecks in the orthopedic center	Med	Med	0	14	9	5
Streamline endoscopy throughput	Low	Med	1	17	9	8
Turnaround						
Improve lab turnaround	Low	Med	1	18	17	1
Improve operating room turnaround	Low	High	2	1	1	0
Standard Work						
Improve pre-op patient readiness	Low	Med	1	4	4	0
Standardize congestive heart failure treatment protocols	Med	High	1	7	13	6
Standardize emergency department sepsis protocols	High	High	0	7	13	6
Standardize stroke treatment protocols	Med	High	1	7	13	6
Waste Elimination/Process Analysis						
Improve inpatient bed assignment	Med	Low	1	11	2	9
Improve outpatient imaging diagnostic time	Med	Low	1	11	5	6
Improve women's center intake processes	Med	Low	1	14	6	8
Reduce outpatient registration wait time	Med	Low	1	20	7	13
Streamline operating room instrument tracking	Med	Low	1	3	2	1
Streamline outpatient rehabilitation processes	Low	Low	0	19	9	10

FIGURE 7.14 Comparison of the examples for the four prioritization techniques (Cudney, Furterer, & Dietrich, 2014).

the time they have to prioritize, whether they want to prioritize based on criteria critical to the organization or align with the business strategies. This chapter presented four different techniques. Organizations should try each one and apply the one that best fits the needs of the organization's Lean program.

PROJECT REVIEW

As with every project, regular reviews are crucial to ensure that Lean projects will deliver the anticipated results. Senior management will be involved in the review process to identify the stumbling blocks and potential pitfalls associated with the projects. Moreover, regular reviews also enable the Lean project, champions, and team members and learning problem-solving and methodologies of potential barriers to the successful completion of the project and share some of the rudimentary challenges in the execution and timely completion.

Lean project champions have a considerable role to play in the success or failure of a project. Although the role is not to solve the problem, they facilitate problem-solving through regular interactions with the Lean project, the Lean leader, usually a Black Belt or Green Belt, and team members. Champions, in many cases, encourage creative thinking and challenge the team while ensuring the project is on track and achieved within a given timeline. Additionally, they ensure that the team has access to the necessary resources to complete the project and then communicate success across the business.

There are two types of reviews organizations should perform for each Lean project. An individual completes the first review with top management and a Lean project champion. The second review is by the Lean expert, an experienced Master Black Belt or Black Belt. Focus on the first type of review is to gauge the project's overall progress toward project objectives, project timeline, and alignment with the business objectives. The review should take place at each stage of the problem-solving phase of the methodology. The review can include the following questions (Antony, Vinodh, & Gijo, 2016):

- Is the project executed to the planned schedule?
- Can team members provide the time required for the project?
- Is the overall progress made in a specific phase acceptable?
- Is there a problem with the current budget and resources?
- Are there any perceived risks associated with the project?

The Lean expert's review should focus on the application tools and techniques utilized in each phase of the problem. In addition, the data collection strategy analysis of data and interpretation of key findings are the main focus of this review. The review can use the following questions as checkpoints (Antony et al., 2020):

- Is the project addressing all critical steps in different phases of the problem-solving methodology?
- Is the plan for data collection appropriate and sound?
- How correctly is the analysis being performed?
- Are the right tools being used at the right stage of the methodology for analysis?
- Are the conclusions from each phase or stage of the methodology and the resulting actions appropriate?
- Are there reasonable control measures in place for sustaining improved performance?
- Who will be the process owner after the completion of the project?
- What are the roles and responsibilities of the process owner?

CONCLUSION

The identification and selection of suitable projects remain a challenging task. Many organizations struggle with project selection, even in the best-managed and best-performing organizations. Poor project selection can undermine the success and credibility of the Lean and Sustainability program. This chapter provides an overview of Lean project selection, what constitutes a good project, and how to select and prioritize Lean Sustainability projects. In addition, it covers the people who are responsible for project selection, their roles and responsibilities, and how to manage project reviews effectively. The next chapter discusses value stream mapping, often one of the first Lean tools implemented for a project.

REFERENCES

Antony, J., Sunder, M. V., Laux, C., & Cudney, E. (2020). *The ten commandments of Lean Six Sigma: A practical guide for practitioners*. Bingley, UK: Emerald Publishing.

Antony, J., Swarnakar, V., Gupta, N., Kaur, J., Jayaraman, R., Tortorella, G., & Cudney, E. (2022). Critical success factors for operational excellence initiatives in manufacturing: A meta-analysis. *Total Quality Management & Business Excellence*. doi: 10.1080/14783363.2022.2157714

Antony, J., Vinodh, S., & Gijo, E. V. (2016). *Lean Six Sigma for small and medium sized enterprises: A practical guide*. Boca Raton, FL: CRC Press.

Barclay, R., Cudney, E., Shetty, S., & Antony, J. (2022). Determining critical success factors for lean implementation. *Total Quality Management & Business Excellence*, *33*(7–8), 818–832.

Bertels, T. (2003). *Rath and Strong's Six Sigma leadership handbook (edited)*. Hoboken, NJ: John Wiley & Sons.

Cudney, C., Cudney, E., & Materla, T. (2022). Integrating project management principles into Lean Six Sigma: A systematic review of the literature. *IISE Annual Conference & Expo*, Seattle, WA.

Cudney, E., & Agustiady, T. (2016). *Design for Six Sigma: A practical approach through innovation*. New York, NY: CRC Press.

Cudney, E., & Elrod, C. (2011). Quality function deployment in continuous improvement. In A. Coskun (Ed.), *Six Sigma projects and personal experiences* (pp. 45–78). Rijeka, Croatia: InTech.

Cudney, E., & Furterer, S. (2012). *Design for Six Sigma in product and service development: Applications and case studies*. New York, NY: CRC Press.

Cudney, E., Furterer, S., Dietrich, D. (2014). *Lean systems: Applications and case studies in manufacturing, service, and healthcare*. New York, NY: CRC Press.

Dale, B. (1994). A framework for quality improvement in public sector organizations: A study in Hong Kong. *Public Money & Management*, *14*(2), 31–36.

Evans, J. R. & Lindsay, W. M. (2007). *The management and control of quality* (7th Edition). UK: Thomson South-Western.

Furterer, S. (2012). *Lean Six Sigma in service: Applications and case studies*. New York, NY: CRC Press.

Furterer, S. (2008). Lean Six Sigma program success factors in a retail application. *International Conference on Industry, Engineering, and Management Systems*.

Furterer, S. (2009). Blazing the trail to operational excellence: Leveraging information systems business architecture methods to enable operational excellence, IIE Magazine, Norcross, GA.

Furterer, S. (2022). *Systems engineering holistic life cycle architecture, modeling, and design with real-world applications*. Boca Raton, FL.: CRC Press.

Gillis, W., & Cudney, E. (2014). A new methodology for eco-friendly construction – utilizing quality function deployment to meet LEED requirements. In S. Azevedo, M. Brandenburg, H. Carvalho, & V. Cruz-Machado (Eds.), *Eco-innovation and the development of business models: Lessons from experience and new frontiers in theory and practice* (pp. 245–273). New York, NY: Springer.

Hoffman, J., & Mehra, S. (1999). Management leadership and productivity improvement programs. *International Journal of Applied Quality Management*, *2*(2), 221–232.

IBM Corporation. (2005). *Component business models, making specialization real*. Somers, NY: IBM Business Consulting Services, IBM Institute for Business Value.

Jach, P., Antony, J., Thomson, S. P., Cudney, E., & Furterer, S. (2022). Voice of the customer as a tool for service quality analysis in public transport. The TQM Journal, 34(3), 448–475.

Kumar, M., Antony, J., & Cho, B. R. (2009). Project selection and its impact on successful deployment of Six Sigma. *Business Process Management Journal, 15*(5), 669–686.

Newman, J. (1994). Beyond the vision: Cultural change in the public sector. *Public Money & Management, 14*(2), 59–64s.

Porter, M. (1985). *Competitive advantage: Creating and sustaining superior performance.* New York: Free Press.

Snee, R. D., & Hoerl, R. W. (2018). *Leading holistic improvement with Lean Six Sigma 2.0* (2nd Edition). North York: Pearson Education.

Sureshchandar, G., Chandrasekharan, R, & Anantharaman, R. (2001). A holistic model for total quality service. *International Journal of Service Industry Management, 12*(4), 378–412.

Swarnakar, V., Singh, A. R., Antony, J., Tiwari, A. K., Garza-Reyes, J. A. (2022). Sustainable Lean Six Sigma project selection in manufacturing environments using best-worst method. *Total Quality Management & Business Excellence.* DOI: 10.1080/14783363.2022.2139675

8 Mapping the Value Stream for an Eco-Friendly Flow of Material and Information

With regard to the environment and Sustainability, organizations can use value stream mapping to understand the environmental waste throughout a product life cycle to guide an organized approach to achieve sustainable circular production. As organizations strive to become more sustainable and environmentally sound, it is also essential to identify wastes associated with the environment and evaluate the value stream accordingly. This chapter will provide an integrated approach to value stream mapping to document flow and identify waste. Value stream mapping enables an environmental approach to support business improvement through enhanced value.

OVERVIEW OF VALUE STREAM MAPPING

Value stream mapping (VSM) is a flow-charting method created in the Toyota Production System (TPS) to document an entire process (of a company or a department) on a single sheet of paper to encourage dialogue and understand the process better (Cudney, 2010). The first step is to create a current state map of how value presently flows through a process. Then, utilizing Lean principles, the team visualizes a better state for how value should flow optimally through the process, which is the future state value stream map. Kaizen activities, which are events to overcome performance deficiencies in the current state, allow the company to reach the future state, identified for implementation on the current state map (Cudney, 2013). The future state map illustrates the ideal state after implementing kaizen changes and represents how the processes should flow (Cudney, Furterer, & Dietrich, 2013). Figure 8.1 provides the overall steps for VSM.

VSM captures the flow of a product from the point that raw material enters the process to the moment the customer receives the final product. A VSM includes all value-added and non-value-added activities accepted as necessary to produce the

FIGURE 8.1 Value stream mapping steps.

 DOI: 10.1201/9780429506192-8

product (Cudney, 2013). Organizations can apply VSM to any product or service; therefore, it is finding widespread applications in non-manufacturing processes, such as designing a product, and in business processes, such as purchasing, billing, and selling (Cudney, Furterer, & Dietrich, 2013).

Value stream mapping comprises all the value-added and non-value-added activities required to manufacture a product. The essential process flow can include bringing a product from raw materials through delivery to the customer or designing a product from concept to production (Cudney, Furterer, & Dietrich, 2013). A value-adding activity is any activity that transforms raw materials to meet customers' requirements. Non-value-adding activities take time, resources, or space but do not add value to the product or service (Hundal et al., 2022). A customer is not willing to pay for non-value-adding activities. Typically, non-value-adding activities account for approximately 95% of process time and only 5% of the time spent adding value to the product or service (Cudney, Furterer, & Dietrich, 2013).

Value stream mapping also provides a common platform for applying various Lean principles and tools and allows an organization to create an integrated plan for implementation. Further, because the VSM captures delays caused by material and information flow on the same page, it is possible to tackle both, creating an optimized process of both information and material flow (Cudney, Furterer, & Dietrich, 2013).

BENEFITS OF VALUE STREAM MAPPING

Value stream mapping, used as a tool, provides several benefits. A primary benefit is enabling people to see an entire process systematically. The flow of the entire process becomes apparent, making the waste sources in the value stream more evident. With a clear process flow and identified sources of waste, decisions needed to improve the flow emerge.

Another significant benefit to VSM is that it utilizes a format that provides a common language for the process, which ties together Lean concepts and techniques. VSM is also the only tool that currently provides a link between information and material flow and is conducive to any environment that contains a process required to meet a desired objective.

As mentioned at the beginning of this chapter, VSM stems from the Toyota Production System (TPS) method called "Material and Information Flow Mapping." TPS used this method more as a means of communication by individuals learning through hands-on experience, used to illustrate the current and future states of a process to implement Lean systems. The focus at Toyota is to establish a flow, eliminate muda (the Japanese word for waste), and add value. Toyota teaches three flows in manufacturing:

1. including the flow of material,
2. the flow of information, and
3. the flow of people and processes.

Two of these three, material and information flow, form the basis of VSM.

INTEGRATING SUSTAINABILITY INTO VALUE STREAM MAPPING

The principle of Lean to manage the expenditure of resources is also shared with Sustainability. The integrated VSM may be called differently, depending upon the organizational context and Lean and Green strategy. These include some version of an enhanced VSM model utilizing environmental-related measures (Garza-Reyes et al., 2018). Environmental objectives are to improve productivity in using natural resources while reducing environmental impact through activity assessment of inputs and outputs (EPA, 2022). Inputs, such as energy, and outputs, such as emissions, support an integrated VSM approach. VSM goals for environmental purposes could include (1) energy, (2) water, (3) materials, (4) garbage, (5) transportation, (6) emissions, and (7) biodiversity (Garza-Reyes et al., 2018). Adopting an integrated Lean and Green VSM approach is a more holistic assessment of the product life cycle.

Integrating Green and Lean in VSM takes the principles of Lean waste through the perspective of wasteful resource consumption (EPA, 2022). For example, the Norwegian dairy industry focused on reducing material usage in production by creating a value stream map to integrate Lean and Sustainability thinking (Hundal, 2022). The results were improved product yield, the Lean premise, improving Sustainability by raw material reduction (Hundal, 2022).

Typically, environmental value focuses on reducing waste that harms the environment, thus protecting the environment (EPA, 2022). Increasingly, incorporating sustainable production into Lean practice requires a mindset of a circular economic approach, extending product life and reducing waste. As stated above, including energy in the VSM is a more sustainable industrial position for conservation and a reduction in wasteful production (Garza-Reyes et al., 2018). A primary qualifier of energy reduction is quantifying carbon emissions, reducing the negative Lean and Green impact of a production process. To date, the primary examples of integrating Sustainability into VSM have been in food production, where the waste streams represent a significant environmental challenge (Hundal, 2022). Nevertheless, the environmental concerns presented in this chapter describe the fundamentals shared across industries: energy and carbon footprint.

CREATING CURRENT STATE AND FUTURE STATE MAPS

The goal of Lean is to get one process to make only what the following process needs, when it needs it, by linking the processes from raw material to the final customer (Cudney, Furterer, & Dietrich, 2013). By implementing a future state value stream, value stream mapping aims to identify and eliminate waste sources. The customer defines value as a product delivered at the right time, with the defined specifications, and at the right price (Cudney, 2010). The initial step is to map the current process in a brainstorming process. This step is often more effective when involving several cross-functional stakeholders with varying opinions and perspectives. Taking an initial Gemba walk is generally helpful in documenting the process and kick-starting creative ideas. While evaluating the current state of a process, the team may typically identify several improvements, including cellular manufacturing, one-piece flow, and single-minute exchange of dies (Chapter 13) through kaizen events whenever possible (Cudney, 2010). The current state map's purpose is to represent the production situation by drawing the material and information flows. For the current state map, the team should calculate the takt time and focus on leveling the demand upstream from the customer. It is helpful to create a supermarket downstream from each facility and implement cells in each facility to create flow and pull (Cudney, 2010). If the team is having difficulty mapping the process flow, a helpful tip is to start at the customer, in the upper right portion of the value stream map, and detail the process moving upstream to define the process clearly. Next, a team should map the improved process to represent the desired future state. The first pass of implementing a future state value stream should ignore the inherent waste from product design, current processing machinery, and the location of some activities. These changes may require considerable work and will not be changed quickly through kaizen (Cudney, 2010). The team should address these features in later iterations of future state VSM. Remember that the first future state mapping activity will not be the last. Organizations should continue to expand upon their future state mapping through iterative activities held periodically (Cudney, 2010). Figure 8.2 provides common value stream mapping symbols as well as primary environmental symbols.

Figure 8.3 provides an example of a hospital's value stream map for emergency services. It shows the patient coming into the hospital. Patients go through the same activities until the hospitalist or a physician determines whether the patient should be admitted to the hospital as an inpatient or discharged from the emergency department (ED). A nurse triages and registers the patient. A physician treats, orders tests, and then diagnoses the patient. Finally, the physician determines a disposition for the patient. If admitted to the hospital, a hospital transporter moves and admits the patient to an inpatient floor or unit. If discharged, after disposition, a nurse discharges the patient from the hospital. The value stream map shows the timeline of the value activities versus the wait time between the value activities and the total time spent within the value system. There were multiple areas of opportunity identified, as shown by the kaizen bursts on the VSM, in the area of testing/diagnosing and moving the patient into the admitting process for inpatient admissions (Furterer, 2018).

STEPS OF VALUE STREAM MAPPING

In value stream mapping, it is essential to walk the process with a process map of how the current process works. Walk a product's production path from beginning to end, and draw a visual representation of every transportation, storage, and overall production process in the material and information flows. When starting, it is

Type	Symbol	Description
Processes	Process	Process box
	Shared	Shared process box
	Supplier	Supplier
	Customer	Customer
	C/T= C/O= # Shifts = Takt =	Databox
		Data/database
		Operator
Inventory	I	Inventory box
	S	Safety stock
	– FIFO →	First in first out (FIFO) sequencing
		Supermarket
		Buffer or safety stock
Material Flow		Push arrow

FIGURE 8.2 Value stream mapping icons.

(Continued)

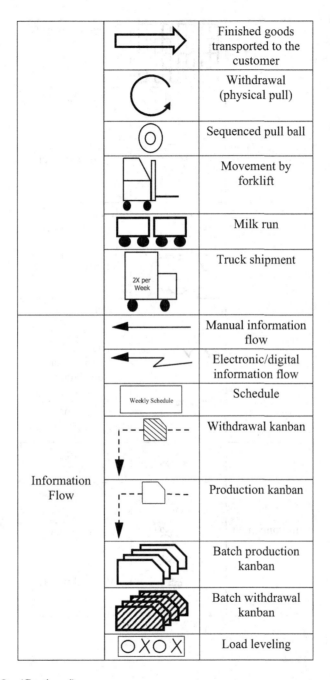

		Finished goods transported to the customer
		Withdrawal (physical pull)
		Sequenced pull ball
		Movement by forklift
		Milk run
	2X per Week	Truck shipment
Information Flow		Manual information flow
		Electronic/digital information flow
	Weekly Schedule	Schedule
		Withdrawal kanban
		Production kanban
		Batch production kanban
		Batch withdrawal kanban
	O X O X	Load leveling

FIGURE 8.2   (Continued)

(Continued)

	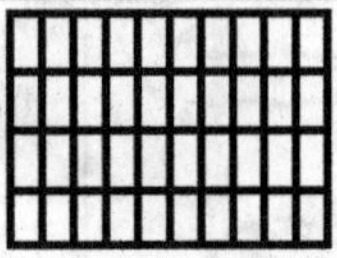	Leveling board
	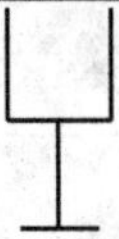	Kanban post
		Signal kanban
Other symbols	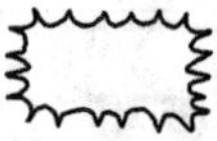	Kaizen lightening burst (waste)
	 Idea	Improvement idea
	 Q	Quality problem
		Go see the production scheduling or manual observation
		Document
Environmental	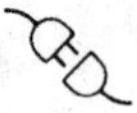	Energy consumption
		Water consumption
		Emissions (carbon)
		Material (waste)

FIGURE 8.2   (Continued)

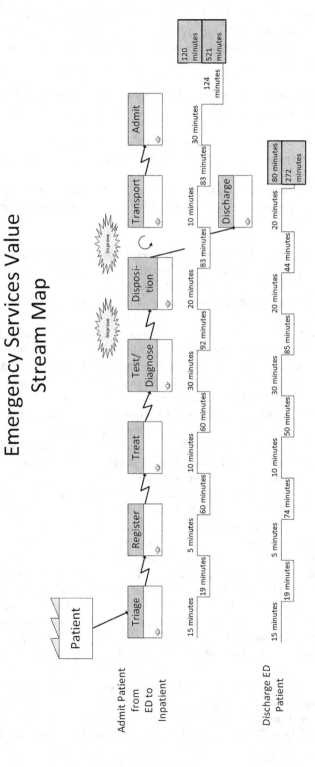

FIGURE 8.3 Value stream map for emergency services in a hospital.

preferable to hand draw/sketch a VSM first when walking a product's production path. Once everyone agrees on the appropriate process, then formally draw, using the VSM icons, a future state map of how value should flow. The main steps to value stream mapping are:

1. Select the product family. The product family shares similar process steps and equipment in production. Start with the most customer-critical product for VSM.
2. Define the boundaries. Focus on the VSM by limiting the scope of the map. Identify the initial starting and ending points to bound the process for analysis.
3. Define the value. Determine the problem for the value stream from the customers' perspective. By identifying the waste defined by the Lean and Green strategy, organizations can address customer/consumer concerns before mapping.
4. Walk the process. Go to the Gemba. The team should perform the VSM walk at the process to directly experience to outline flows (e.g., material, information) required for production and identifying tasks. Sometimes this is accomplished by starting in reverse, with the customer. Fill in gaps by multiple iterations.
5. Gather data. Identify the resources through consumption for each task and flow for overall process performance. Collect process data on the Gemba walk. As the team walks the process, they should collect data on the process to add to the map. Make sure to differentiate between human and machine efforts. During the assessment, answer a few fundamental questions: (1) How long does each step take? (2) What is the queue time between each step? (3) What are the inventory levels? (4) What are scrap and rework rates? While these are conventional to VSM, the team should differentiate the inputs and outputs for each task for Lean and Green integration. For instance, conventional VSM overlooks environmental wastes, such as energy and water consumption used in excess in each task, with pollutants and material waste released as outputs to the environment. During this step, the team needs to recognize where environmental impacts occur in a product line and quantify Lean and Green wastes. These could result in finding efficiencies and cutting waste. Add process data to the data boxes to the VSM.
6. Create the current state map. Understand how the process currently operates. Create a current state map by walking the flow and including the process owners or those who do the work. Clarify misconceptions to come up with a shared understanding of the current state. Collect the data and information by "walking the flow" and interviewing the people who perform the task. While each map is slightly different, utilize a VSM template based on context.
7. Analyze current conditions. Identify value-added and wastes. VSM enables the visualization of an entire process as a holistic set of operations rather than as a disjointed material movement through separate and discrete operation steps. Therefore, VSM supports interaction among operators in

visualizing entire process improvement rather than seeking only local optimization for specific operations. Integration of Lean and Green should support a sustainable growth strategy. In this analysis, the eight wastes become more evident. Examples from Chapter 5 include defects, overproduction, waiting, non-utilized resources/talent, transportation, inventory, motion, and excess processing.

8. Visualize the ideal state. Reconfigure the process to eliminate waste and maximize value. The future-state map should portray the improvements that a process value stream can attain by incorporating the elimination of wastes and Lean and Green strategies formulated in the previous step. Design for Lean flow: takt time improvements, reduction/elimination of bottlenecks, inventory reduction/elimination, and other improvements noted from the previous step.

9. Develop and track action plans. Observe and record the flow of orders, materials, and information for a product family. Then identify non-value-added activities. It is essential to visualize areas of waste and areas that generate value. In value stream mapping, it is crucial to understand the takt time. Based on the takt time, focusing on the future state map is on developing continuous flow, sending the schedule to only one process, leveling the production mix evenly, and producing every part daily.

FUTURE STATE MAPS

In developing future state maps, it is critical to revisit the five Lean fundamentals developed by Womack and Jones (2003):

1. Specify value: The customer defines value in terms of specific products and services

2. Identify the value stream: Map out all end-to-end linked actions, processes, and functions necessary for transforming inputs into outputs to identify and eliminate waste.

3. Make value flow continuously: Having eliminated waste, make the remaining value-creating steps flow.

4. Let customers pull value: Customer's pull cascades back to the lowest level supplier, enabling just-in-time production.

5. Pursue perfection: Pursue a continuous process of improvement, striving for perfection.

The goal is to make value flow. To create flow, focus on the product or service flowing through the process. It is essential not to be limited by organizational or functional boundaries. In addition, the team should rethink work practices and the tools used to get the job done by reducing or eliminating bottlenecks and stoppages. Finally, the team should focus on controlling the process.

Part of determining and achieving the future state is locating the pacemaker. The pacemaker is the point in the process where the customer's order enters the process, as shown in Figure 8.4. The location of the decision point is governed by customer

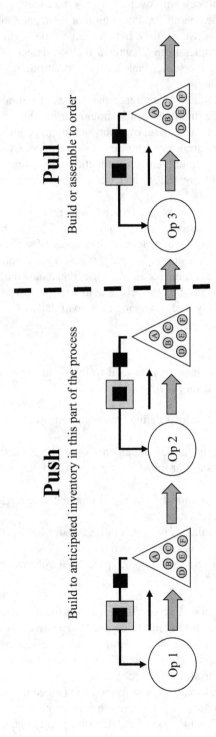

FIGURE 8.4 Pacemaker process.

expected response time and build time. If the response time is very long, the process does not need any WIP inventory and can have a complete build-to-order. By cutting waste, the team should be able to move the decision point upstream.

MACRO VALUE STREAM MAPPING

VSMs should extend beyond a single facility in a Lean enterprise. Macro value stream maps extend beyond single-level locations to the supply chain vital to sustainable goals and circular economic activity. Macro value stream maps identify who does what across the supply chain to systematically capture the product life cycle. For example, purchased materials are the process's single most significant cost driver. Finally, costs from downstream activities can negate any internal cost savings realized from process improvements. The organization uses this information for major asset reconfigurations impacting the entire supply chain. A current state macro VSM should focus on a product or partner important to the business and include practical limits. The team should draw the current state by mapping the facility closest to the customer and then work backward to create the map. The team should collect data for each activity just as in the process or plant-level value stream map. Once VSM initiatives have gained success within companies, it is essential to transplant VSM efforts across a single company and eventually beyond the company walls. Known as an "extended value stream map" (EVSM) (Womack & Jones, 2003), value stream mapping should eventually engage multiple sites and suppliers up and downstream from the targeted facility. This transparency and partnership among suppliers enable the organization to conduct numerous mapping activities among several companies, all working together to produce a good or service. Garza-Reyes et al. (2018) describe the conditions for an extended value stream mapping effort.

CONCLUSIONS

As one of the powerful tools of the Lean journey, the value stream map helps the practitioner to visualize the information and material flow in mapping the value stream. The steps in creating a value stream map start with how the current value stream operates for improvement in managing the process end to end, removing muda from the system. Integrating sustainable principles into the value stream requires an additional waste assessment from the production process, including energy expenditures. A future state of the value stream can then be created for the holistic evaluation from a Lean and Green perspective to improve sustainable business performance.

REFERENCES

Cudney, E. (2010). *Using Hoshin Kanri to improve the value stream*. New York, NY: Productivity Press.
Cudney, E. (2013). Value stream mapping: Hoshin planning at Carjo manufacturing. In D. Kudernatsch (Ed.), *Hoshin Kanri: Enterprise strategy implementation of lean management tools* (pp. 197–210). Stuttgart, Germany: Schäffer-Poeschl.
Cudney, E., Furterer, S., & Dietrich, D. (2013). *Lean systems: Applications and case studies in manufacturing, service, and healthcare*. New York, NY: CRC Press.

EPA (2022). Lean and clean value stream mapping. Retrieved from: https://www.epa.gov/e3

Furterer, S. L. (2018). Applying Lean Six Sigma methods to reduce length of stay in a hospital's emergency department. *Quality Engineering*, *30*(3), 389–404. DOI: 10.1080/08982112.2018.1464657

Garza-Reyes, J., Torres, R., Govindan, K., Cherrafi, A., & Ramanathan, U. (2018). A PDCA-based approach to environmental value stream mapping (e-VSM). *Journal of Cleaner Production*, *180*, 335–348.

Hundal, G. (2022). Exploring Lean & Green internet of things (IoT) wireless sensors framework for the adoption of precision agriculture practices among Indiana row-crop producers. [Doctoral dissertation, Purdue University].

Hundal, G., Thiyagarajan, S., Alduraibi, M., Laux, C., Furterer, S., Cudney, E., & Antony, J. (2022). The impact of Lean Six Sigma practices on supply chain resilience during COVID-19 disruption: A conceptual framework. *Total Quality Management & Business Excellence*, *33*(15–16), 1913–1931.

Womack, J., & Jones, D. (2003). *Lean thinking: Banish waste and create wealth in your corporation*. New York, NY: Simon & Schuster.

9 Using a Lean Sustainability Lens for Business Process Mapping

INTRODUCTION

Business process mapping is essential to ensuring the Sustainability of processes and systems and incorporating ideas for integrating Sustainability into business process mapping methods. The Strategic Business Process Architecture model developed by Furterer (2022) uses a foundation for creating a Lean Sustainable system view of the organization. The model incorporates value stream mapping, business function decomposition, and process architecture mapping into a model for Lean Sustainability. The process and Sustainability metrics model integrate Sustainability metrics collected at the process level. This integration provides numerous benefits to business process mapping and integrating Sustainability into the organization's continuous improvement initiatives.

The value system and business process metamodels derive from the Strategic Business Process Architecture models. Organizations can use the integrated model as the basis of business process modeling and the design of sustainable business process maps. These process maps are integrated with value stream maps and business functions to provide documentation and connectivity across the value stream and the organization's Lean program initiatives. This chapter provides examples of how organizations may use the models to integrate value stream maps, business function decomposition, and process architecture maps.

OVERVIEW OF BUSINESS PROCESS MAPPING

The value system and business process models provide an understanding of how a business provides products or services to its customers. Chapter 8 details value stream mapping, a specific process mapping type. The value system and process models ensure that organizations meet their strategic tactics and provide value to satisfy the customers across all defined segments. This chapter first describes the value system and how the value system map identifies the high-level business functions that consist of the value stream activities. Continuous improvement teams use business functions to identify the business processes, which contain work activities within the business process maps. Then the chapter discusses the value system, business function, and business process models.

DOI: 10.1201/9780429506192-9

BENEFITS OF BUSINESS PROCESS MAPPING

A process map helps continuous improvement teams document, understand, and gain agreement on a process. Organizations can use the process map to document the current or future state processes to designate the process after improvement. A typical process map uses rectangles to represent an activity or task, diamonds to represent decisions, and ovals or circles to connect to an activity on the same or another page. Flow usually moves from left to right and top to bottom. Sometimes swim lanes or rows of activities are set between boundary lines and represent activities performed by the same roles or departments. Process maps help process owners understand the work tasks, how all processes transform inputs into outputs, how small processes combine to form more extensive processes, and how processes are connected and interdependent. They help process owners understand a systems view of processes. Process maps also help process owners see how their work affects others, how other roles affect their work, how even minor improvements make a difference, and how process improvement requires communication and teamwork. Process maps are also great tools to train process owners on the process. Organizations can use a process map to generate information systems requirements and develop an information model such as a class diagram.

INTEGRATING SUSTAINABILITY INTO BUSINESS PROCESS MAPPING

Business process mapping enables continuous improvement teams to document and understand any process. The Sustainability aspects are integrated quite seamlessly within business process mapping. Organizations can map specific Sustainability processes using the same techniques discussed in the rest of this chapter. The value system and process metamodels provide a systems view and create the connectivity between the value system through the high-level activities of the value stream map (discussed in detail in Chapter 8). The business function decomposition model provides a more detailed view of the business functions, with the integration of the detailed process maps that enable continuous improvement of processes. The methodology adds specific Sustainability requirements related to the processes into the process metamodel. Figure 9.1 provides an example of a process metamodel. Sustainability requirements help ensure that the organization considers them as they relate to their processes. Sustainability requirements could include elements related to the following:

- Waste disposal,
- Recycling,
- Technology maintenance, upkeep, retirement, and disposal,
- Use and disposal of materials, hazardous waste, chemicals, and greenhouse gases,
- Environmental impact,
- Energy type, use, and management,
- Carbon footprint,

Value System and Process Meta Model

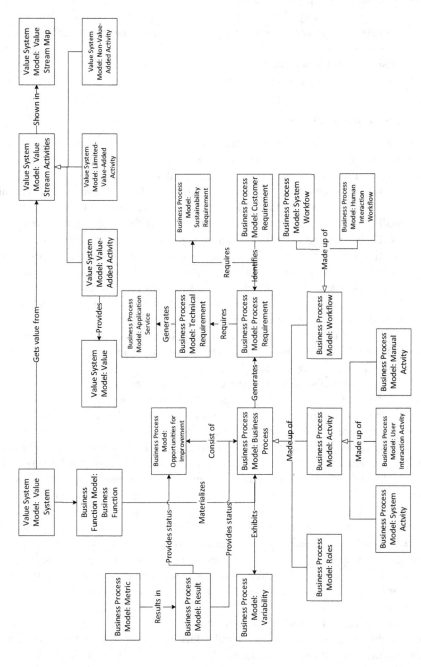

FIGURE 9.1 Value System and Process Meta Model. (adapted from Furterer, 2022)

- Economic analysis and decisions related to Sustainability,
- Societal, community, and social requirements related to Sustainability,
- Use and consumption of water,
- Business continuity planning, as regards developing processes to deal with climate change and severe weather conditions, pandemics, and natural disasters,
- Risk assessment and controls, and
- Process metrics for Sustainability.

VALUE SYSTEM AND PROCESS MODELS

The value system is an interconnected system of value chains (activities), or in a Lean system, the value system (Porter, 1985). Value systems consist of activities including value-added, limited-value, and non-value-added activities. Value activities are critical to providing value to the customer and can differentiate an organization from its competitors. Limited-value activities are necessary but are not core to providing value to customers. Instead, they support the value activities required, such as regulations and compliance requirements, or because the processes should be more efficient. The previous chapter discussed the value system activities shown in the value stream map. The activities within the value stream decompose into business functions. The activities within the value stream map are the first-level business functions in the business function decomposition model. The first-level business functions decompose into second-level functions and sometimes into third-level functions. There are typically no standard or set functions; therefore, it becomes an art learned by those who apply the business function model to determine the number of levels and names of the functions.

Process and value system knowledge are critical to generating a complete set of business functions. The business process model consists of more detailed activities than in the value stream map, as well as roles that perform the activities and a workflow or sequence of the activities. A business process activity can be performed entirely by an automated information system, a manual activity performed by a user, or a user interacting with an information system. The workflow can be performed entirely by technology, an information system, or humans interacting with information systems. The process model generates process requirements identified by the customers, which relate to technical requirements. The process requirements require Sustainability requirements, while the technical requirements require application services to achieve the technical requirements within the process. The business process generates opportunities for improvement. The business process metrics provide results that provide status for the business processes and opportunities for improvement as implemented by a continuous improvement team. Business processes also represent variability.

As discussed in the previous chapter, the macro value systems provide a broader view of the value system, perhaps broader than one service. Chapter 8 provided a value stream map showing an emergency services value stream (see Figure 8.3). Each hospital healthcare service would have its value stream as part of the value system. To further illustrate the distinction, a healthcare organization's value system could consist of value streams for providing emergency services, inpatient services, outpatient services, surgical services, women's services, supply chain services, human resources services, and infrastructure services. Some of these value streams show activities outside the hospital's boundaries, moving into the supply chain and to other facilities that send or receive patients. Figure 9.2 illustrates the value stream activities for the emergency services provider (Furterer, 2014).

There are several essential definitions for a value system model. A value system is an aggregation of the value streams that provide value to the customers. Value stream activities are the activities that provide a specific service or product line to the customer. A support activity supports the value activities in a value stream. It does not directly add value to the customer. Finally, a value activity within a value stream provides value to the customer (Furterer, 2022).

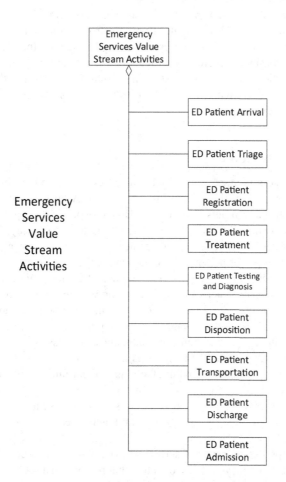

FIGURE 9.2 Emergency services value stream activities. (adapted from Furterer, 2013)

Business Function Decomposition

The business function decomposition model is used to identify business functions and the processes that comprise them. A business function consists of those operations performed in the organization. The functional decomposition diagram does not depict process flows but the hierarchical organization of functions and the processes they include. Then, the business function decomposition model is a taxonomy of business functions in that each top-level function generalizes from its lower-level functions. Traditionally, organizations use a business function decomposition model to identify the functions, which allows teams to define the processes and business systems. The business function decomposition model is related to the value stream. It helps teams capture and understand the current state structure of business functions and their relationship to business processes. A business function decomposition model also relates to the business process model through the set of business processes identified at the lowest levels of the hierarchy. At some level, business functions break down into business processes.

The conceptual dividing point is somewhat arbitrary; however, continuous improvement teams can differentiate a process from a function by the amount of activity it represents. A process represents a tangible activity that occurs within the organization. A business function is a noun–verb pairing always in that order, such as "patient registration." The business function decomposition starts with the high-level functions in the value stream. Figure 9.3 illustrates a business function decomposition for emergency services.

Business Process Model

A business process is a sequence of activities performed in coordination and in a specified sequence to achieve some intended result. A business process is a set of activities transforming inputs into outputs. Business processes typically cross traditional organizational boundaries or departments (Evans & Lindsay, 2020). A single organization or department enacts each business process, but it typically interacts with business processes performed by other organizations or departments. Activities can be performed by a person manually, without the use of technology or information systems. Individuals perform activities by interacting with technology or an information system, while some are entirely automated by technology or information systems.

A business process model has three primary purposes: communication, knowledge capture, and analysis. When using a business process model for communication, it is imperative to convey a rigorous understanding of the business process and the ability to manage personnel change. Continuous improvement teams should study the process for optimization, improvement, and transformation purposes in the analysis. Finally, teams use business process models to understand the associations of business processes and activities in knowledge-gathering (Furterer, 2022).

A business process consists of activities. Continuous improvement teams should use swim lanes to identify the roles or actors that perform that set of activities. Cross-functional hand-offs are where the process flow crosses the swim lanes, where a business process may exhibit the most variability. Understanding and controlling the

Emergency Services
Business Function Decomposition

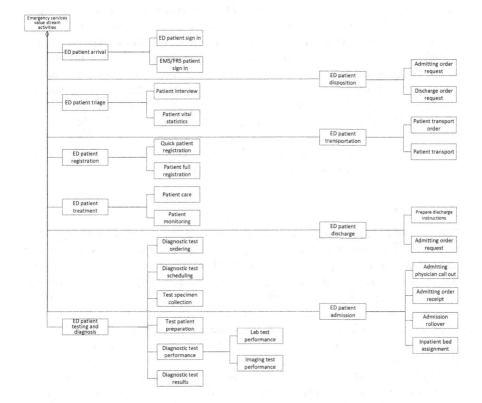

FIGURE 9.3 Emergency service business function decomposition model.

factors contributing to the variability enables the processes to provide a competitive advantage. The technical requirements identify process requirements.

In contrast, continuous improvement teams identify process requirements through different business processes. This step ensures traceability from customers' expectations to customers' requirements, the technical requirements to process requirements, and the business processes that enable process requirements.

Continuous improvement teams identify opportunities for improvement from the business process metric model results. The metrics measure business processes. The team assigns an organizational role to the processing activity. The activities of a process consist of three types depending upon how they are performed, by the system, with a user and a system interacting, and entirely manual activities (Furterer, 2022).

There are several key definitions for the business process model. First, a business process is a sequence of activities performed in coordination to achieve some intended result. A business process is a set of activities transforming inputs into outputs, while a workflow is a sequence of activities performed within a business process to meet the stated objectives. There are two kinds of workflows: system and human interaction workflows. An information system performs a system workflow; therefore, it is automated.

In contrast, a human performs a human interaction workflow by interacting with an information system or automation. An activity is a step in a process. An activity model encapsulates several activities, a grouping of activities. An information system performs a system activity and is, therefore, automated. User interaction is an activity a person performs with an information system or automation. While a manual activity is an activity, a person performs without using an information system or automation. A technical requirement is a design characteristic that describes the customer's requirements in the language of the designer or engineer. These are "how" the organization should produce a product or deliver a service to meet customer expectations (Evans & Lindsay, 2020; Cudney & Furterer, 2012). A process requirement is a process performed to meet technical requirements. An improvement opportunity is an area or idea that can be enhanced, streamlined, or made more efficient. Finally, variability is how a process may or does vary, such as a variable feature or factor (Furterer, 2022).

PROCESS ARCHITECTURE MAP

Furterer (2022) developed a process architecture map that incorporates process architecture elements, including the role that performs each activity and the information and technology used to perform the activity. There are separate lanes for the activities, roles, information, and technology used with each activity. Teams use a process architecture map as the foundational tool to document the current process, perform a Lean and waste analysis, identify improvement opportunities, and document the future process after implementing improvements. The process architecture map template allows the creation of a cover page that summarizes the high-level process steps from the value stream map to provide the connection to the system view of where this process fits within the system. A system here refers to the set of processes that interconnect to achieve a work system. The cover page also provides an inventory of the process architecture roles or process stakeholders, information, and technology.

The following section provides the steps for using the process architecture map and examples.

STEPS AND EXAMPLES OF BUSINESS PROCESS MAPPING

There are six steps to creating a process map. First, the continuous improvement team should identify the level of detail to map and document. When implementing Lean tools, the teams start with developing the value stream. The teams develop the business function decomposition model to identify which process maps are needed to document the work system.

Next, the process analyst developing the process maps should define the process boundaries for the value stream map. Continuous improvement teams should use the purpose of the process mapping activity to define a boundary, such as the goal of the particular process improvement project or Lean improvement effort. The boundary could be identified based on the kaizen blitzes from the value stream mapping effort.

In the third step, the process analyst identifies the major activities within the process, beginning with identifying the activities and sequence of those activities. In the following step, the continuous improvement team should identify the process steps

Business Functions

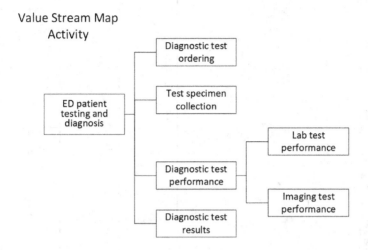

FIGURE 9.4   Value stream map activity and related business functions.

and uncover complexities using brainstorming and storyboarding techniques, where different process scenarios are generated and mapped. Next, the team arranges the steps in a time sequence and differentiates operations by identified symbols. Finally, the team validates the process map by a "walk through" of the actual process and by having other process experts review it for consistency.

Figure 9.4 provides an example value stream map for emergency department patient testing and diagnosis with the related functions from the business function decomposition.

Figure 9.5 provides an example of the process architecture map for the hospital lab emergency department. The process architecture map provides a lower level of detail that organizations can use to perform Lean and waste analyses, which leads to the generation of process improvement ideas. Chapter 10 provides several examples of Lean, value, and waste analyses. Figure 9.6 shows the cover page, which illustrates the process architecture.

METRIC MODEL

A metric model is the generalization of all models intended to measure things in the organization. Figure 9.7 illustrates a general metric model from Furterer's Strategic Business Process Architecture.

Since a metric model is a generalization, this leads to the conclusion that there must be specializations of metric models. A metric provides a quantifiable measure that organizations use to assess their performance. For example, if a metric is associated with a business process, then cycle time could be a measured aspect of the business process. Measuring a metric and collecting data provides results. A regulating organization or requiring authority may require reporting specific metrics (Furterer, 2014).

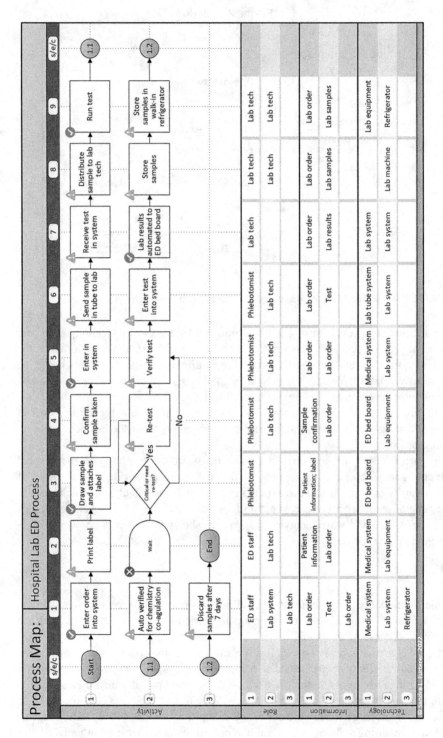

FIGURE 9.5 Process architecture map for a hospital lab emergency department process.

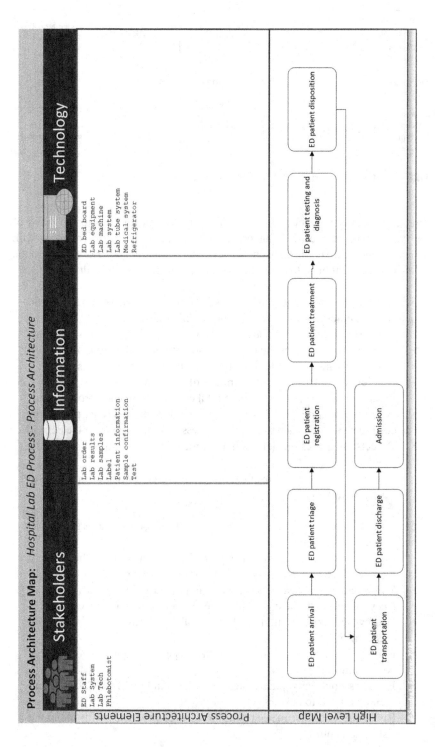

FIGURE 9.6   Cover page of process architecture for a hospital lab emergency department process.

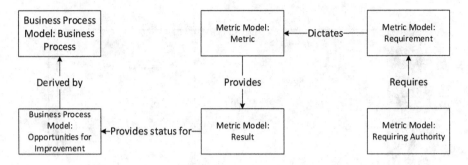

FIGURE 9.7   General metric model. (adapted from Furterer, 2014)

Furterer (2022) also developed a specialized metric model of potential types of metric types to be measured in an organization, which this book enhances with Sustainability metrics. The specialized metric model defines the types of metrics in the following categories aligned to the Baldrige Performance Criteria (Baldrige, 2022):

- *Service line metrics*. These metrics assess the success, volume, growth, quality, and outcomes of the service or product lines.
- *Process metrics*. These are metrics used to measure the processes, such as:
  - Throughput: measures the capacity and volume of the organization.
  - Cycle time: measures the time to move one unit through the system.
  - Efficiency: measures the efficient use of resources.
  - Process times: measures the time it takes to perform each process step.
  - Wait times and delays: measures the time that the unit (e.g., product or customer) waits at each step of the process and the reasons for the delays.
  - Defects: measures the defects in the process to assess the quality of the processes.
  - Process metrics for Sustainability: Measures processes related to Sustainability goals.

- *Sustainability metrics*. These are metrics used to assess if the organization and processes are green, such as:
  - Carbon footprint: measures the effect of an organization on the environment related to greenhouse gases and carbon-related metals and minerals.
  - Waste reduction: measures the reduction in waste in landfills.
  - Recycling of materials: measures the amount of materials recycled.
  - Wastewater consumption and disposal: measures the impact on wastewater.
  - Energy consumption: measures the type and amount of energy consumption.
  - Business continuity plans: measures the number of processes documented related to business continuity.
  - Risks and controls: measure the percent of processes with identified risks and controls.

- *Leadership metrics*. These are metrics used to measure leadership effectiveness, such as:
  - Strategic initiatives metrics: measures how well an organization meets its strategic goals.
  - Governance metrics: measures the effectiveness of the organization's governance or system of management.
  - Societal metrics: measures the ability of the organization to meet the community and societal needs.
  - Operational initiatives metrics: measures how well the organization meets its operational goals.
  - Compliance metrics: measures whether the organization complies with rules, regulations, and accreditation requirements.
  - Ethics metrics: measure whether the organization is adhering to ethics and ethical decisions. These metrics can also include alignment with organizational core values.
  - Sustainability leadership metrics: measures metrics related to achieving Sustainability goals.

- *Customer metrics*. These are metrics used to measure customer-related metrics, such as:
  - Customer satisfaction: measures customer satisfaction, usually based on survey questions.
  - Quality: measures the quality indicators of the processes. Organizations also include these within the process metrics.
  - Safety: measures the safety of the processes, workforce, and environment.

- *Financial metrics*. These are the traditional financial measures to assess the organization's financial viability.

- *Workforce metrics*. These are measures of the organization's development, engagement, and satisfaction such as:
  - Workforce development metrics: measures how effectively the workforce can meet expected process competencies.
  - Workforce satisfaction metrics: measures the level of the associates' satisfaction, usually based on a survey.
  - Engagement metrics: measures the degree to which the organization is engaged in the mission and meeting the organizational goals.
  - Productivity: measures how productive the organization's resources are in meeting the needs of the organization.
  - Workforce climate: measures the culture and climate of the organization.

- *Market metrics*. These assess the market share and growth of the organization. Organizations often include these in the service line metrics.

Figure 9.8 illustrates the specialized metric metamodel.

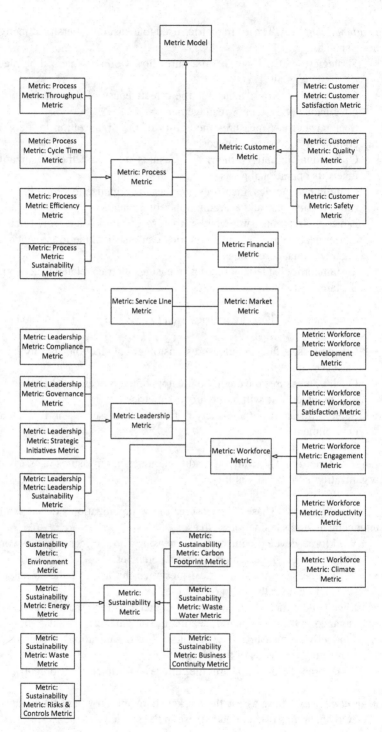

FIGURE 9.8 Specialized metric model.

CONCLUSION

This chapter covered the integration of the value system with the business functions, process maps, and metrics. The chapter also discussed the integration of Sustainability into these models and tools through example metrics. The next chapter will cover Lean analysis, which includes value and waste analysis, and extends nicely from the process architecture map tool to identify inefficiency and waste in processes.

REFERENCES

Baldrige Excellence Framework (2022). https://www.nist.gov/baldrige/publications/baldrige-excellence-framework. Accessed: 1/22/2023.

Cudney, E., & Furterer, S. (2012). *Design for Six Sigma in product and service development: Applications and case studies*. New York, NY: CRC Press.

Evans, J., & Lindsay, W. (2020). *Managing for quality and performance excellence* (11th Edition). Independence, KY: Cengage Press.

Furterer, S. (2013). *Lean Six Sigma Case Studies in the Healthcare Enterprise*. New York, NY: Springer.

Furterer, S. (2014). *Lean Six Sigma case studies in the healthcare enterprise*. London, UK: Springer.

Furterer, S. (2022). *Systems engineering holistic life cycle architecture modeling and design with real-world applications*. Boca Raton, FL: CRC Press.

Porter, V. C. M. . What Is Value Chain. 1985 Available online: http://www.dspmuranchi.ac.in/pdf/Blog/What%20is%20the%20 First%20Mover%20Advantage.pdf (accessed on 22 August 2023).

10 Analyzing Lean, Value, and Waste for Sustainable Continuous Improvement

INTRODUCTION

This chapter provides an overview of Lean analysis, which incorporates value and waste analysis. Teams can use the process architecture map developed by Furterer (2022) to perform the Lean, value, and waste analyses based on the activities within the process map. This chapter also discusses the integration with Lean Sustainability.

LEAN ANALYSIS

Lean analysis consists of an integrated value and waste analysis, leveraged within the context of the process architecture map. This chapter describes Lean and waste analysis with an example from the lab hospital process map shown in Chapter 9.

VALUE ANALYSIS

Value analysis categorizes each activity on the process maps as either value-added, limited-value-added, or non-value-added activities. The symbols on the process architecture map to designate these categories are value added (green check mark circle), limited value (yellow triangle with an exclamation point), and non-value added (red X circle). Figure 10.1 provides an example. Figure 10.2 also illustrates the symbols on the sample process architecture map. In traditional applications from manufacturing processes, where the value analysis tool originated, the activities are either value-added or non-value-added.

Once organizations adopt value analysis to improve their service and administrative processes, the next concept to introduce is a limited value-added activity. The value-added activity is one that, from a customer perspective, helps create the end product or service. For the emergency services example, this activity moves the patients through the emergency department's processes and would be something the customer would be "willing to pay for" or value. Limited value-added activities do not add value to the process or progress quickly without defects or delays. However, they are necessary to perform due to either regulatory reasons or the current process

DOI: 10.1201/9780429506192-10

Process Architecture Map Symbol		Value Analysis Meaning
Green check mark circle	✓	Value-added activity
Yellow triangle with an exclamation point	⚠	Limited-value-added activity
Red X circle	✗	Non-value-added activity

FIGURE 10.1 Value analysis symbols and meaning from the process architecture map.

design. For example, patients probably do not care whether the nurse records their vitals in the medical record or whether a staff member registers them in the system. Patients want to be treated and provided a disposition as to their illness and get better. However, a hospital would violate regulations that ensure the privacy of the patient's medical information, or they could only bill the patient for services if registered in the emergency department. Thus, the non-value-added activities, which often do not add value to the process, and ones the customer would not want to pay for, often include delays or defects that do not progress the work (in this case, patient) success-fully through the process. In this example, these non-value-added activities can include waiting for the physician to see the patient, waiting for a test, or running the wrong test.

In the example of the emergency services processes, the team designated each step of the lab process after the team used the process architecture map to develop the detailed process maps. The team categorized the steps into one of the three categories of value: value-added (VA), limited-value-added (LVA), or non-value-added (NVA). The percent of value-added activities versus non-value-added and limited-value activities is calculated and summarized in Figure 10.3 for the hospital lab in the emergency department. The percent of value-added activities compared to all activi-ties is 28%. Sixty-seven percent of the activities on the process maps were limited-value-added, and almost 6% were non-value-added, as shown in Figure 10.4. The limited-value activities include printing the label, confirming the sample, sending the sample in the tube to the lab, receiving the test in the system, distributing the sample to the lab tech, auto-verifying the test, re-testing and verifying the test, entering the test manually into the system, storing samples and then discarding them after seven days. The non-value-added activity waits for the test to run and the results. The value-added activities are entering the lab order into the system, drawing the sample, attaching the label, entering the lab into the system, running the test, and presenting the results from the lab system to the bed board system in the emergency department in an automated fashion. These all add value by getting the labs ordered, run, and the results provided.

Continuous improvement teams may use value stream mapping (VSM) to assess the value-added activities compared to the limited-value and non-value-added

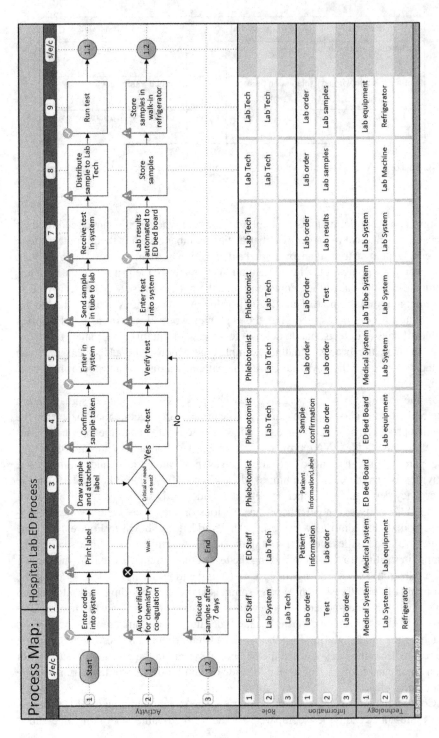

FIGURE 10.2 Process architecture map for a hospital lab emergency department process.

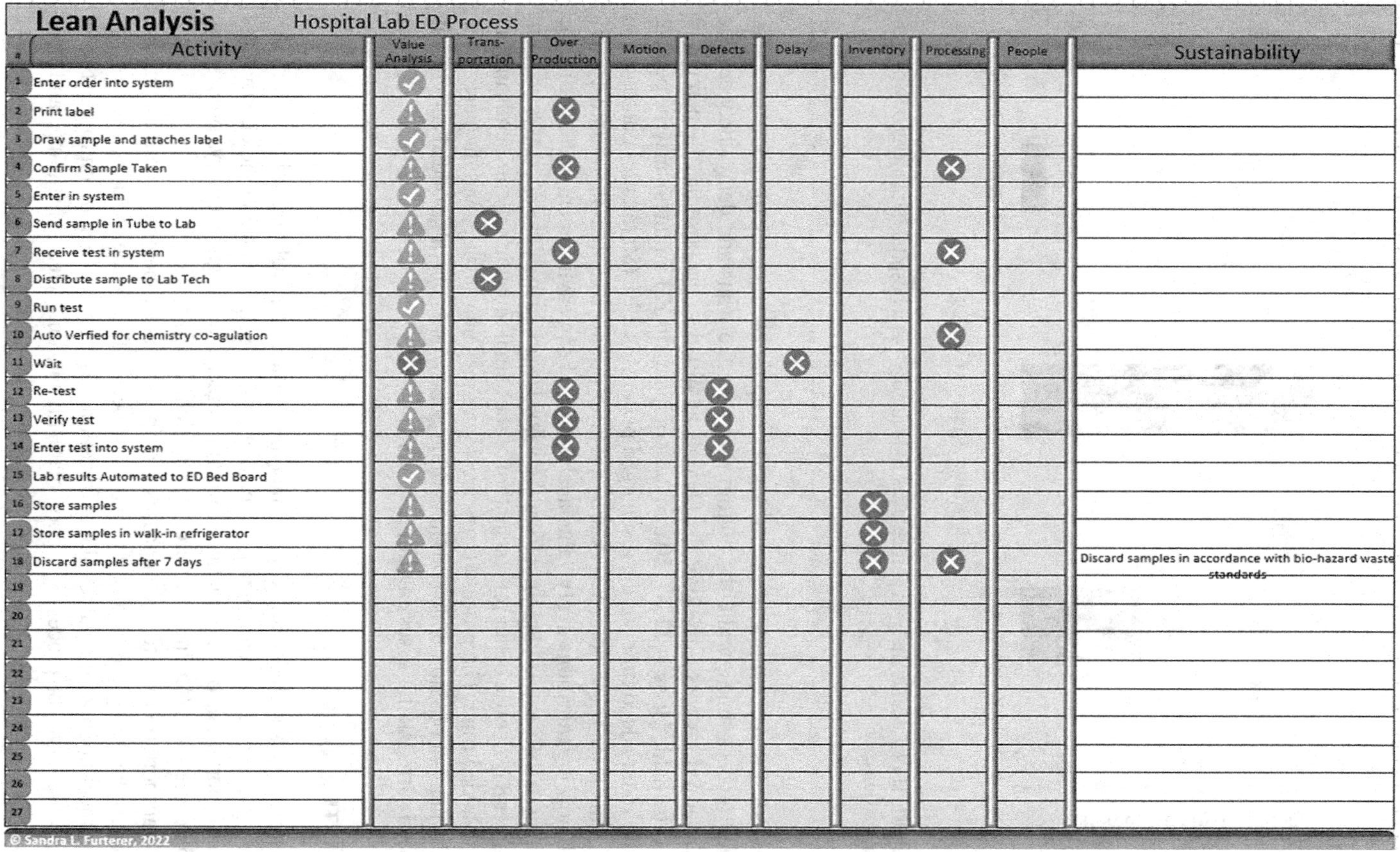

#	Activity	Value Analysis	Trans-portation	Over Production	Motion	Defects	Delay	Inventory	Processing	People	Sustainability
1	Enter order into system	✓									
2	Print label	◁									
3	Draw sample and attaches label	✓		✕					✕		
4	Confirm Sample Taken	◁		✕							
5	Enter in system	✓									
6	Send sample in Tube to Lab	◁	✕								
7	Receive test in system	◁		✕					✕		
8	Distribute sample to Lab Tech	✓	✕						✕		
9	Run test	◁									
10	Auto Verified for chemistry co-agulation	✕									
11	Wait	◁					✕				
12	Re-test	◁		✕		✕					
13	Verify test	◁		✕		✕					
14	Enter test into system	◁		✕		✕					
15	Lab results Automated to ED Bed Board	✓						✕			
16	Store samples	◁						✕			
17	Store samples in walk-in refrigerator	◁						✕	✕		
18	Discard samples after 7 days										Discard samples in accordance with bio-hazard waste standards

Lean Analysis — Hospital Lab ED Process

© Sandra L. Furterer, 2022

FIGURE 10.3 Lean analysis with value analysis and waste analysis for a hospital lab emergency department process.

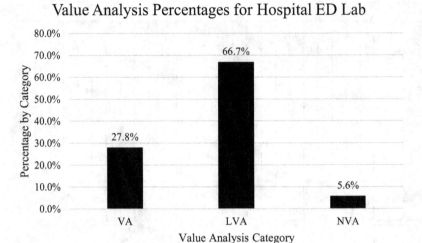

FIGURE 10.4   Value analysis percentages by category for a hospital lab emergency department process.

activities. For the timeline within the VSM in Figure 10.5, the top times are the value-added process times, while the bottom times are the waits and delays between the value-added process times. For the patients admitted to the hospital, the percent of the value-added time is 23% (120 minutes compared to 521 minutes), and the percent of the value-added time for the discharged patients is 29% (80 minutes compared to 272 minutes). These percentages are shown in Figure 10.5 and align more closely with how organizations apply value analysis in a Lean environment. Calculating the percent of the value-added time from the value stream map of emergency services in Chapter 8 is likely a better representation of the actual time the patient spends in non-value-added time. The process times are sometimes unavailable, and the percentage of the number of value-added, limited-value-added, and non-value-added activities is a good surrogate for assessing improvement.

WASTE ANALYSIS

Waste analysis includes identifying the type of waste for each limited-value or non-value-added activity. Organizations may categorize activities using the eight wastes of transportation, overproduction, motion, defects, waiting, inventory, processing, and people skills (Cudney, Furterer, & Dietrich, 2013).

Transportation waste encompasses moving products, materials, and documents, among other things, manually through the process. This waste includes any material movement not part of a value-added operation. Root causes include multiple storage locations, large lot processing, poor plant layout, unleveled scheduling, and poor workplace organization. An example is moving the patient to the X-ray room instead of bringing the X-ray machine to the patient.

Emergency Services Value Stream Map

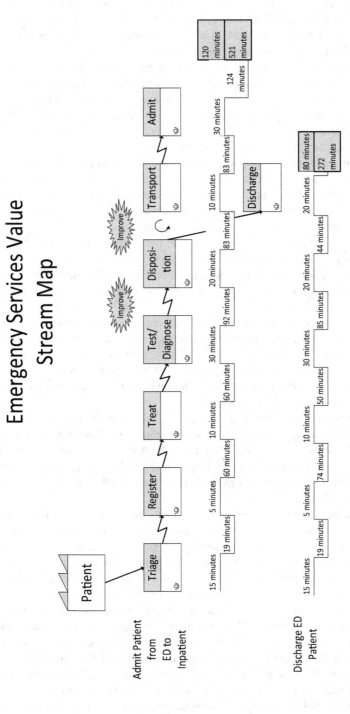

FIGURE 10.5 Value stream map for emergency services in a hospital.

Overproduction waste stems from producing more products or services than required or faster than needed to achieve the process goals. Root causes of overproduction include incapable processes, long changeovers, just-in-case logic, insufficient preventive maintenance, and lack of level schedules. An example is giving the patient an X-ray and CT scan when an ultrasound exam would do.

The waste of motion represents smaller motions within a person's workplace. This waste includes any movement of people or machines that does not add value to the product or service. Root causes include poor workplace organization, poor plant layout, and inconsistent work methods. An example is needing to turn away from the patient multiple times to type into the medical record on the computer table.

Defects are any failure to meet the specifications or requirements of the product or service. Defects require inspecting or repairing a product or service to fulfill the customer's requirements. Root causes of defects include poor process control, insufficient preventive maintenance, lack of training, and inadequate tools or equipment. An example is a person misdiagnosed with a urinary tract infection because the physician misreads the results.

Waiting is any delay in the process before performing the next step. Idle time is when people wait on machines or wait on people. Root causes include unbalanced workloads, unplanned downtime, long changeovers, insufficient preventive maintenance, and quality problems. An example is waiting for the phlebotomist to take a blood sample for lab tests.

Inventory waste includes storing materials, products, information, and paperwork in excess of the customer's just-in-time demand. Root causes include incapable processes, incapable suppliers, unleveled schedules, poor communication, long changeovers, insufficient preventive maintenance, and low uptime. An example is storing extra linens in the patient's room that the hospital must clean after the patient leaves, even if the patient did not use the linens.

Processing waste is any non-value or limited-value activity not identified as another type of waste. This waste includes human or machine effort, which adds no value (only cost) to the product or service. Root causes include product changes without process changes, just-in-case logic, undefined or unclear customer requirements, and lack of training. An example is needing to help the patient sign into the kiosk because it is not user-friendly.

Finally, the waste from people skills is due to the organization not leveraging the skills and knowledge of people to perform or improve the process, which can include poor utilization of employees' abilities, talents, skills, and ideas. Root causes include lack of training, lack of teamwork, poor management involvement and understanding, and poor communication. An example is not including the nurses and physicians on the process improvement team to improve the process.

Figure 10.3 provides a waste analysis example for the hospital lab in the emergency response department. The wastes include transportation, overproduction, defects, delays, inventory, and processing. Two examples of waste are sending the sample to the lab via the lab tube system and moving the tube to the lab tech to process. Overproduction waste for these activities includes labeling the tubes, confirming the sample, receiving the test in the system, re-testing and verifying the test, and entering the results into the system. Although many of these activities are necessary, these steps could be streamlined or revised. Verifying the test and re-testing and entering the re-test results again into the system are all examples of defect wastes. Waiting for the test results and for the test to run is an example of delay waste. Storing samples and then discarding them are inventory wastes. Processing or over-processing waste includes confirming the sample in the tube, receiving the tube in the system, verifying the sample, and discarding the samples. Again, those activities are necessary with the current process design, especially for regulatory and identification purposes, but could be improved and streamlined. The process analysis team may select the waste type as they update the process map during the value analysis for each limited-value and non-value-added activity. The process architecture map template provides a macro program that generates the Lean analysis report, shown in Figure 10.3.

BENEFITS OF LEAN ANALYSIS

The Lean analysis is beneficial to identify activities teams can reduce or eliminate that do not add value to the process from a customer perspective. There is a synergistic relationship between the value analysis and waste analysis that identifies how the limited-value-added and non-value-added activities are inefficient and the potential root causes of these activities and wastes. Categorizing the activities by their value helps prioritize where to start improving the process, starting with non-value-added activities. These activities can be eliminated or significantly reduced by identifying and removing the root causes of these inefficiencies or incorporating technology that better automates the process. The limited-value activities can then be reduced and eliminated through the identification and removal of the root causes of the wastes and incorporating further automation. Teams can then improve value-added activities by incorporating further process improvements to reduce the time spent on these activities. Figure 10.6 illustrates this improvement prioritization strategy.

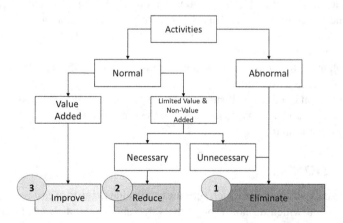

FIGURE 10.6 Value analysis prioritization and improvement strategy.

INTEGRATING SUSTAINABILITY INTO LEAN ANALYSIS

Identifying value from a customer perspective to identify value-added, limited-value, and non-value-added activities is sound from an efficiency perspective of what the customer is willing to pay. However, the analysis may only encompass part of the impact of Sustainability on the process activities. For example, an organization may take more time to dispose materials and waste because they are incorporating sustainable ways to limit their environmental impacts, such as water consumption and waste reduction. For example, in the hospital lab case, the process example used in the value and waste analyses, discarding biohazard lab samples, must be done safely. This analysis may add activities and time to the value stream and process. The Lean analysis model adds a Sustainability category to the Lean analysis report to enable the process analysis team to incorporate notes for Sustainability aligned to specific process activities (Furterer, 2009). As an example (Figure 10.3), for discarding the samples, the process analysis team could add a note, "Discard samples per bio-hazard waste standards," to ensure alignment with Sustainability requirements.

STEPS FOR LEAN ANALYSIS

The steps for performing a Lean analysis are as follows:

1) Understand the process by observing it and documenting the process.
2) Create the process map in the process architecture map or another process mapping tool.
3) Identify each activity in the process as value-added, limited-value-added, and non-value-added.
4) For each limited-value-added and non-value-added activity, identify which wastes exist for each. Multiple wastes can be associated with each activity.
5) Generate improvement ideas that eliminate abnormal activities that should not be part of the process.
6) Generate improvement ideas that can reduce the time or number of limited value or non-value-added activities that are a normal part of the process.
7) Generate improvement ideas that can improve the value-added activities through further automation, reducing lengthy approval processes and documentation of processes.
8) Implement the improvement ideas, measure, and verify that the improvements made a difference.
9) Implement control mechanisms to maintain the improved process.
10) Redo the value and waste analyses for the improved process via the process architecture map.

CONCLUSION

The Lean analysis identifies which activities add value to the process from a customer perspective and which do not through the value and waste analyses. Organizations can and should integrate Sustainability into value analysis and waste analysis. The next chapter covers the 5S and Sustainability, which can further identify waste and housekeeping issues in an organization.

REFERENCES

Cudney, E., Furterer, S. L., & Dietrich, D. (2013). *Lean systems applications and case studies in manufacturing, service, and healthcare.* Boca Raton, Florida: CRC Press.

Evans, J., & Lindsay, W. (2020). *Managing for quality and performance excellence* (11th Edition). Independence, KY: Cengage Press.

Furterer, S. (2009). Enabling enterprise Six Sigma through business process architecture modeling techniques. *Quality Management Forum, 35*(3), 7–10.

Furterer, S. (2014a). *Lean Six Sigma case studies in the healthcare enterprise.* London, UK: Springer.

Furterer, S. (2014b). Building a conceptual business process modeling architecture repository. *Journal of Management and Engineering Integration, 7*(2).

Furterer, S. (2022). *Systems engineering holistic life cycle architecture modeling and design with real-world applications.* Boca Raton, FL: CRC Press.

11 Using 5S to Reduce the Environmental Footprint

OVERVIEW OF 5S

5S is a Lean tool that improves quality and productivity by providing a clean, organized, and manageable work environment. 5S builds upon a foundation for a company to deliver high-quality products and services in the correct quantity and at the right time to satisfy and exceed customer requirements. 5S is critical to creating a work environment that focuses on quality by making it possible to increase productivity and improve quality. 5S also creates a safer and more pleasant place to work for employees (Cudney, Furterer, & Dietrich, 2013). However, current 5S methods need to address Sustainability aspects. 5S and Sustainability are closely related with respect to environment, economy, and social aspects.

Lean practices foster sustainable principles. Lean and Sustainable practices converge among common aspects such as waste reduction, shortening lead times, and embedding Sustainability in business decision-making, such as 5S. As 5S is a Lean technique, Sustainability enables organizations to conserve resources and minimize waste. Organizations can achieve substantial savings by reducing resource consumption, including materials, energy, and water, and recovery of waste materials. In addition, both methods provide organizations with an organized, safe, and healthy working environment. In addition, organizations may realize significant environmental, economic, and social gains by conserving resources and eliminating waste streams resulting from integrating Sustainability aspects into 5S. These efforts eventually help organizations shift from a linear to a circular, regenerative economy toward a waste-free economy. This chapter presents an integrated 5S and Sustainability methodology.

There are five steps in the 5S methodology, defined briefly here and discussed in more detail in the rest of this chapter. Western organizations often translate the five Japanese terms into similar English terms that also begin with the letter "S".

Step 1 *is* **Seiri** *or* **Simplify (or Sort)**. In this step, the team must determine what is necessary and unnecessary. The teams must then dispose of the unnecessary items.

Step 2 *is* **Seiton** *or* **Straighten (or Set in Order)**. The team organizes the necessary items to be easily found, used, and returned to the proper location.

Step 3 *is* **Seiso** *or* **Scrub (or Shine)**. This step not only includes cleaning the equipment but also cleaning the floor and furniture in all areas of the workplace.

Step 4 *is* **Seiketsu** *or* **Stabilize (or Standardize)**. This step aims to maintain and improve the first three steps.

Step 5 *is* **Shitsuke** *or* **Sustain**. The discipline or habit of properly maintaining the correct 5S procedures is maintained.

DOI: 10.1201/9780429506192-11

For a 5S program to be successful, management must support 5S efforts. Management must give guidance, coordination, support, and proper communication and provide a suitable environment for employees to utilize their skills properly (Agustiady & Cudney, 2022). An essential element is management's support to encourage the team to focus on value-added activities to expose problems and respond accordingly (Antony et al., 2019).

BENEFITS OF 5S

There are numerous benefits to implementing 5S principles. First, quality is improved by clearly identifying all necessary objects in an area, reducing production lead times, and enhancing Sustainability. 5S reduces waste by eliminating unnecessary steps to search for the required materials, tools, or equipment, where a specific inventory reduction is a sustainable benefit. Safety is also improved by providing a place for everything and having everything in its place (Cudney, Murray, & Pai, 2012). Maintenance is more manageable by having all the needed tools in a specific location (Agustiady & Cudney, 2015). Overall, 5S improves profitability by reducing waste, improving quality, and eliminating all unnecessary equipment.

5S also provides benefits that directly relate to the employee. Employees take more pride in their workplace when the area is clean and organized. Respect is gained from associates and customers after they visit the area. Employees also keep a more positive mental attitude working in this environment. 5S can build trust, remove frustration, and improve morale (Cudney, Furterer, & Dietrich, 2013).

INTEGRATING SUSTAINABILITY INTO 5S

It is a common practice that organizations apply 5S and implement Sustainability principles within their organizations simultaneously through separate teams and efforts. However, 5S and Sustainability have a great deal of overlap to be merged since both eventually pursue a similar goal – improving resource efficiency. As a tool, 5S enables Lean and Sustainability drivers, as shown in Figure 11.1.

On the one hand, current 5S applications do not address environmentally, economically, and socially responsible operations within organizations. Hence, the focus is usually on traditional aspects that the 5S method aims to address – organized, safe, and healthy working environments. In addition, 5S teams need to understand that much of their work aligns with Sustainability principles, most notably conserving resources such as materials. On the other hand, Sustainability teams utilize the most recent tools and approaches such as eco-design, design for the environment, industrial symbiosis, and others to address various issues, including saving resources within organizations. These split efforts of 5S and Sustainability, following similar goals within organizations, could be merged and integrated to achieve better and more robust gains. A substantial benefit of this integration for organizations would be saving human resources, time, and money allocated to implement both 5S and Sustainability approaches. Organizations realize some of these gains by integrating Lean and Sustainability. For example, organizations can focus on production cycle

Lean and Sustainability drivers	Potential 5S application
Low production lead time	**Simplify and Shine** – improved workplace organization may lesson transportation, giving impetus to just-in-time
Low inventory levels	**Sort** – just-in-time deliveries keep the finished goods inventories low and improves inventory management
Low-capacity surplus	**Sort** – improved accuracy of inventory levels may lead to reducing capacity surplus
High information frequency	**Stabilize and Sustain** – through maintenance of 5S, higher information exchange leads to better communication and reduction of waste in operations
Low transportation lead time	**Straighten** – improved organization reduces transportation with items needed for production properly stored

FIGURE 11.1 Lean and Sustainability drivers.

times to reduce the time and improve the agility of firms to respond to customer demand. This effort can lead to reduced inventory levels, recovering the energy required to carry extra goods, requisite space, and reduced carbon footprint to maintain lower good levels. In this regard, respected teams such as EHS and the Sustainability Division should cooperate closely to merge and direct efforts toward better results. For instance, the 5S team may need to determine recovery options for unwanted materials and parts.

In contrast, a Sustainability team supports the implementation of 5S by exploring and identifying recovery options such as recycling, reuse, and other disposal methods. In this way, 5S would adequately address environmental issues as well. Therefore, Sustainability must be integrated into existing 5S methods so that companies may achieve substantial savings by conserving resources and minimizing waste. This chapter explains how to incorporate traditional 5S with Sustainability aspects. This integration will provide companies and practitioners of 5S and Sustainability with a methodology for an environmentally responsible organization.

5S INTEGRATED WITH SUSTAINABILITY

At the intersection of the 5S methodology and Sustainability is resource efficiency. Resource efficiency might be considered different from 5S and Sustainability viewpoints; however, both follow a similar principle: efficient use of appropriate resources. On the one hand, resource efficiency, from the 5S perspective, is about keeping wanted and necessary materials and parts active in use. In other words, 5S emphasizes the elimination of waste and unused materials from the working area, which eventually leads to the efficient use of resources. However, repurposing, reusing, or recycling unwanted and unnecessary materials and parts is often an afterthought. The team can move unnecessary items to another department that needs the item, or it is sold or scrapped. Resource efficiency converts input materials and energy into finished products and services from a Sustainability definition. The more input an organization transforms materials and energy into a finished product or service, the fewer waste materials and byproducts are generated. Therefore, it is also only using necessary resources to reduce waste. Further, this simple but fundamental principle underlying 5S and Sustainability aligns with circular economy principles. Therefore, 5S can be considered a solid foundation for Sustainability and circular economy initiatives within organizations.

5S and Sustainability closely interconnect with respect to including environmental, economic, and social aspects. From an environmental standpoint, 5S helps companies conserve resources and minimize waste. From the economic perspective, organizations can achieve substantial savings by reducing resource consumption, including materials, energy, and water, and recovery of waste materials. From a social viewpoint, 5S provides organizations with an organized, safe, and healthy working environment. As shown in Figure 11.2, organizations gain considerable bottom-line benefits by implementing the 5S methodology.

Sustainability Triple Bottom Line		
Environment	Economy	Social
• Reduce waste (minimize waste disposal) • Reduce raw materials consumption (improve resources efficiency) • Reduce defects • Improve energy efficiency by reducing space required for the operation	• Reduce operational costs by not purchasing new materials and parts, and instead using unwanted materials (improve the company's profits)	• Improve work safety • Improve hygiene • Increase safe operating conditions • Improve employee morale and commitment improvement • Increase employee awareness about environmental, health, and safety issues

FIGURE 11.2 Bottom line benefits for organizations implementing 5S.

5S Steps Integrated with Sustainability

Step 1: Seiri or Simplify the Workplace

The first step of 5S is to Simplify (Seiri). In the first step, the team should sort all items in the work area. The team must distinguish between items that are necessary and unnecessary. The unnecessary items are disposed of and recovered properly based on Sustainability principles. Seiri means separating the necessary equipment, such as tools, parts, and instructions, from the unneeded materials and disposing of, recovering, or removing the latter.

Simplifying the area reduces crowding and clutter, which improves the workflow. The wasted time searching for tools is eliminated, and worker safety improves due to debris removal and potential trip hazards (Mousavi et al., 2020). Decreasing the unneeded inventory and equipment also reduces costs. Excess stock can hide other problems, such as quality defects and increasing time for sorting good from bad items. Unneeded items make improving process flow difficult. For example, organizations realize efficiency improvements by reducing unnecessary movement when individuals spend less time and energy looking for items necessary for production. This improvement also reduces production lead time, a key performance driver for Lean and Sustainability adoption, and gives the organization a better ability to adopt just-in-time production. The organization also benefits from improved quality.

An example of how simplifying improves quality is when a process uses two different but similar parts to make two different products. An operation could use the wrong part in an assembly. The parts were color-coded along with their container and work order to reduce confusion. Simple color-coding can be an easy way to eliminate unnecessary confusion in daily activities.

This step is essential and at the core of the integrated 5S with Sustainability because it identifies waste, improves quality, and explores ways to dispose of and recover them appropriately. It also makes the workplace safer by eliminating clutter. Floor space is gained by disposing of all unnecessary items. This step makes the necessary items that remain much easier to visualize.

Seiri establishes a solid foundation for practicing Sustainability in different ways. First, Seiri helps eliminate potential fire hazards, chemicals, contaminants, and other hazardous materials and substances in the workplace. Simplifying reduces the potential of accidents that could lead to leak or spill incidents and associated hazardous wastes. Second, it could make a bridge between the disposal of those unnecessary items separated from necessary ones and the waste recovery practices of a company. For instance, instead of ending up in a trash bin that would go to a recycling company or added to landfills, those unnecessary items could be shared to be reused by other facilities within the organization or cross-industry facilities. This practice would extend the life cycle of materials, components, and products by reusing them. This practice conserves resources, including materials, and saves the energy required to make those materials and components.

Separating Necessary from Unnecessary Items. The team must thoroughly examine the area. All unnecessary items should be discarded and recovered correctly. Teams should reassess items considered necessary for their use to address why and how often the process uses them. The team should evaluate components, documentation, supplies, tooling, gauges, parts, and machines in a production area. When using 5S in an office area, the team should evaluate such items as records, forms, books, supplies, equipment, computers, shelving, reports, and parts. When using 5S in a healthcare environment, the team should evaluate such items as medical equipment, supplies, furniture, beds, storage cabinets, forms, computers, printers, office equipment, pharmaceuticals, and instruments. Items thought to be unnecessary should be recovered. One useful source is Material Safety Data Sheets (MSDS) which provide necessary information about the disposal of materials. If the materials are hazardous, the team should consider careful condensation while disposing of the materials. Non-hazardous items should be reused, shared, or recycled. Depending on the item's conditions, such as excess raw material, the most preferred option from a Sustainability standpoint is to either reuse it as it is in another department of the same organization or share it with an outside company. As a last option, unnecessary items such as scrap should be recycled either by the company itself or by a recycling company to restore valuable materials. Nonetheless, for a better implementation of the disposal of materials, Lean implementation teams must have close cooperation with the environmental team of the organization in waste and materials handling to ensure they follow the best and most feasible recovery methods to dispose of unnecessary items.

Using Red Tags for Identification. An essential part of the "simplify" step is red-tagging any items that are unnecessary or in question. The red tag should be a large piece of red paper, typically 8.5 x 11 inches. The lower portion of the tag should be perforated to keep a record of the tag's location. Figure 11.3 provides an example of a red tag.

Area:	RED TAG	Tag #:
Category (Circle):		
Supplies	WIP	Tools
Office Materials	Raw Material	Equipment
Furniture	Finished Goods	Other:
Books/Magazines/Files		_____
Date Tagged:		Tagged By:
Item:		Quantity:
Reason:		
Disposition (Circle):		
□ Hazardous		□ Non-hazardous
Recovery: □ Reuse □ Share □ Recycle		Sell
Store in Dept.		Transfer
Long Term Storage		Other: _____
Action Taken:		Date:

- Perforated Line -

Area:	RED TAG LOCATOR	Tag #:

FIGURE 11.3   Red tag.

To organize the red tag materials, create a red tag board for tracking purposes. Then move all red-tagged items into a temporary red-tag area and set up a time to dispose of the items. This tracking allows other teams to remove items for their use instead of buying new material.

After the predetermined time is up, dispose of and recover all remaining items promptly. Continue this process regularly to ensure that more unnecessary items do not begin to clutter the area again. The steps in a red tag effort include the following:

1. Identify red tag target/area,
2. Establish criteria for evaluation,
3. Make the red tags,
4. Attach tags and separate the lower portion for traceability, and
5. Evaluate the tagged items.

Step 2: Seiton or Straighten the Workplace

In the second step, the entire workplace is organized/straightened. Seiton means arranging and identifying parts, materials, and tools for ease of use. Items should be placed in the best location for point of use and visually organized. This step improves quality by visually identifying all products and creating a specific location for that item, which makes it easier for employees to find, use, and easily return all items to their proper place. It helps the team implement Sustainability by tightening up the space required for production or operations by organizing and arranging materials or disposing unused or unwanted machines, equipment, and supplies. This practice reduces energy consumption for heating, cooling, and lighting and improves energy efficiency in plants, buildings, and other areas. Regarding Lean and Sustainability drivers, straighten helps the organization reduce transportation costs with items needed for production only properly stored and visible to all involved in the production cycle.

First, the team should decide where to place items for more accessible organization. The team must ensure the locations and systems are easily understood and clearly labeled. When selecting a storage method, the team should pay careful attention to these details: their goal should be to minimize inventory and space and improve the visual management of items. Again, the team should incorporate visual management (see Chapter 12) so employees can quickly return items, minimizing travel and searching for needed items. Visual management also promotes readily identifying missing items. Items that should be determined using visual controls include shadow boxes for tools, tooling/fixtures, movable objects, documentation control, storage area for common tools, raw material, finished material, discrepant material, and packaging material (Cudney, Dietrich, & Furterer, 2013).

Step 3: Seiso or Scrub the Workplace

The team should thoroughly clean all work areas in the third step, including floors, equipment, and furniture. Seiso means performing a cleanup campaign, which is important because a clean work environment promotes quality work. Seiso contributes to Sustainability through waste reduction, a critical Sustainability pillar.

Implementing Seiso reduces the accumulation of various substances, such as clippings, shavings, debris, and other materials, potentially resulting in defects. Defect equals waste. Therefore, reduction in defects has Sustainability benefits, including saving materials, avoiding waste generation, and conserving energy. Additionally, eco-friendly and toxic-free cleaning materials and detergents should be used for cleaning machines, floors, and areas, improving workers' health by limiting exposure to material compounds that, with cumulative exposure, may result in chronic illness.

While cleaning, the team should consider how the area became dirty to help maintain a clean environment. The team should inspect for safety hazards or leaks, and before continuing with the cleaning, the team should fix or repair any items (Mousavi, Cudney, & Trucco, 2017). Cleaning equipment should also have an identified location to ensure that employees can easily find them. Teams should integrate these activities into daily maintenance. Teams should also clean the areas in the workplace, including floors, ceilings, walls, computer equipment, furniture, cabinets, desks, production equipment, and unnecessary computer files.

Step 4: Seiketsu or Stabilize the Workplace Standards

Stabilize consists of maintaining and improving the first three 5S standards by implementing needed changes. Seiketsu means performing Seiri, Seiton, and Seiso at specified frequency intervals to maintain and enhance the well-organized and clean work environment. This step is essential in all quality improvement efforts. Moreover, developing and stabilizing workplace standards through Seiketsu aligns with the underlying concept behind Sustainability – a systems approach. Seiketsu creates a system to ensure the team performs all tasks as specified to maintain the first three pillars.

Teams should perform Seiketsu by creating a daily checklist of cleaning and organizing activities. This step leads to more frequent and better communication of what operations should sustain for 5S. This step leads to better communication in general for reducing environmental waste. The team can also perform 5S patrols and spot checks to monitor the progress of the 5S efforts. During this step, the team can make changes to existing equipment to make cleaning quicker and easier, and they can use the "five-why?" method to determine the root causes. The 5-Whys is a simple method of asking "why" five times to get to the root cause of a problem. A 5S question could be, "Why does the workplace become so cluttered?" The team can then modify equipment and systems to improve the cleanliness of the area. Standardized problem analysis, such as the 5-Why's, supports employee productivity and development and a more fundamental focus on quality. Teams should also eliminate flat storage areas and excess storage areas.

During Step 4, the team schedules time and resources for 5S activities. The team can create model areas to demonstrate the 5S philosophy, and use check sheets to provide feedback, another fundamental quality improvement technique. The team should arrange for management walk-throughs to maintain the 5S culture. Finally, training on 5S is required to occur on a specified schedule, supporting worker development.

Step 5: Shitsuke or Sustain

The final step of 5S instills the discipline or habit of adequately maintaining the 5S procedures. 5S must become a habit in the team's daily life. Shitsuke means forming a habit of following the first four Ss. The team must develop a routine of simplifying, straightening, scrubbing, and stabilizing the work environment. This step focuses the entire team on the goal of 5S.

This step is the most difficult "S" to maintain. It means maintaining self-discipline and practicing 5S until it is a way of life. Focusing on continuous improvement is essential. An important part of any 5S program is also sharing the lessons learned. By sustaining the effort, organizations improve employee spirit. Management involvement is critical for the success of the 5S effort to continue to grow and maintain. Shitsuke and Sustainability follow a similar philosophy – creating a discipline that would survive, prosper, and sustain indefinitely (Agustiady & Cudney, 2022). By maintaining the first 4S, Shitsuke lays a sound foundation for implementing Sustainability principles, which are indeed continuous improvements.

USING VISUAL BOARDS TO DOCUMENT 5S STATUS

Teams can use several forms to document the 5S status of their workplace visually. These forms may exist in paper form or be displayed using digital monitors posted in workplace areas. The first form is the 5S wheel, which gives a visual overview of the level of 5S an area has obtained. Teams fill in each "S" as they obtain each 5S level. The team leaves the remaining 5S levels unfilled. Figure 11.4 shows an example of a 5S wheel.

The second form is a series of questions the team should address to obtain each level. Figure 11.5 provides a checklist of the questions that teams can ask for each S. Post these forms in each area on the shopfloor or work area.

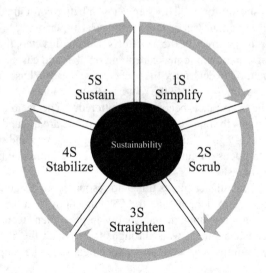

FIGURE 11.4   5S wheel.

5S - Evaluation Sheet	Year:		Area:																						
Manufacturing / Shop Floor	JAN		FEB		MAR		APR		MAY		JUN		JUL		AUG		SEP		OCT		NOV		DEC	
	Y	N	Y	N	Y	N	Y	N	Y	N	Y	N	Y	N	Y	N	Y	N	Y	N	Y	N	Y	N

1S Simplify (Seiri) - clearly distinguishing between what is needed and what is unneeded.

1 Are only necessary items present?																									
2 Are defective materials identified?																									
3 Are unneeded items marked with a red tag?																									
4 Are red tagged items in the red tag area?																									
5 Are unneeded hazardous items separated from non-hazardous ones?																									
6 Are recovery options explored and identified for defective materials?																									
6 Are recovery options identified for unneeded items?																									
7 Is standard work present and current?																									

2S Straighten (Seiton) - organizing the necessary items, making it easy for anyone to find and use them.

6 Are areas and walkways marked for location?																									
7 Are materials visually controlled and at the point of use?																									
8 Are maximum and minimum allowable quantities on materials indicated?																									
9 Is nonconforming material segregated, identified & documented?																									
Are disposal options identified for nonconforming material?																									
10 Is product clearly identified?																									

3S Scrub (Seiso) - cleaning floors and equipment; finding ways to prevent dirt and debris from accumulating in the work area.

11 Are floors and areas free of trash, liquids, or dirt?																									
Are toxic free cleaning materials used?																									
12 Is the work area lighting sufficient, ventilated, and free of dust and odors?																									
13 Are cleaning operations visually managed?																									
14 Are cleaning supplies and equipment easily available and stored in a marked area?																									

4S Standardize (Seiketsu) – maintaining the first three S's.

15 Are machines equipped with removal systems for waste or chips?																									
16 Are there records defective material entries with corrective action?																									
17 Are equipment TPM procedures in place and current?																									
18 Are waste and recyclable material receptacles emptied regularly?																									
Are recyclable and non-recyclable materials separated for proper disposal options?																									
19 Are scrap and product nonconformance areas cleared on a regular basis?																									
Are scrap and product nonconformance recovered through reusing or recycling?																									

5S Sustain (Shitsuke) - adopting the discipline of properly maintaining correct 5S procedures.

* The 5th S-Sustain, is awarded when a minimum of 3 consecutive months of																									
1-S, 2-S, 3-S and 4-S have been sustained.																									

FIGURE 11.5 Integrated 5S – Sustainability evaluation check sheet.

INTEGRATED 5S AND SUSTAINABILITY: A PATHWAY TO A CIRCULAR ECONOMY

The integrated 5S and Sustainability approach supports the circular economy by practicing resource efficiency within organizations. The circular economy is a resource-efficient and regenerative economy that does not generate waste; therefore, all waste materials and byproducts are cycled back into the economy. By applying this integrated methodology, companies can reuse and share unnecessary materials within their organizations or across industries to give those materials a second life. Closing the materials loop this way helps companies shift from a linear to a circular economy, as shown in Figure 11.6.

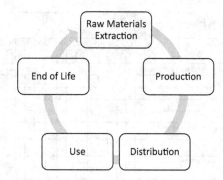

FIGURE 11.6   Circular economy for materials.

CONCLUSION

5S is a powerful tool for improving workplace organization. Organizations can use the forms to implement 5S in their workplace. Integrating Sustainability principles into 5S enables organizations to use resources more effectively. Further, this promotes the circular economy by allowing organizations to reuse and share unnecessary materials within their four walls or across the supply chain. Reusing and sharing unnecessary materials gives these materials a second life creating a resource-efficient and regenerative economy. The next chapter will expand upon the integration of 5S and Sustainability to improve visual management practices throughout the organization and supply chain.

REFERENCES

Agustiady, T., & Cudney, E. (2015). *Total productive maintenance: Strategies and implementation guide*. New York, NY: CRC Press.

Agustiady, T., & Cudney, E. (2022). *Building a sustainable Lean culture: An implementation guide*. New York: NY: CRC Press.

Antony, J., Laux, C., Cudney, E., & Sundar, V. (2019). *Ten commandments of LSS: A practical guide for senior executives and business leaders*. Bingley, UK: Emerald Publishing.

Cudney, E., Furterer, S., & Dietrich, D. (2013). *Lean systems: Applications and case studies in manufacturing, service, and healthcare*. New York, NY: CRC Press.

Cudney, E., Murray, S., & Pai, P. (2012). An analysis of the impact of lean on safety. In J. C. Spohrer, & L. E. Freund (Eds.), *Advances in the human side of service engineering* (pp. 420–432). New York, NY: CRC Press.

Mousavi, S., Cudney, E., & Trucco, P. (2017). Towards a framework for steering safety performance: A review of the literature on leading indicators. In P. Arezes (Ed.), *Advances in safety management and human factors* (pp. 195–204). New York, NY: Springer.

Mousavi, S., Khani Jazani, R., Cudney, E., & Trucco, P. (2020). Quantifying the relationship between lean maturity and occupational health and safety: Antecedents and leading indicators. *International Journal of Lean Six Sigma, 11*(1), 150–170.

12 Tracking Sustainability Efforts through Visual Management

INTRODUCTION

Visual management is an excellent tool to provide visibility to the organization at all levels, starting at the Lean Sustainability program level, the project initiatives, through processes and daily control. Metrics are developed, defined, and tracked using dashboards to control the processes and activities and scorecards to assess and identify opportunities for improvement (Swarnakar et al., 2022).

OVERVIEW OF VISUAL MANAGEMENT

A key focus of Lean is incorporating simple, yet powerful, visual management to assess and control the organization, Lean Sustainability program, processes, and daily activities, as shown in Figure 12.1.

Organizations commonly use scorecards and dashboards to provide visual management. They can be electronic or physical, depending on how they are to be analyzed. A dashboard is similar to a vehicle's dashboard, where the driver can see how they are performing as they drive. A scorecard is a view of critical metrics after completing the process. Scorecards assess how the team or unit performed over a certain period. This visualization is similar to a baseball scorecard that shows how many runs occurred in each inning. Both are useful. A dashboard helps to manage activities as they occur, while a scorecard helps to identify and assess improvement opportunities.

Key performance indicators (KPIs), as the name indicates, help shed light on the organization's success and departments within the organization. While most KPIs transcend to every level of the organization, there can be KPIs specific to departments, depending on their roles and goals for the year (Cudney, 2009). Typically, KPIs should be ways to measure the organization's success and a guide for how they are meeting their goals.

Organizations should develop operational definitions for the KPIs and metrics to ensure consistent measurement (Agustiady & Cudney, 2022). Each should contain a target and a trigger point for the team to take corrective action. Organizations often use color coding based on these trigger points. Green indicates the metric is good or on track. Yellow indicates concern. Red indicates that action is required. Once a measurement reaches a trigger point, the team should initiate problem-solving and implement appropriate countermeasures to avoid recurrence (see Chapter 15 on mistake proofing).

Visual management can include scorecards of the key Lean and Sustainability metrics at an organizational level, as shown in Figure 12.2 for a hospital. The

DOI: 10.1201/9780429506192-12

FIGURE 12.1 Visual management focus.

Hospital Lean Sustainability Organizational Scorecard					
Metric	Definition	Actual	Target	% Improvement from Baseline	Desired Direction
Efficiency					
Length of stay – inpatient	Time from admission to discharge	5.5 days (R)	4.5 days	11%	↓
Length of stay – ED	Time from arrival to discharge	4.5 hours (G)	4.8 hours	38%	↓
Patient Care					
Readmission rates	Percentage of patients re-admitted for the same condition (or complication)	21% (Y)	15.5%	5%	↓
Mortality rates – average heart attack mortality rate	Percent of patients who die under hospital care	11.6% (G)	12.6%	3%	↓
Incidents	Number of incidents per 1,000 patient days	12 (G)	17	50%	↓
Patient and Employee Satisfaction					
Inpatient satisfaction	Average % of positive patient satisfaction survey rates	75% (R)	85%	0%	↑
ED patient satisfaction		89% (G)	80%	32%	↑
Outpatient satisfaction		85% (G)	80%	18%	↑
Employee satisfaction	Average % of positive employee satisfaction survey rates	94% (G)	90%	16%	↑
Financial Performance					
Bed utilization rate	Percentage of hospital beds used	45% (R)	57%		↑
Operating margin	Revenue less operating costs / revenue	-12% (R)	2%		↑
Average cost per day	Average cost per patient per day	$12,000 (Y)	$10,400		↓
Bad debt ratio	Average bad debt to net patio revenue ratio	6% (G)	7.2%		↓
Sustainability Performance					
Linen use – soil to clean ratio	Soil to clean ratio: (1 – (Clean / Soiled)) * 100%	3.9% (R)	10%		↑
Recycling percentage	Percentage recycling	12% (R)	60%		↑
Contamination waste	Contaminated items per bag	3 (R)	1		↓

FIGURE 12.2 Hospital Lean Sustainability organization scorecard example.

scorecard allows leadership to track several categories of metrics, including efficiency, patient care, patient and employee satisfaction, financial performance, and Sustainability (No author, 2022). The red (R) is the darkest gray, the green (G) is the middle gray, and the yellow (Y) is the lightest gray. For example, efficiency measures include the length of stay for inpatients and emergency department patients (No author, n.d.). Patient care metrics include readmission rates, mortality rates, and the number of incidents where unintended events occur to patients. Hospitals measure patient and employee satisfaction through surveys and the percentage of positive responses to specific survey questions. Hospitals assess financial performance through the bed utilization rate, operating margin, average cost per day per patient, and bad debt ratio. In addition, hospitals assess Sustainability performance through linen loss, recycling percentages, and waste contamination of recycled materials. The scorecard shows the metrics, their definitions, the actual results, the targets, the percent improvement from the baseline, and the desired direction that the metric should move to demonstrate improvement.

Organizations can use scorecards to quickly assess the status of Lean Sustainability initiatives and the program, as shown in Figure 12.3. This scorecard shows, for each initiative, the expected and actual percent completion of the project, estimated due date, and actual completion date. Organizations should shade 100% complete items in green shading, while those that the team did not complete on time are in yellow or red, depending on how far past the due date. The red (R) is the darkest gray, the green (G) is the middle gray, and the yellow (Y) is the lightest gray.

At a process level, both scorecards and dashboards help assess the performance of the process. Figure 12.4 shows a scorecard for the Emergency Department's (ED) length of stay metric by activity (Furterer, 2018). The process improvement team can quickly identify where lengthy processes can cause bottlenecks. Figure 12.4 shows each step in the sequence and the average length of time during that time period in minutes. The team separated the process by patients discharged from the ED and admitted to the hospital from the ED since the times vary significantly between the two types of patient dispositions. Another example of a scorecard for the ED process was providing improvement status to senior leadership after three months of implementing improvements, as shown in Figure 12.5. This scorecard shows the baseline for each major process step in the ED, the targets, the improved metrics, and the percent improvements for both discharged and admitted patients. This scorecard can also be used to identify improvement areas. Most of the improvement in this project was realized in the up-front processes versus the middle and final steps (Furterer, 2018).

The goal of daily control related to visual management is to understand within five minutes of walking into the facility what has happened today with respect to production from both an efficiency and quality perspective (Agustiady & Cudney, 2022). Organizations typically use dashboards to monitor and control activities daily, hourly, or by the minute. The dashboard shown in Figure 12.6 shows a dashboard that was used in the ED to control the patient flow and ensure that no patient was stalled in the process (Furterer, 2018). Staff monitored each patient/room through alerts connected to the ED Bed Board data that tracked each step of the patient's activities. If the patient waited too long for lab results, an alert would

Hospital Lean Sustainability Program Scorecard				
Initiative	Expected Percent Completion	Actual Percent Completion	Estimated Due Date	Actual Completion Date
In Progress Projects				
ED throughput	80%	85% (G)	2/20	
OR turnaround	60%	40% (R)	4/1	
Inpatient discharge	70%	70% (G)	6/1	
Outpatient scheduling	60%	55% (Y)	8/15	
Waste contamination of recycling	40%	35% (Y)	12/22	
Increase recycling	35%	40% (G)	12/22	
Completed				
Diagnostic scheduling	100%	100% (G)	7/6	7/1 (G)
Operating room patient readiness	100%	100% (G)	11/1	10/22 (G)
CT scan appropriate use	100%	100% (G)	4/22	5/12 (Y)
Sepsis protocols	100%	100% (G)	12/22	9/1 (R)

FIGURE 12.3 Hospital Lean Sustainability program scorecard example.

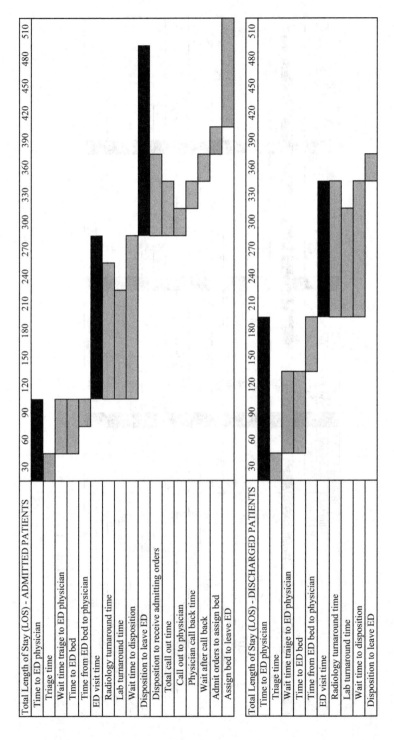

FIGURE 12.4 Emergency department process scorecard.

	Baseline		Target		Improved		% Improvement	
	Admitted	Discharged	Admitted	Discharged	Admitted	Discharged	Admitted	Discharged
Total length of stay	8.7 hours	5.8 hours	5 (43%)	3 (48%)	6.1	4.1	30%	29%
% leave without being seen	6.50%		3.50%			0.60%		91%
Total time to ED physician	93	109	35	35		32		66%
- Triage time	34	34	15	15		13		62%
- Wait time triage to ED physician	65	79	20	20		25		62%
- Time to ED bed	61	81	35	42		16		74%
- Bed to physician	34	55	20	20		16		53%
Treat/Diagnose to disposition time	192	175	109	91		166		14%
- Radiology diagnostic time	138	270	154	154		170		-23%
- Lab time	119					57		109%
- ED physician time: visit	192	175	109	91		175		9%
Disposition to leave ED	223	64	127	33	171	47	23%	27%
Disposition to get admit orders	103		59		70		32%	
- Total call out time	41		23		24			
- Call out to physician	13		7		5			
- Physician call back	29		17		19			
- Wait after call back	37		21		46			
- Admit orders to assign bed	42		24		44		-5%	
- Assign bed to leave ED	112		64		67		40%	

FIGURE 12.5 Emergency department process scorecard for improvement.

Bed	Status	Triage	Regis-tration	Waiting EDP	Orders Pending	Phleb. Pending	EKG	Meds. Pending	Respi-ratory	LAB Resuls	X Ray	CT	US	To Be DC / Adm	Callout Pend Ans	Bed Request	Bed Assigned	Report
ED-01																	42	
ED-02	LABS not resulted									>2H								
ED-03	Empty																	
ED-04	Waiting to be discharged																58	
HW-1H	Empty																	
ED-05	Empty																	
ED-06														>2 H				
ED-07														>3 H				
ED-08	Waiting EDP disposition													>6 H				
ED-09	Empty																	
ED-10	Empty																	
ED-11																		
ED-12											57							
HW-32H	Waiting EDP disposition													>6 H				
HW-13H	Empty																	
ED-15																		
ED-16													36					45	

FIGURE 12.6   Emergency department daily control dashboard.

show first in yellow, then in red. This dashboard was delivered to monitors throughout the ED so anyone could attend to a stalled activity. The dashboard development was Excel-based. The left rows of the dashboard list each patient room with an overall status summary and appropriate color coding to address whether the patient spent too much time waiting on an activity. The top of the dashboard shows each activity with green fill within the cells where the activity is complete. The dashboard also provides the time spent on the activities past the specification time when the activity was past due. The darker gray in Figure 12.6 represents green in real-time and the lighter gray with numbers shown in yellow. A very dark cell would show in red as very past due. There are no examples of that alert in this example.

Another example of a dashboard provides different charts to assess the ED process average, variability (control charts), defects (p-chart), and distribution of average and variation (histogram and box plot), shown in Figure 12.7 (Furterer, 2018). An x-bar and R control chart for the Length of Stay over time shows if the process is in control and stable from a length of stay perspective. The p-chart shows a patient's percent length of stay that is considered out of specification or greater than one standard deviation from the mean (greater than 360 minutes). The histogram shows the distribution of the length of stay per patient, the average, the variation, and whether it is a normal distribution, which it is. Moreover, the bottom right chart is a box plot to show the median, quartiles, and any outliers for the length of stay by a patient.

BENEFITS OF VISUAL MANAGEMENT

Visual management ensures that the organization's Lean Sustainability program, processes, and daily activities are monitored and controlled. Organizations can also use these metrics to identify areas for improvement and put initiatives together to enhance Lean and Sustainability in the organization.

STEPS TO IMPLEMENT VISUAL MANAGEMENT

Implementing visual management is no small task. Leaders, middle management, and process owners must be involved in developing the KPIs, metrics, dashboards, and scorecards, as well as reviewing and taking action when needed (Antony et al., 2022). Organizations can use the following steps to develop visual management.

1) Define the metrics at each level: organizational, program, process, and daily activities. Leaders, middle management, and process owners should be engaged in the brainstorming of KPIs and metrics. Information technology and data analytics analysts should also be engaged, as they will build, provide, and use the dashboards to generate the data, metrics, dashboards, and scorecards.
2) Develop the operational definitions for each metric.
3) Develop the technology or mechanisms to deliver the dashboards and scorecards.

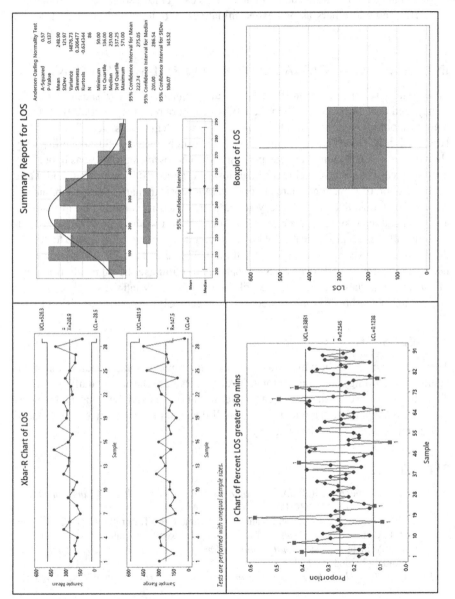

FIGURE 12.7 Emergency department dashboard for average, variability, defects, and outliers.

4) Implement appropriate use by defining the visual management usage's who, what, where, and when.
5) Take action when improvements are necessary at the four levels of the organization.
6) Enhance metrics as needed. Organizations can remove some KPIs and metrics and add others as processes, initiatives, activities, and organizational strategies evolve.

INTEGRATING SUSTAINABILITY INTO VISUAL MANAGEMENT

Traditional visual management focuses on safety, quality, delivery, satisfaction, efficiency, and cost as performance metrics (Cudney, Furterer, & Dietrich, 2013). These metrics should flow down from the organization's strategic goals (see Chapter 19 on Hoshin Kanri). However, as organizations increasingly focus on Sustainability, they should incorporate additional Green performance metrics and initiatives, as in our hospital scorecard examples, including linen loss (Furterer, 2011), recycling, and waste contamination of recycling. There are considerable costs in many industries related to waste of materials that could be recycled and prevented from ending up in landfills. The US healthcare system generates 7,000 tons of solid waste daily, costing $10 billion annually. Estimates indicate that hospitals could divert or eliminate 40% to 70% of their waste to recycling, equating to $4 billion to $7 billion annually. All organizations need more visibility and focus on Sustainability to eliminate the tremendous amount of waste in materials not reused or recycled within facilities and the supply chain (No author, 2021). Dashboards and Scorecards are great tools to provide this visibility.

CONCLUSION

There are four levels in which dashboards and scorecards can enact visual management, including the organizational level, program, process, and daily activities. This chapter showed examples of each level for a hospital and the important aspects of visual management. The next chapter will discuss total productive maintenance and its integration with Sustainability.

REFERENCES

Agustiady, T., & Cudney, E. (2022). *Building a sustainable Lean culture: An implementation guide.* New York: NY: CRC Press.
Antony, J., Swarnakar, V., Gupta, N., Kaur, J., Jayaraman, R., Tortorella, G., & Cudney, E. (2022). Critical success factors for operational excellence initiatives in manufacturing: A meta-analysis. *Total Quality Management & Business Excellence.* DOI: 10.1080/14783363.2022.2157714
Cudney, E. (2009). *Using hoshin kanri to improve the value stream.* New York, NY: CRC Press.
Cudney, E., Furterer, S., & Dietrich, D. (2013). *Lean systems: Applications and case studies in manufacturing, service, and healthcare.* New York, NY: CRC Press.
Furterer, S. (2011). Applying Lean Six Sigma to reduce linen loss in an acute care hospital. *International Journal of Engineering, Science, and Technology, 3*(7), 39–55.

Furterer, S. (2018). Applying Lean Six Sigma methods to reduce length of stay in a hospital's emergency department. *Quality Engineering*, *30*(3), 389–404.

No Author (2021). The high cost of poor waste management in healthcare, https://www.zabbleinc.com/blog-post/the-high-cost-of-poor-waste-management-in-healthcare. Accessed: 2/15/2023.

No Author (2022). Top 10 hospital performance metrics you need to know, Definitive Healthcare https://www.definitivehc.com/blog/top-10-hospital-performance-metrics-you-need-to-know. Accessed: 2/15/2023.

No Author (n.d.). Decreasing the patient length of stay, https://centrak.com/resources/blog/decreasing-patient-length-of-stay

Swarnakar, V., Singh, A. R., Antony, J., Tiwari, A. K., & Cudney, E. (2022). Prioritizing indicators for Sustainability assessment in manufacturing. *Sustainability*, *14*(6), 3264.

13 Utilizing Single-Minute Exchange of Dies for an Environmentally Friendly Changeover Process

OVERVIEW OF SMED

Shigeo Shingo initially developed SMED to improve die press and machine tool setups. Shingo introduced SMED after 19 years of observing factory setup operations. Setup time is the time between completing the last good piece of product A and completing the first good piece of product B. Setup time includes changing materials, tools, fixtures, and dies and stabilizing the process to make good parts (Cudney, Furterer, & Dietrich, 2013).

In developing his methodology, Shingo (1985) discovered two main points. First, setup operations include two categories:

1. Internal setups occur while the machine is not operating. An example is changing the tooling in the machine. A hospital operating room turnover example is the surgeons waiting for staff to clean and setup the room. During this time, surgeons cannot perform surgery in that room.
2. External setups occur while the machine is running. An example of this is setting tools for a different product. A hospital operating room turnover example is ensuring that the instruments and supplies are available before turning over the room. Otherwise, time is lost looking for instruments and supplies while preparing the room for the subsequent surgery.

Shingo's second point is that converting internal setups to external setups substantially reduces changeover times. Reducing internal setup time also increases the time the machines can operate. Shigeo Shingo believed organizations could reduce setup time by 59/60ths (Shingo, 1985). Figure 13.1 provides examples of changeover applications within manufacturing, healthcare, and financial services organizations.

Though rarely achievable, the theoretical goal of SMED is zero setups, in which changeovers are instantaneous and do not affect continuous flow. The purpose of SMED is to standardize setups and create routine operations, achieved by detailed analysis of a continuous process. In practice, SMED setup should take fewer than ten minutes, where the term "single minute" originated. SMED helps to reduce inventory, improve flexibility, increase capacity, and provide better customer service (Cudney, Furterer, & Dietrich, 2013). Current SMED practices, though, do not consider Sustainability principles. SMED and Sustainability focus on the effective use of

 DOI: 10.1201/9780429506192-13

Manufacturing	Healthcare Services	Financial Services
Changing over a plastic cup extrusion line from one cup size or color to another	Changing over an operating room from one patient's surgical procedure to the next	Processing financial statements and reports from one period to the next, including identifying and reducing transaction errors
Changing over a machine from one product size to another	Changing over an emergency department room from one patient to the next	Providing service to banking customers in a banking center, going from one customer to the next
Changing over a car assembly line from one make and model to another	Discharging an inpatient and preparing the room for the next patient	Processing mortgage loan applications, moving from one application to the next
Changing over an engine plant from making combustion engineers to electronic vehicles	Sterilizing surgical instruments from one case to ready them for the next case	Performing quality control inspections of new bank accounts, moving from one account to the next
	Changing imaging equipment from one procedure to the next, sometimes within one patient or across patients	

FIGURE 13.1   Applications of changeovers across three industries.

resources and can impact the triple bottom line (TBL). Considerable waste can occur during a changeover process concerning resource consumption (e.g., materials, energy, water) that impacts the environment. Labor gains affect the social impacts of TBL. Sustainable SMED also impacts economic gains. Organizations can realize significant environmental, economic, and social gains by streamlining changeover processes and conserving resources. Integrating Sustainability principles into SMED enables organizations to shift from a linear to a circular economy that is regenerative and waste-free.

BENEFITS OF SMED

As mentioned, implementing SMED provides many benefits. SMED also includes benefits Sustainability and the TBL. Figure 13.2 notes select SMED benefits and area classification according to TBL (Helleno et al., 2017).

INTEGRATING SUSTAINABILITY INTO SMED

All setup operations consist of five main steps:

1. Before beginning SMED, the team must determine the setup operation.
2. The next step includes preparation, after-process adjustments, checking of materials and tools, and Sustainability analysis.
3. The third step is mounting tools necessary for the changeover at point-of-use.
4. Next, the SMED team must perform measurements, settings, and calibrations.
5. The final step is a trial run and adjustments.

Next, let's look at each step in more detail.

SMED Benefit	TBL Pillar	Area
There are fewer physical adjustments in process changes, which means less chance for error.	Economic, Social	Cost Management, Quality, Health
Increased flexibility in scheduling because the setup is less than takt time.	Economic, Environmental	Operational Efficiency, Consumption
Reduced expense of excess inventory which, in turn, increases capacity by reducing the time lost during a changeover.	Social, Environmental	Human Resources, 3R's (Reduce, Reuse, Recycle) Culture
Reduced material wasted due to scrap during setup.	Environmental, Economic, Social	3R's (Reduce, Reuse, Recycle) Culture, Consumption, Economic
Improved product quality by reducing variation between each setup.	Social	Quality, Health, Satisfaction Level
Decreased chance of considerable defects in inventory from producing smaller runs.	Social, Environmental	Quality, Health, Responsibility
Reduction in defects from setup errors and eliminating trial runs.	Social, Environmental	Quality and Health, Environmental aspects
Improved customer service because of the ability to change over quickly and meet changing customers' needs.	Social, Environmental, Economic	Quality and health, Consumption, Customers
Increased productivity by performing changeovers quicker and reducing the amount of downtime.	Economic, Social	Human Resources Cost Management
Safer work environment and reduced risk of physical strain or injury by simplifying setups.	Social	Quality and Health
Reduced physical space, or footprint, provides more efficient use of floor space and reduces clutter.	Environmental, Economic	Environmental Aspects, Infrastructure

FIGURE 13.2   SMED benefits and corresponding TBL pillar.

STEP 1: DETERMINING THE SETUP OPERATION

In observing the current setup, the first step is selecting the improvement area. When selecting an area, the team should not consider the machines or processes independent from each other. Instead, the team should consider setup time reduction as part of a complete production flow. A holistic perspective of SMED incorporates sustainable principles into the manufacturing process. The US Department of Commerce defines sustainable manufacturing as "the creation of manufactured products that use processes that minimize negative environmental impacts, conserve energy and natural resources, are safe for employees, communities, and consumers, and are economically sound" (Ebrahimi et al., 2021). The manufacturing or service process should consist of the continuous flow from raw materials to finished products and include a holistic perspective of the four primary phases of manufacturing processes: processing, inspection, transport, and storage. When evaluating process SMED candidates, often, process improvement specialists locate the largest monument machine within the production facility and use that as a starting point to assess upstream and downstream impacts of the machine operations. The largest machine may or may not be the SMED to be analyzed; however, it provides a starting point for process evaluation.

For evaluating sustainable manufacture, a more holistic approach incorporating the product's life cycle helps assess TBL and create sustainable solutions to overcome barriers to adoption (Ebrahimi et al., 2021). For a service process, improvement is selected based on where the most significant time, inefficiencies, or quality defects exist in going from one customer (patient) to another. Utilizing the TBL perspective allows the practitioner to look beyond the immediate economic benefits toward a more holistic approach that incorporates environmental and social impact for identifying potential candidates for SMED adoption (Helleno et al., 2017).

STEP 2: PREPARATION, AFTER-PROCESS ADJUSTMENTS, AND SUSTAINABILITY ANALYSIS

Once the SMED evaluation candidate is selected, this next step aims to ensure that all necessary tools and materials are in place and functional. The team should perform this step external to the machine operating as this is the primary source of streamlining the setup process. In addition, the team should perform a Sustainability analysis. TBL criteria should include the environmental (energy consumption, material usage, emissions, water consumption, handling), the social (operator health/safety, operator setup muda, teamwork, and skill), and economic (material setup costs, indirect material costs, manpower costs, energy consumption (setup), inventory costs, handling costs, buffer stock costs, overhead costs (Ebrahimi et al., 2021). The organization may identify other specific criteria and may do so by utilizing the table above through TBL classification.

STEP 3: MOUNTING AND REMOVING BLADES, TOOLS, AND PARTS

Once Step 2 is complete, the next step consists of removing parts and tools after processing a part and then attaching the parts and tools for the next part. To perform this step, typically, the team must stop the machine. Therefore, the team should identify this step as an internal setup. This step also applies in non-manufacturing environments. In an operating room turnover, hospital staff clean the room, instruments, supplies, and materials, remove the patient from the room, and prepare the room for the next case by bringing in the case cart and patient and setting up the room for the next case.

STEP 4: MEASUREMENTS, SETTINGS, CALIBRATIONS

In this step, the team should perform the necessary measurements and calibrations during production operations. These operations are typically internal, but the team can convert them to external. For example, in an operating room, the surgical team must count instruments and materials to ensure that they are present and removed after the surgery (i.e., do not get thrown in the trash or lost in the patient).

STEP 5: TRIAL RUNS AND ADJUSTMENTS

The final step in a changeover is to make adjustments after machining the first piece. Adjustments are more straightforward if the team has taken accurate measurements and calibrations during the previous step. The team considers this an internal setup element during traditional setup because changeover is only complete once the process is producing good parts. In an operating room example, this is where any missing instruments, materials, supplies, and equipment are retrieved or adjusted, and perhaps the patient on the operating room table is also re-positioned. For example, setting up a surgical robot or adjusting anesthesia controls.

ANALYZING SETUP

Three stages of SMED simplify changeover (Cudney, Furterer, & Dietrich, 2013):

1. separating internal and external setup,
2. converting internal setup to external setup, and
3. streamlining the setup operation.

Figure 13.3 outlines the three stages.

The first step to implementing SMED improvements is for the team to analyze the current operation. The team should observe the setup by using video capture techniques for easy reference. The team should watch each person's movements (e.g., hand, eye, and body). The team can then show the video to those involved with the setup and normal operations. Finally, the video allows the continuous improvement team to record the time and motion on a setup analysis chart, as shown in Figure 13.4. This worksheet includes traditional SMED calculation for time. It also includes a Sustainability assessment of select criteria of the triple bottom line. Depending on the organization, the TBL criteria can incorporate a more holistic assessment of SMED (Ebrahimi et al., 2021).

Figure 13.5 illustrates an operating room setup analysis chart. Again, the organization should include TBL criteria per operational environment and the organization's strategic Sustainability goals.

Chart each category in Pareto format. Figure 13.6 provides an example of the format for the manufacturing example, including the economic criteria and time. The breakdown includes several time categories: searching, fixture change, walk time, first-piece inspection, gaging, tool change, and programming. Figure 13.7 illustrates a Pareto chart for the operating room turnover. In addition, Figure 13.8 provides a Pareto chart for the setup of a manufacturing process for energy consumption.

The key to successful SMED implementation is properly distinguishing between internal and external setups in a proper sustainable manner (i.e., greenwashing, see below). The team should perform as many changeover tasks as possible while the machine is running, such as preparation and transport, which can typically reduce

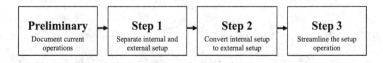

FIGURE 13.3   Stages of SMED implementation.

Setup Analysis Chart TBL Pillar					Machine	1000				Date	
		Economic	Environmental	Social	From:	A	To:	B			
		Time	Energy	Op. Skill	Changeover Categories				The goal of the Improvement Plan		
Step #	Changeover Element	Min.	kwh	%	Internal	External	Waste	Improvement Plan	Eliminate	Internal to External	Reduce
1	Remove fixture (Fixture change)	12	40	3.5	12			Eliminate bolts – install quick release			X
2	Search for tools (Search)	13	---	4.5	13		X	Mount tools at the machine	X		
3	Clean fixtures (Fixture change), remove used supplies such as oil, parts, or products and dispose of them properly, and recycle if necessary	10	---	5.0	10			Standardize procedure to externalize step		X	
4	Put on the fixture (Fixture change)	17	40	3.5	17			Eliminate bolts – install quick release			X
5	Load tools (Tool change)	15	9.9	4.5	15			Standardize tooling on all models	X		
6	Machine first part (First piece)	3	377	3.5		3		Introduce energy efficiency			
	Totals	70	466.9	31.5	67	3					

FIGURE 13.4 Setup analysis chart for manufacturing process.

Setup Analysis Chart TBL Pillar					Machine 1000 From: A To: B				Date		
		Economic	Environmental	Social	Changeover Categories				The goal of the Improvement Plan		
Step #	Changeover Element	Time Min.	Inventory waste in handling %	Teamwork Min.	Internal	External	Waste	Improvement Plan	Eliminate	Internal to External	Reduce
1	Wake up and remove patient	20	---	---	20						
2	Search for instruments, equipment, tables, and supplies (Search)	20	---	---	15	5	X	Case cart preparation, standardize, preference cards.	X	X	X
3	Clean the room, discard waste and biohazards, and clean instruments and equipment	20	5	5	20		X	Standardize procedure, eliminate or reduce non-value to reduce time		X	X
4	Prepare room (instruments, equipment, tables, supplies)	15	1	5	15		X	Eliminate or reduce non-value-added activities, standardize the process		X	X
5	Bring in the patient and adjust	10	---	1	10		X	Standardize process			X
6	Start surgery	3	5	3	3	5					
Totals		88	11	14	83						

FIGURE 13.5 Setup analysis chart for operating room turnover.

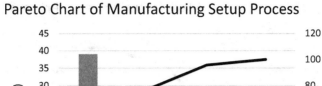

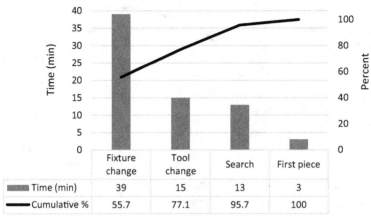

FIGURE 13.6 Setup Pareto analysis for a manufacturing process.

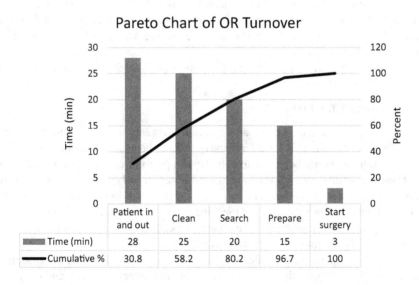

FIGURE 13.7 Setup Pareto analysis for an operating room turnover.

internal setup time by 30% to 50%. Another way to reduce internal setup is to reexamine operations assumed to be internal. The team may assume that some steps are internal but could perform these steps externally. The team can also convert internal setup to external setup by looking at the function of steps and breaking them down into sub steps during the setup process. The continuous improvement team can also

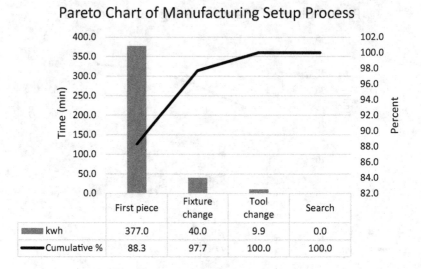

FIGURE 13.8   Setup Pareto analysis for a manufacturing process (TBL).

analyze the internal setup steps to identify ways to shorten or break up tasks. Standardizing the procedure is critical so everyone can perform the standard and repeatable process. Standardization helps to eliminate waste and non-value-added activities in the process.

The following sections describe the three steps of analyzing setup in more detail.

STEP 1: SEPARATE THE ELEMENTS

The team must separate internal and external elements to identify improvement areas. The goal of SMED is for all necessary tools to be available at the point of use so the operator does not need to leave the area to perform any of the external tasks. The team should also identify the separation of internal and external elements on the setup analysis chart using changeover categories, as in Figure 13.5. The team performs internal activities while the machine is not operating or the surgeons are not performing surgeries. However, the team should perform external elements while the operator runs the machine or the patient is in surgery.

The machine operators can efficiently perform several tasks while the machines are running: for example, they can call the proper personnel, set tools, and get parts. However, many operators often begin these tasks once the machine stops. As mentioned earlier in this chapter, by performing these tasks external to the setup, the team can reduce setup time in the organization by 30% to 50%. An emphasis on teamwork, a social area, could improve externalization. Surgical techs can begin moving case carts while the prior surgery is occurring, as well as ensuring surgical techs are available before the surgery is complete. External setups require standardizing alerts and communication to align staff to case completions.

Practical techniques to separate internal and external tasks include checklists, function checks, and improving transport.

Using Checklists. Checklists should include everything required to setup and run the next operation, including equipment, tools, specifications, people, operating conditions, and measurements. By checking off items on the list before stopping the machine, operators can correct missed steps and errors prior to the internal setup. The checklist should also be specific for each machine or operation because general checklists can be confusing and are, therefore, often ignored.

Using Function Checks. Function checks are also important before beginning the internal setup because they verify that the parts are in working order and allow repair time before the changeover. If the operators do not find broken equipment until setup, there may be a large delay during internal setup.

Improving Transport. Another way to reduce the time the machine is down is to move the parts and tools to the machine during external setup. Machine operators should transport all necessary tools and equipment to the machine or operation before they shut down the machine for a changeover. On the other hand, employees should not move the parts and tools from the previous operation to storage until they have installed the new parts and the machine is running. In the operating room, case carts can be staged directly outside the room while the patient is recovering in the room.

STEP 2: CONVERT INTERNAL SETUP TO EXTERNAL SETUP

In the previous step, the team separated internal and external tasks. To reduce the setup time, the team needs to convert the internal setup to an external setup. The first stage is to evaluate each task's true functions and purposes in the current internal setup. The second stage is to convert the internal steps to the external setup. With regard to Sustainability, Ebrahimi et al. (2021) note that the conversion of internal to external tasks may have positive or negative impacts on TBL. For instance, conversion to external may increase externalities, or costs that are indirect to the organization, such as emissions, and have a negative impact beyond the immediate producer and consumer to the wider environment (Goodstein, 2014). Such activity may be called "greenwashing," where the appearance of sustainable or environmentally sound activity is less than perceived (Delmas & Burbano, 2011). Truly sustainable production should avoid externalizing environmental costs as indirect costs and social burdens.

There are three methods to convert internal setup to external setup, described in the following paragraphs.

Technique #1: Prepare the Operation Conditions in Advance. Advance preparation means having the parts, tools, and conditions ready before starting the internal setup. An example is preheating the die molds in advance instead of heating the molds after the setup. Preheating could impact the economic pillar (time) and the environmental pillar (energy). For the operating room, preparation ensures the case carts have all the instruments, supplies, materials, tables, and equipment ready to move and use.

Technique #2: Standardize the Essential Functions. Standardization means keeping characteristics the same from one operation to another. If tools or parts vary between operations, the operators must typically make adjustments while the machine is down, which is time-consuming. In contrast, the team can reduce internal setup time by standardizing the parts and tools. In the operating room, this is standardizing the equipment, tables, supplies, materials, and instruments as much as possible. In operating rooms, each surgeon may prefer slightly different supplies, equipment, materials, and instruments, whereas standardizing these may have little to no effect on the procedure's safety.

Functional standardization focuses on only standardizing elements essential to the setup, such as securing the mold or fixture, centering, and dimensioning. Functional standardization involves two steps:

1. First, evaluate each function in the setup process and determine which can be standardized.
2. Next, evaluate each function again to determine if a more efficient means is possible by using fewer parts. An example is standardizing the tooling for each model to eliminate changing the tools during setup or standardizing the procedure cart for similar procedures across surgeons.

Technique #3: Use Intermediary Jigs. These standard dimension plates or frames are removable from the machinery. The purpose is to externalize as much of the setup as possible. The current fixture is attached to an intermediary jig on the machine. The team can install the next fixture onto an intermediary jig as an external setup procedure. Therefore, the jig is ready for installation onto the machine. An example is standardizing the fixture subplate for similar installation of all fixtures. All fixtures are designed and built with an intermediary jig.

STEP 3: STREAMLINE THE SETUP OPERATION

In the final step of SMED, the team can improve the remaining internal and external setup operations by evaluating each task's functions and purpose again. The team separates the methods for implementing improvements into external and internal setup improvements. In developing the improvement plan, consider the nine forms of waste/*muda*:

1. Defects,
2. Overproduction,
3. Waiting,
4. Non-utilized resources/talent,
5. Transportation,
6. Inventory,
7. Motion,
8. Excess processing, and
9. Wasted resources (e.g., materials, water, energy)

Refer back to the wastes discussed in Chapter 7 for a complete description of each type of waste. The improvement plan should convert internal to external setup, eliminate or reduce internal and external setup, and eliminate adjustments.

Streamlining External Setups. The external setup improvements focus on streamlining the storage and transportation aspect of the setup. To refine these areas, tool and part management are key. 5S is essential to a successful changeover. 5S will ensure that employees do not lose time searching for tools and materials because the required materials will be in the proper place and clean and working. The team can often cut setup times in half just by organizing materials. Staff can spend considerable time in an operating room environment looking for instruments or supplies unavailable on the case cart. Procedures to standardize instrument cleaning and organization, as well as inventory storage of materials and supplies can be implemented. Consistent communication with the vendor who brings medical devices and equipment is also critical.

Streamlining Internal Setups. There are a few techniques for streamlining the internal setup:

- **Implementing parallel operations:** Certain changeovers require performing tasks at the front and back of the machine. Parallel operations reduce the time lost by walking back and forth from the front and back of the machine. Instead, divide the setup operations between two people, one for each side of the machine or different activities in the operating room; this eliminates the walk time and reduces the internal setup time. However, the team must carefully develop a detailed procedural chart to maintain safe and reliable operations during a changeover. The procedural chart should list the task sequence for each person, the time it will take, and when safety signals are required. The signal should be a buzzer, a whistle, or a light to notify the other person. Much time is wasted in an operating room because the staff is not available to change over the room immediately when the prior case is complete.
- **Using functional clamps:** Another technique to streamline internal setups is to use functional clamps. Bolts are considered an enemy in SMED because they slow down internal setups. Bolts often get lost, mismatched, and take too long to tighten. In contrast, functional clamps attach items in place with minimal effort and can be loosened or tightened quickly. Also, because they are typically attached to the machine, operators cannot lose or mismatch them. Types of functional clamping systems include one-turn, one-motion, and interlocking.
- **Eliminating adjustments:** Eliminating adjustments also reduces the time spent during internal setup. Trial runs and adjustments typically account for 50% of the total time in a changeover. By eliminating these adjustments, the team can avoid any time lost due to machine downtime. The key is to have the proper settings before starting the machine for the new operation. Trial runs and adjustments depend on the accuracy of centering, dimensioning, and condition setting. Positioning the patient once reduces re-adjustment time.

Eliminating adjustments can be achieved in several ways:
- Using numerical scales and standardized settings – for example, the team can make a graduated scale with marks that indicate the proper settings.
- Identifying imaginary reference planes and centerlines – for example, by placing V-blocks and rods on the machine table parallel to the centerline and then aligning the center of the cutter.
- And by using the least common multiple (LCM) system, which considers operations with elements in common but different dimensions, patterns, or functions.
- Standardizing operating room tables and setups can reduce the number of patient re-adjustments.

- **Mechanization:** This is the final attempt to streamline setups because it will not significantly reduce the setup time as much as the other techniques. Another reason is that mechanization will reduce inefficient operations but not improve the process. Techniques in mechanization include:
  - Using forklifts for inserting large dies or molds into machines,
  - moving heavy dies,
  - tightening and loosening dies by remote control, and
  - using the energy from presses to move heavy dies.

DOCUMENT THE NEW SETUP

The final step of SMED is to document the new setup on a new setup analysis chart. Videotape the setup procedure again and record the time for each element. Develop a new improvement plan. This process will continue until the elimination of the setup or the setup is within takt time. The setup analysis chart is now the basis for the setup procedure because it contains the necessary steps for a successful changeover. Any other detailed work instructions not included must also be posted and the personnel trained. Remember that continuous improvement is a cycle. So now the team should go back and try to streamline the setup process even more.

INTEGRATED SMED AND SUSTAINABILITY: A PATHWAY TO A CIRCULAR ECONOMY

SMED focuses on reducing non-value-added activities and waste in processes to changeover from one product or service to another. This chapter presented manufacturing and hospital operating room examples for applying SMED. Although service applications do not include manufacturing dies (the D in SMED), the concepts still are extremely valuable to eliminating wastes and improving and standardizing service processes. Services are changed over. For example, operating rooms change from one surgical case to another. In addition, an inpatient or emergency department room must be ready for the next patient when discharging a patient from the hospital and getting ready for the next.

Referring to organizational strategies for SMED and Sustainability, various performance measures within the TBL framework have been incorporated into SMED assessment, depending upon particular Lean and Sustainable strategies (Kalemkerian et al., 2022). Continuous improvement teams should perform SMED analysis in a more holistic and sustainable manner. Nevertheless, organizations can infer generalities such as cost in the economic pillar, consumption (energy, water, material) in the environmental pillar, and health and safety in the social pillar. Methods for improvement rely upon a variety of Lean techniques, namely kaizen, life cycle assessment, 5S, VSM, and 3-R (Kalemkerian et al., 2022). As a circular approach, 3-R is most utilized, with 6R (recover, remanufacture, redesign) gaining interest.

From a Sustainability perspective, many particular elements of turnovers apply to SMED. For example, efficiently using linen in a hospital can help reduce the environmental impact from laundering linens that are left in a patient room, not used, but that must be removed and laundered. Decreasing the items laundered impacts the environment, from water and energy usage to using resources in the laundry facility (Furterer, 2011). When changing over a manufacturing product, there could be harmful chemicals that must be appropriately disposed of when changing from one product to another, such as machine oils or food products, when changing over and cleaning a food production line. There are many bio-hazards in a hospital, especially in cleaning an operating room. Strict regulations and procedures for cleaning must be adhered to, as well as discarding bio-hazardous waste. If not disposed of safely, these bio-hazards could negatively impact the environment, employees, and patients in a hospital.

To put this in perspective, Walker Stockert and Langerman (2014) found the average instrument use rates ranged from 13% for otolaryngology procedures to 21.9% for neurosurgery procedures. Although this is an older study, this demonstrates the potential reduction in cost related to re-processing and re-sterilizing instruments that are sent to the operating room but not used. Further, a study in the Netherlands found potential cost savings between $48,843 and $81,360 and up to $156,461 each year for a non-academic 13-room operating room (Kroes, 2009). Another study estimated savings of up to $2.8 million yearly from a 70% reduction in instrument processing through the sterile supply (Farrokhi et al., 2015). In a study by (Ebrahimi et al. 2021), setup time (economic) reduction was 87%, energy consumption (environmental) was 20%, and operator waste (social) was 99%.

CONCLUSION

SMED enables significant reductions in changeover time, enabling organizations to be more flexible for changes in customer demands and requirements. A large part of providing services is seamlessly transitioning from one customer to the next while providing the organization's services. Considering the integration of the entire process, such as how efficiently a bank account is opened, impacts the speed with which the next customer can receive their services. A holistic TBL assessment is needed to impact sustainable process improvement through SMED. How quickly a hospital can safely discharge a patient impacts the ability to admit and serve the next patient, especially in the emergency room and the surgical suite. Many hospitals use repeatable processes that continuous improvement teams can streamline and remove. Ensuring that processes around changing from one product or customer to the next impacts the Sustainability of the environment through properly discarding or recycling supplies, materials, equipment, and waste.

The next chapter will discuss total productive maintenance moving from a fix when it's broken to one of preventing machine breakdowns by incorporating planned or preventive maintenance integrated with the elements of Sustainability.

REFERENCES

Cudney, E., Furterer, S., & Dietrich, D. (2013). *Lean systems: Applications and case studies in manufacturing, service, and healthcare*. New York, NY: CRC Press.

Delmas, M. A., & Burbano, V. C. (2011). The drivers of greenwashing. *California Management Review, 54*(1), 64–87.

Department of Science, Technology, Health, and Policy Studies (STeHPS). University of Twente, Enschede, The Netherlands. February 2009.

Ebrahimi, A., Khakpour, R., & Saghiri, S. (2021). Sustainable setup stream mapping (3SM): A systematic approach to lean sustainable manufacturing. *Production Planning & Control.* DOI: 10.1080/09537287.2021.1916637

Farrokhi, F. R., et al. (2015). Application of lean methodology for improved quality and efficiency in operating room instrument availability. *Journal for Healthcare Quality, 37*(5), 277–286. doi: 10.1111/jhq.12053

Furterer, S. L. (2011). Applying Lean Six Sigma to reduce linen loss in an acute care hospital. *International Journal of Engineering, Science and Technology, 3*(7), 39–55.

Goodstein, E. (2014). *Economics and the Environment*. Hoboken, New Jersey: Wiley. ISBN 9781118539729.

Helleno, A. L., de Moraes, A. J. I., & Simon, A. T. (2017). Integrating Sustainability indicators and Lean manufacturing to assess manufacturing processes: Application case studies in Brazilian industry. *Journal of Cleaner Production, 153*, 405–416.

Kalemkerian, F., Santos, J., Tanco, M., Garza-Reyes, J. A., & Viles, E. (2022). Analysing the alignment between the Green Lean and Circular strategies: Towards a circular Lean approach. *Journal of Manufacturing Technology Management, 33*(6), 1059–1079. https://doi.org/10.1108/JMTM-11-2021-0480

Kroes, L. (2009). Creating more efficiency and patient safety by changing processes and contents of instrument trays. Master thesis Health Science. School of Management and Governance.

Shingo, S. (1985). *A revolution in manufacturing: The SMED system*. Portland, ME: Productivity Press.

Walker Stockert, E., & Langerman, A. (2014). Assessing the magnitude and costs of intraoperative inefficiencies attributable to surgical instrument trays. *Journal of the American College of Surgeons, 219*(4), 646–655.

14 Employing Total Productive Maintenance for Eco-Friendly Equipment Maintenance

OVERVIEW OF TPM

Traditional manufacturing operates under the "we fix it" mentality in which the maintenance department performs all maintenance activities. These activities are "firefighting" maintenance when a machine breaks down. The maintenance department performs some preventative maintenance; however, there is limited time for this because it occurs around regular machine operating times. In the traditional manufacturing environment, the manufacturing department functions under the "we operate" and "run it until it breaks" mentality. The operators generally do not perform any maintenance activities. Instead, the operators contact maintenance when a machine breakdown occurs. In addition, the operators are inactive during the maintenance activities.

The goal of productive maintenance is to maximize the effectiveness of plants and their equipment to incur the most optimum life cycle of production machinery (Agustiady & Cudney, 2015). In 1951, an idea came to Japan from Dr. W. Edwards Deming. Dr. Deming was an American statistician, professor, author, lecturer, and consultant who promoted the Shewhart Cycle, also known widely as Plan-Do-Check-Act, named after Dr. Walter A. Shewhart. The company Nippondenso, part of Toyota, introduced a maintenance program plant-wide in 1960 based on preventative maintenance for their automated processes. This program had employees utilizing machines. In addition, the company dedicated the maintenance department to maintaining those machines. However, the plan assigned many maintenance personnel to these machines.

Instead of hiring more personnel, management decided it was more logical to use existing labor. Management decided to use operators working on the machine to maintain these machines. Management realized that the labor cost would be much lower than hiring skilled engineers and would also help ensure the operators thoroughly understood the machine they were operating throughout the day. These operators quickly detected if an issue occurred, the machines were performing well, or the product quality was decreasing due to the machinery. This concept now freed up maintenance to focus on more complex problems and determine long-term upgrades and fixes for machines focusing on reliability. The communication between operators and maintenance allowed changes to the machines on an ongoing basis, allowing for

DOI: 10.1201/9780429506192-14

the prevention and detection of issues while increasing the quality of the machines. Product quality improved, and there were fewer scraps and defects. Through communication and group effort, the teams worked on preventative maintenance, prevention of maintenance, and maintainability improvement, which became known as total productive maintenance (TPM).

These developments were well known and developed Toyota as the first company to obtain "TPM" and become certified in the methodology. Nippondenso received the distinguished plant prize for developing and implementing TPM from the Japanese Institute of Plant Engineers (JIPE).

The TPM concept became an innovative Japanese concept in the 1950s. The preventive maintenance concept portion of TPM stemmed from the United States. The concept added autonomous maintenance, and the maintenance crew improved equipment reliability by modifying equipment. These modifications then led to maintenance prevention. Thus, preventive maintenance combined with maintenance prevention and maintainability improvement came to a new concept called productive maintenance. The goal of productive maintenance is to maximize plant and equipment effectiveness and achieve optimum life cycles of production equipment. The involvement of all employees helped make the program a well-established and sought-after system.

Total productive maintenance (TPM) is a Lean tool for equipment maintenance. TPM includes maintenance personnel and operators working in teams to eliminate equipment breakdowns and defects. The three main goals of TPM are to reduce unplanned equipment downtime, eliminate barriers between departments, and reduce equipment-related defects. In addition, the three main objectives of TPM are total employee involvement, a hands-on approach, and improving the organization's competitiveness (Cudney, Furterer, & Dietrich, 2013).

BENEFITS OF SMED

There are numerous benefits to incorporating SMED and how SMED and Sustainability go together in Chapter 13. First, unplanned breakdowns are frustrating to employees. By reducing breakdowns, organizations can increase job satisfaction and increase throughput. Unplanned breakdowns also increase costs from staffing areas that cannot run production and expediting equipment and materials needed for emergency machine maintenance. Further, improving equipment function also improves the quality of products, which provides a competitive advantage (Agustiady & Cudney, 2018). When equipment is maintained correctly, organizations can reduce equipment leaks (e.g., oil, coolant), reducing safety and environmental incidents and impacting the triple bottom line (TBL).

INTEGRATING SUSTAINABILITY INTO TPM

The initial focus of TPM is to return the equipment to like new condition and prevent further deterioration. Implementing preventive maintenance (PM) schedules is the first step toward eliminating deterioration. Figure 14.1 presents the four-phased approach to PM schedules.

PHASE 1
- Inspect equipment for problem areas via the electrical, hydraulic, mechanical, and pipefitter checklists
- Tag all abnormalities
- Document abnormalities using "Tag Log"

PHASE 2
- Prioritize abnormalities via "Tag Log"
- Identify causes of abnormalities

PHASE 3
- Develop PM standards for abnormalities via "Inspection Standards" worksheet
- Identify PM frequency based on priority ranking
- Build PM schedules based on inspection standards

PHASE 4
- Training maintenance and operators on PM standards and PM schedules
- Implement PM schedules
- Monitor PM schedule and usage and effectiveness (i.e., OEE)
- Update standards to reflect changes in requirements

FIGURE 14.1 Four-phased preventive maintenance approach.

The first phase of the four-phase PM schedule development consists of inspecting target equipment, utilizing customized checklists, and tagging and documenting problems. The second phase involves prioritizing identified issues and identifying causes of the highest-priority problems. Commonly used tools in this phase include brainstorming, data collection, and maintenance/operator experience. In phase three, the focus is to develop inspection standards and build PM schedules. The inspection standards should be written standards. These are essential for developing accurate PM schedules. The personnel should communicate the procedure necessary to carry out effective PM. Finally, the fourth phase is to deliver training, implement PM schedules, and monitor and adjust. Appropriate training should be developed and delivered to targeted operators and maintenance personnel. Effective PM implementation requires adequate training. In addition, implementing monitoring measurements provides the vehicle to adjust and change the performance of the equipment. Therefore, overall equipment effectiveness (OEE) is an effective monitoring tool.

The total productive maintenance methodology consists of four key phases, as outlined in Figure 14.2. The methodology starts by returning equipment to almost new conditions. Next, the focus is on zero breakdowns through proper maintenance. The third phase focuses on consolidating information for future use. The final phase of TPM is zero defects.

Complete TPM implementation centers on autonomous maintenance, equipment improvement, maintenance prevention systems, and quality maintenance, as shown in Figure 14.3. Autonomous maintenance involves developing preventative maintenance practices. For equipment improvement, the equipment activities should focus on eliminating all breakdowns through physical equipment analysis (PEA) techniques to target zero breakdowns. The organization should develop an information system for maintenance prevention systems that consists of all TPM activities.

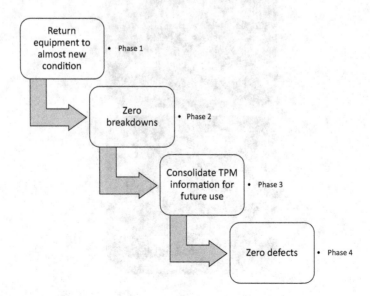

FIGURE 14.2 Total productive maintenance phases.

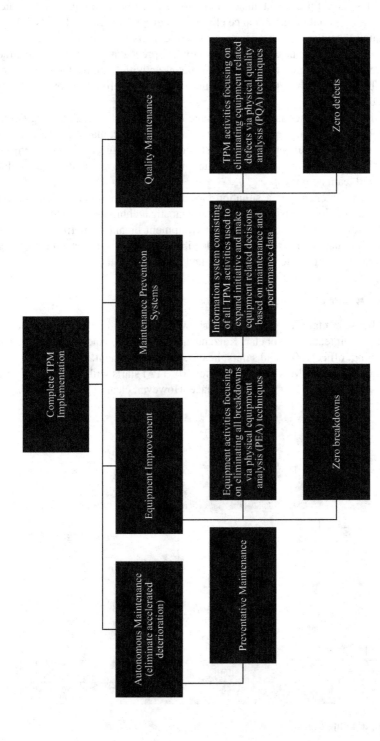

FIGURE 14.3 Total productive maintenance implementation.

Organizations should use maintenance and performance data for equipment-related decisions. Finally, quality maintenance eliminates equipment-related defects through physical quality analysis (PQA). The goal is zero defects.

Autonomous maintenance involves developing preventative maintenance practices. For equipment improvement, the equipment activities should focus on eliminating all breakdowns through PEA techniques to target zero breakdowns, though PQA for zero defects.

Preventive maintenance is a time or usage-based method of maintaining equipment. Much like maintenance of oil changes in an automobile, maintenance activities are performed on equipment based on defined time or usage intervals to prevent equipment breakdowns from occurring. Examples of preventive maintenance are PM schedules and team activities.

Predictive maintenance is a situation-based method of maintaining equipment. Organizations should use visible signals or diagnostic techniques to perform maintenance activities on equipment and prevent equipment breakdowns from occurring. Examples of predictive maintenance include vibration analysis, ultrasound, thermography, laser measuring, generator analysis, and oil analysis.

PILLARS OF TPM

The TPM house contains seven pillars, as shown in Figure 14.4. The pillars include autonomous maintenance, Kobetsu Kaizen, planned maintenance, quality maintenance, training, office TPM, and safety, health, and environment.

The foundation of TPM is 5S (see Chapter 10). TPM starts with 5S because issues cannot be seen clearly in an unorganized place. However, cleaning and organizing an

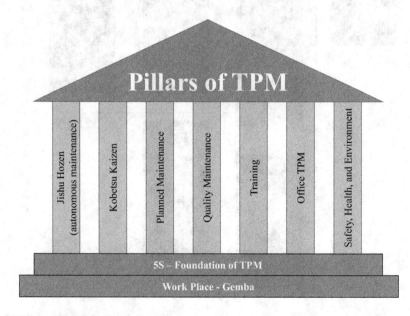

FIGURE 14.4 Pillars of TPM.

area uncovers problems. The first step in making improvements is to make problems visible. 5S consists of five steps: sort, straighten, shine/sweep, standardize, and sustain. In addition, Gemba is a critical concept of TPM. The team must go to the Gemba, or the place where the equipment is, to improve the equipment. Finally, it is essential to understand the concept of maintenance with the minimum environmental impact because of increased maintenance requirements, creating an inefficient use of material, potentially discarded into the environment (parts and materials, discarded into the environment and degrading) (Samadhiya & Agrawal, 2020). Overall maintenance requirements for Sustainability can include: (1) environmental impact (2) energy efficiency, and (3) human-related risks (Samadhiya & Agrawal, 2020).

The first pillar of TPM is autonomous maintenance or jishu hozen. Autonomous maintenance empowers and develops operators to take care of minor maintenance tasks. Operators are responsible for keeping up their equipment and preventing it from deteriorating. Operator-performed maintenance often includes operators performing daily inspections for leaks, oil levels, and oil quality. Preventing environmental losses is important, with machine upgrades reducing maintenance requirements and using non-toxic materials (Samadhiya & Agrawal, 2020). This maintenance frees skilled maintenance people to spend time on more value-added activities and technical repairs.

The second pillar is Kobetsu Kaizen, which is small incremental improvements. *Kai* means change and *zen* means for the better. Kaizen is a concept of continuous improvement. The philosophy is that these minor incremental improvements add up over time.

The third pillar is planned maintenance. By scheduling maintenance, the aim is to eliminate unplanned downtime, eliminate defects, and increase customer satisfaction. Planned maintenance requires the organization to be proactive rather than reactive. Organizations should use trained maintenance staff to help train operators to maintain their equipment and perform daily inspections properly. Common goals of planned maintenance are zero equipment failure and breakdown, improving reliability and maintainability by 50%, reducing maintenance costs by 20%, and always ensuring the availability of spares. There are six key steps to planned maintenance, which include (1) evaluating equipment and recording the present status, (2) restoring the equipment to like new condition, (3) building an information system with equipment data, (4) preparing a time-based information system, select equipment and parts, and map a maintenance plan, (5) develop a predictive maintenance system by introducing equipment diagnostic techniques, and (6) evaluate the planned maintenance.

The fourth pillar of TPM is quality maintenance. This pillar aims to improve customer satisfaction by producing the highest quality product through defect-free manufacturing. The focus is on systematically eliminating non-conformances or defects. The TPM team needs to understand what parts of the equipment affect product quality and begin to eliminate current and then potential quality concerns. Focusing on quality maintenance enables the TPM team to move from reactive to proactive. The goals of quality maintenance are to eliminate customer complaints, reduce in-process defects by 50%, and reduce the cost of quality by 50%.

The fifth TPM pillar is training. TPM training aims to have multi-skilled and energized employees who have high morale and are eager to come to work to perform all their required functions independently and effectively. The training focuses on essential equipment maintenance, such as looking for leaks or cloudy oil. Operator maintenance activities help the organization achieve and sustain downtime at zero on critical machines. The goal is to have 100% of operators trained and engaged in basic mainte- nance activities. The six key steps for training include (1) setting policies and proce- dures and checking the status of education and training, (2) establishing a training system for operations and maintenance skills, (3) training employees in operations and maintenance skills, (4) preparing a training calendar, (5) kicking-off training, and (6) evaluating training activities and adjusting as needed. Organizations should conduct Green training to orient employees around green activities related to training, which involves the proper use of materials, the right movement to minimize safety risks and productivity loss, and less energy consumption (Samadhiya & Agrawal, 2020).

The sixth pillar is office TPM. Organizations should start office TPM after the other pillars of TPM. Office TPM should improve productivity, efficiency, and flow in the administrative functions while identifying losses. Losses are determined by analyzing processes and procedures for office automation. The 12 major losses include processing loss, cost loss, communication loss, idle loss, setup loss, accuracy loss, office equipment breakdown, communication channel breakdown, time spent on retrieval of information, non-availability of correct online stock status, customer complaints due to logistics, and expense on emergency dispatches/purchases.

The seventh and final TPM pillar is safety, health, and environment. This pillar focuses on creating a safe workplace and a surrounding area. This pillar plays an active role in each of the other pillars regularly.

OVERALL EQUIPMENT EFFECTIVENESS

Overall equipment effectiveness (OEE) measures the percentage of time a piece of equipment produces a product that meets or exceeds customer expectations. OEE measures the six big losses: breakdowns, setup, idling, minor stoppages, quality fac- tors, and rework, as shown in Figure 14.5. These six big losses fall under the three categories of availability level, operating level, and quality level. The availability level consists of breakdowns and set up when the equipment is unavailable to run pro- duction. The operating level consists of idling and minor stoppage when the equip- ment is not running; however, these are regular stoppages during the operation for activities such as unloading a part from a machine or malfunctions that are less than ten minutes. The quality level consists of quality factors and rework, which relate to activities to ensure the product meets the customer's quality requirements or rework.

Overall equipment utilization and utilization are related concepts. Utilization shows only an asset's black-and-white utilization from a financial standpoint. However, OEE defines equipment effectiveness by capturing load/unload time and minor stoppages (i.e., operating level) and quality factors and rework (i.e., quality level). OEE measures the actual time the equipment is producing a quality product. OEE is similar to utilization; however, OEE is a more detailed measure.

OEE is essential because it helps to prioritize improvement projects and reflect results. OEE combines the equipment's utilization, operation, and quality aspects into one mea- sure. OEE provides a benchmark for changes to capacity, productivity, and quality. Figure 14.6 provides the OEE calculation, and Figure 14.7 provides a sample calculation.

Availability Level	Operating Level	Quality Level
Breakdowns Malfunctions causing equipment to stop processing product for more than a set time (e.g., 10 minutes)	**Idling** Load/unload time for product on a piece of equipment and/or operators waiting for activities outside of their control	**Quality Factors** Activities related to ensuring the quality of the product produce on the equipment
Setup Any activity related to equipment changeover, setup, and adjustments	**Minor Stoppages** Malfunctions causing equipment to stop processing product less than a set time (e.g., 10 minutes)	**Rework** The time taken to process product of rework

FIGURE 14.5   Major equipment losses.

Loading Time (LT)	Total hours available for equipment operation			
Availability Level (AL)	$\dfrac{LT - (\text{Adminiatrative} + \text{Setup} + \text{Breakdown})}{LT}$		Breakdowns & Admin.	Setup & Adjust
Operating Level (OL)	$\dfrac{AL - (\text{Idling} + \text{Minor Stoppages})}{AL}$	Idling	Minor Stoppages	
Quality Level (QL)	$\dfrac{OL - (\text{Quality} + \text{Rework})}{OL}$	Quality Factors	Rework	
OEE	AL x OL x QL			

FIGURE 14.6   Overall equipment effectiveness calculation.

Loading Time (LT)	Total hours available for equipment operation =168 hrs			
Availability Level (AL)	$\dfrac{168 - (12.3 + 12.4 + 12.5)}{168} = 78\%$		Breakdowns & Admin.	Setup & Adjust
Operating Level (OL)	$\dfrac{131 - (15.4 + 1.1)}{131} = 87\%$	Idling	Minor Stoppages	
Quality Level (QL)	$\dfrac{114 - (3.1 + 0.1)}{114} = 97\%$	Quality Factors	Rework	
OEE	78% x 87% x 97% = 66%			

FIGURE 14.7   Sample overall equipment effectiveness calculation.

CONCLUSION

Total productive maintenance is an innovative approach that reduces equipment breakdowns and defects. TPM is a critical adjunct to Lean. When machine reliability or uptime of the machine is not predictable or sustainable, the process must keep extra stocks to buffer against this uncertainty, and flow through the process will be interrupted. Breakdowns or poorly performed maintenance lead to unreliable uptime. Correcting maintenance will allow uptime to improve and speed up production through a given area, enabling a machine to run at its designed production capacity and minimizing environmental impacts. The next chapter dives into producing quality products and services by implementing mistake-proofing or poka-yoke devices.

REFERENCES

Agustiady, T., & Cudney, E. (2015). *Total productive maintenance: Strategies and implementation guide*. New York, NY: CRC Press.

Agustiady, T., & Cudney, E. (2018). Total productive maintenance. *Total Quality Management & Business Excellence*. Advance online publication. DOI: 10.1080/14783363.2018.1438843

Cudney, E., Furterer, S., & Dietrich, D. (2013). *Lean systems: Applications and case studies in manufacturing, service, and healthcare*. New York, NY: CRC Press.

Samadhiya, A., & Agrawal, R. (2020). Achieving Sustainability through holistic maintenance-key for competitiveness. Proceedings of the International Conference on Industrial Engineering and Operations Management, Dubai, UAE.

15 Integrating Sustainability Principles into Mistake Proofing to Prevent Waste

OVERVIEW OF POKA-YOKE/MISTAKE PROOFING

Poka-yoke is a technique to prevent simple human error. A poka-yoke device is the most effective means of reducing defects because it prevents a defect from occurring. However, implementing poka-yoke devices to detect mistakes and immediately stop the action is also a valuable part of the continuous improvement effort.

The concept of poka-yoke has existed for a long time in various forms. Shigeo Shingo, a Japanese manufacturing engineer, developed the idea into a tool to achieve zero defects. The poka-yoke concept focuses on taking over repetitive tasks and actions to free people's time and mind for more creative and value-adding activities (Cudney, Furterer, & Dietrich, 2013).

Zero Quality Control is an approach for achieving zero defects. This approach controls process performance to prevent defects even when a machine or person makes mistakes. Zero Quality Control is a blameless approach recognizing that people sometimes make mistakes.

BENEFITS OF POKA-YOKE/MISTAKE PROOFING

Poka-yoke devices offer numerous benefits, mainly increasing quality. Implementing poka-yoke devices is essential to maintaining customer satisfaction and loyalty. Since poka-yoke devices prevent or catch defects, defective products or services do not reach the customer. Therefore, the customer only receives good products or services, which increases customer satisfaction. Poka-yoke devices also promote a culture of continuous improvement. Continuous improvement teams should strive to identify and eliminate the root causes as defects occur. Spending time upfront correcting defects before they happen helps change the culture from reactive to proactive (Antony et al., 2022). While organizations often implement poka-yokes to improve quality, poka-yokes are also helpful in improving safety by preventing unsafe situations (Cudney, Murray, & Pai, 2015; Mousavi et al., 2017; Trakulsunti et al., 2022). When organizations reduce the number of defective products, they also waste fewer materials and reduce the resources used to produce defective products, such as water, oil, energy, and other materials. Cost is another reason to focus on eliminating defects. Defects result in costs from scrapping a product, reworking, or repairing damaged equipment.

DOI: 10.1201/9780429506192-15

In these ways, mistake proofing can support an organization's Sustainability efforts with a focus on waste reduction/avoidance. In addition, reducing defective products increases productivity, which can impact an organization's social aspects for Sustainability. Zero defects are also vital for a company to achieve Lean production and smaller inventories (Qin, Cudney, & Hamzic, 2015). Reducing defects allows a company to decrease buffer inventories built with anticipation of problems. The organization does not have to produce more products to replace the defective products. Companies can produce the exact quantity of products ordered by the customer.

INSPECTION TECHNIQUES

Before jumping into the integration of poka-yoke devices and Sustainability, it is essential first to understand the overall goals of poka-yokes and how they are used for inspection to ensure quality products and services. Three primary inspection techniques exist in the field of quality control:

1. Judgment inspection. With the judgment inspection technique, the operator separates defective parts from good parts after processing. This inspection method prevents defects from reaching the customer but does not lower the company's internal defect rate.
2. Informative inspection. Using informative inspection, teams can investigate the cause of the defect and relay that information back to the appropriate process so that the operator can take action to reduce the defect rate.
3. Source inspection. Because simple mistakes typically cause defects, this approach to inspection focuses entirely on the source or root cause. The organization can correct the error by addressing the root cause before it becomes a defect. Organizations can achieve zero defects using source inspection.

Zero Quality Control consists of three main methods leading to eliminating defects. First, source inspection checks for the factors that cause an error rather than inspecting for the resulting defect. It assures that certain conditions exist to perform a process correctly. An example of source inspection is adding a locator pin to prevent a part from being misaligned in a fixture. Source inspection differs from judgment and informative inspection in that it catches errors and provides feedback, enabling the operator to correct the mistake before processing the product.

Second, inexpensive poka-yoke devices, called 100% inspection devices, can provide 100% inspection automatically for errors or defective operating conditions. Zero Quality Control varies from statistical quality control inspections because it requires inspection of every product produced. Statistical quality control only indicates whether a process is in control and does not prevent defects. A limit switch or inexpensive sensing device is an example of a 100% inspection device.

The third component is taking immediate action. Organizations should immediately stop operations when a defect or mistake is made and will not resume until the error is corrected. An interlocked circuit that automatically shuts down a machine when a mistake occurs is an example of taking immediate action.

TYPES OF ERRORS

There are several different types of errors. The first type of human error is forgetfulness. A safeguard to prevent forgetfulness is setting inspections for the operators to perform at regular intervals. Errors due to misunderstanding can happen when people make conclusions before they are familiar with the situation. A lack of suitable work standards or instructions can cause mistakes. Work instructions and work standardization can help avoid these errors. Training and standardizing work procedures can help prevent these situations (see Chapter 16 on standard work). Identification errors are another type of human error. People can misjudge situations when viewed too quickly or from too far away to be visible (see Chapter 12 on visual management). Training and attentiveness can avoid these. Newer operators also make errors due to a lack of experience. Skill building through formal training programs can help prevent these types of mistakes. The fifth type of human error is a willful error when operators decide they can ignore specific rules. Experience, basic education, and corrective actions from management are safeguards against these errors. People can also make inadvertent errors when lost in thought or distracted. Through proper discipline and work standardization, organizations can avoid these defects. Delays in judgment can also cause errors. Again, skill building and work standardization are aspects of avoiding these defects. Occasionally, equipment and machines will run differently than expected, resulting in surprise errors. Total productive maintenance can prevent these errors (see Chapter 14 on total productive maintenance).

TYPES OF DEFECTS

There are various types of defects, including omitted processing (e.g., a missed process), processing errors (e.g., a broken tool), errors in setup (e.g., the wrong machine setting), missing parts (e.g., a missing component in an assembly), wrong parts (e.g., assembling the wrong component), processing the wrong part (e.g., picking up the wrong part), misoperation (e.g., variation in the process), and adjustment errors (e.g., changing the setting incorrectly).

Defects typically occur during one of five situations. First, defects can occur because of inappropriate procedures or standards during process planning. Proper planning to ensure correct standards can avoid this situation. In addition, defects can also occur because of excessive variation in a process. Maintenance can prevent these types of defects (Agustiady & Cudney, 2015). Third, defects can occur when the material is damaged or varies excessively. Implementing inspection on receipt of the materials for defects and variation is a means of eliminating this situation. Next, defects also stem from worn equipment and tools. Again, regular maintenance can prevent these defects. The final situation can occur even when these conditions do not exist. Simple human mistakes result in defective products.

Defects are either about to occur or already exist. Poka-yokes have three main functions: shutdown, control, and warning. Prediction is recognizing that a defect is going to happen. Detection is recognizing that a defect has occurred.

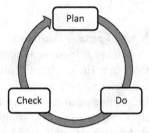

FIGURE 15.1   Plan, do, check cycle of traditional quality improvement.

FIGURE 15.2   Integrated do and check in the zero quality control approach.

QUALITY IMPROVEMENT ACTIVITIES

The traditional quality improvement cycle consists of plan, do, and check, as shown in Figure 15.1. The plan stage is where the continuous improvement team determines the processing conditions. These planned actions then occur in the do stage. Finally, the continuous improvement team monitors the quality in the check stage. The team uses this information to take additional corrective action in the next plan stage, which leads to improving the conditions during the next do stage.

However, organizations cannot completely prevent defects even when continuously repeating the functions in this cycle because the feedback occurs only after producing a defect. There is no means of avoiding the error before it happens.

Zero Quality Control addresses this problem by integrating the do and check stages, as shown in Figure 15.2. Errors can occur between the plan and do functions. In the Zero Quality Control approach, inspection occurs at the point in the process where the error happens. When an error is detected, the operator can correct the problem before completing the work using source inspection.

POKA-YOKE DETECTION SYSTEMS

There are several methods to identify the proper poka-yoke for a situation. Based on the situation, then there are appropriate systems to prevent defects. The first method is to identify an item by its characteristic. The characteristic can be the product's weight, dimension, or shape. Another approach is determining how the defect can deviate from procedures or omitted processes by following the process sequence. Using basic work standardization methods of traveling documentation often provides a living history. A third method is detecting deviations from fixed values using a counter, odd-part-out method, or critical condition detection.

In Zero Quality Control, organizations use true poka-yokes as source inspections to detect errors before the production process creates a defective product. The poka-yoke system detects an error and automatically shuts down the equipment or gives a warning. Control systems stop the equipment when an error is detected. This method is more effective for achieving zero defects because it does not depend on the operator. This type of system may only sometimes be possible or convenient; therefore, the team can also use a warning system. A warning system is used to get the operator's attention and could be a flashing light or a sound. Control systems, however, also typically use lights and noise to direct the operator's attention to the equipment with the problem. Non-automated warning systems, such as color-coding parts and part holders, can also be effective.

There are three main methods for poka-yoke detection devices: contact, fixed-value, and motion-step. Organizations can use these methods with control or warning systems, but each uses a different approach to defects or errors.

Using Contact Methods to Detect Defects or Errors

Contact methods detect if a product makes a physical or energy contact with a sensing device. Microswitches and limit switches are the most commonly used contact devices. However, contact methods do not have to be very technical. Inexpensive contact devices such as guide pins or blocks will only allow an operator to load a part into a fixture in the correct position. These contact methods are passive devices and take advantage of a parts design or uneven shape.

Using Fixed-Value Methods to Detect Defects or Errors

Organizations should use a fixed-value poka-yoke method to detect defects or errors when they have a process with a fixed number of parts that must be attached or assembled in a product. Organizations can also use this method when a process requires a set number of repeated operations at a station.

With fixed-value methods, the device counts the number of times the operator performs a task. The device signals or releases the part only after reaching the required number. Organizations can use limit switches with each movement sending a signal to the counter that, in turn, detects when the necessary number of activities is complete. After reaching the preset number of signals, the device will release the part. For example, if the process requires an assembly with three bolts, that must be set at a specific torque. The assembly fixture would hold the part in place until reaching the count (in this case, three). The device is preprogrammed only to count achieving the proper torque level.

Using Motion-Step Methods to Detect Defects or Errors

Another approach uses the motion-step method to sense when an operator completes a motion within a specific expected time. Organizations can also use this method to detect whether an operator performs a task according to a specified sequence, which is often helpful for assembling the correct parts in a particular product model.

POKA-YOKE PRODUCT DESIGN/RE-DESIGN

Sometimes, it may be necessary to design or re-design a product to be mistake-proof during assembly or installation. This concept is known as design for manufacturing (DFM), design for assembly (DFA), or simply product optimization. This concept includes designing parts so that if a mistake occurs during fabrication and assembly, the part will still be functional and not be considered scrap. This practice uses simple design rules of symmetric design. For example, consider a flat sheet metal formed into a 90-degree bend. The operator can bend the sheet metal in either direction to make a symmetrical bracket, which helps avoid simple fabrication mistakes.

Another design rule includes reducing the number of left-hand-/right-hand-specific designs to eliminate part count numbers and fabrication errors, thus reducing scrap. In addition, designing parts to be multi-functional and multi-use eliminates unnecessary assembly steps that may result in defects and scrap. Also, designing an assembly fixture for a single assembly direction within the assembly process prevents an operator from wasting time and motion and prevents operator fatigue and the propensity for mistakes.

INTEGRATING SUSTAINABILITY INTO POKA-YOKE/MISTAKE PROOFING

The concept of the circular economy is to stop waste from being produced initially by designing systems to eliminate waste and pollution, circulate products and materials at their highest value, and regenerate nature. This concept aligns perfectly with mistake proofing, where continuous improvement teams focus on preventing defects and wastes from occurring in the first place. In the concept of a circular economy, designing Sustainability, refuse, reuse, and recycling into the design of products and services should be the goal so that organizations do not add waste to landfills. This sustainable review of mistake proofing through the design of refuse, reuse, and recycling is critical to Sustainability and sustaining the environment. Organizations can refuse or plan not to use certain materials in the design of their product and incorporate more sustainable production processes, energy, and equipment to enhance environmentally friendly designs. Organizations can reduce the amount of materials, equipment, and overproduction by focusing on Lean efficiency and productivity practices. In addition, organizations can plan to reuse materials, equipment, facilities, and energy sources and then recycle materials internally or externally to keep them out of landfills. Finally, organizations can plan to purchase raw materials as part of the refuse and reflect Sustainability activities.

CONCLUSION

Mistake proofing improves the overall quality of a product or service by increasing awareness, preventing defects, and identifying when defects do occur. Lean mistake proofing prevents errors and defects. Sustainability planning can better design products and services for refuse, reuse, and recycling to reduce waste of material, products, and energy within the incorporation of mistake proofing tools and concepts. The next chapter will discuss standard work, a Lean methodology for consistently performing a task or service.

REFERENCES

Agustiady, T., & Cudney, E. (2015). *Total productive maintenance: Strategies and implementation guide*. New York, NY: CRC Press.

Antony, J., Swarnakar, V., Cudney, E., & Pepper, M. (2022). A meta-analytic investigation of lean practices and their impact on organizational performance. *Total Quality Management & Business Excellence*, *33*(15–16), 1799–1825.

Cudney, E., Furterer, S., & Dietrich, D. (2013). *Lean systems: Applications and case studies in manufacturing, service, and healthcare*. New York, NY: CRC Press.

Cudney, E., Murray, S., & Pai, P. (2015). Relationship between lean and safety. *International Journal of Lean Enterprise Research*, *1*(3), 217–231.

Mousavi, S., Cudney, E., & Trucco, P. (2017). Towards a framework for steering safety performance: A review of the literature on leading indicators. In P. Arezes (Ed.), *Advances in safety management and human factors* (pp. 195–204). New York, NY: Springer.

Qin, R., Cudney, E., & Hamzic, Z. (2015). An optimal plan of zero-defect single-sampling by attributes for incoming inspection in assembly lines. *European Journal of Operational Research*, *246*(3), 907–915.

Trakulsunti, Y., Antony, J., Edgeman, R., Cudney, E., Dumpsey, M., & Brennan, A. (2022). Reducing pharmacy medication errors using Lean Six Sigma: A Thai hospital case study. *Total Quality Management & Business Excellence*, *33*(5–6), 664–682.

16 Ensuring Consistent Performance through Standard Work

OVERVIEW OF STANDARD WORK

Standard work is a Lean tool that defines and documents the interaction between people and their environment. Standard work provides a routine for the consistency of an operation and a basis for improvement by detailing the operator's movement and the sequence of action. First, a continuous improvement team documents the current process to provide a basis or standard for continuous improvement. This baseline enables the team to identify opportunities for improvement. Using time observations of the existing process, the improvement team should make changes to the line to improve working conditions, flow, and the level load of the operators. After implementing improvements, the team should revise the process's standard work to incorporate them. The improved process becomes the baseline for the team to use in the future.

Standard work is a tool to determine maximum performance with minimum waste through the best combination of operator and machine. In addition, standard work helps eliminate variability from the process and functions as a diagnostic device. Furthermore, standard work exposes problems and facilitates problem-solving for both operator and process control monitors. Finally, it helps us to identify waste and drives us to kaizen the process (Cudney et al. (2013)).

BENEFITS OF STANDARD WORK

Standard work is a Lean tool with several benefits. First, standard work establishes a routine for repetitive tasks and makes managing resource allocation and scheduling easier. Further, standard work demonstrates the relationship between a person and the environment. Standard work also forms a basis for improvement by defining the normal process and highlighting areas for improvement by making problems visual and obvious. It prohibits backsliding or relapse into previous bad habits.

INTEGRATING SUSTAINABILITY INTO STANDARD WORK

Before implementing standard work, the operation must be observable, repetitive, and based on human motion. In addition, the process must be standardized. Moreover, the

DOI: 10.1201/9780429506192-16

production manager or supervisor must be responsible for the implementation of standard work. Standard work consists of three elements: takt time, standard work sequence, and standard work-in-process.

Takt time. Takt time is how frequently an organization must complete a product to meet customers' expectations. Teams calculate takt time using customer demand and available time. Takt time sets the rhythm for standard work. Operator cycle time, CT_O, is the total time required for an operator to complete one cycle of operation, including the time needed for walking, loading and unloading, and inspecting products. The machine cycle time, CT_m, is the time between the instant an operator presses the on or start button and the point at which the machine returns to its original position after completing the target operation.

Takt time is equal to the total daily operating time divided by the total daily requirements, as shown in Equation (16.1). The variables include customer demand and available work time. Therefore, teams should recalculate the takt time when customer demand changes or the available work time changes.

$$\text{Takt Time} = \frac{\text{Available Time}}{\text{Customer Demand}} \tag{16.1}$$

The total cycle time, TCT, is the completion rate of a process or operation. TCT is a summation of operator cycle time and machine cycle time for all the processes, as shown in Equation (16.2).

$$\text{TCT} = \sum_{i=1}^{n} i = \left(CT_0 + CT_m \right) \tag{16.2}$$

If takt time is known, computing TCT provides an understanding of how many operators the process needs to balance the line, as shown in Equation (16.3).

$$\text{Number of operators needed} = \frac{\text{TCT}}{\text{Takt Time}} \tag{16.3}$$

Work Sequence. Work sequence is the specific order in which an operator performs the manual steps of a process. The work sequence may be different from the process sequence. Focusing on the work sequence identifies waste and stabilizes the process. Work sequence requires multi-skilled operators. A complete operator cycle is from when the operator begins the sequence to when the operator returns to that same point.

Standard Work-in-Process. Standard work-in-process is the minimum number of parts on the line that will allow an operator to flow product efficiently, minimizing waste in the process. Keeping the number of parts standard is critical to allowing work to continue without the operator waiting.

DOCUMENTING STANDARD WORK

Teams will document standard work using several standard forms. These forms help standardize the process. These forms consist of the takt timesheet, time observation sheet, process capacity table, standard work combination sheet, standard worksheet, and operator loading chart.

Takt Time Sheet. The takt time sheet documents the minutes available, pieces per shift, time allotted for break times, time for washup, and time for cleanup. Figure 16.1 shows the takt timesheet, and Figure 16.2 provides an example of the takt time calculation. Figure 16.3 shows the total cycle time calculation.

```
|                 Calculating Takt Time                          |
|                                                                |
| ____ hours = _____ minutes (based on standard work shift) |
|              - _____ minutes (break time)                   |
|              - _____ minutes (wash time)                    |
|              - _____ minutes (clean-up)                     |
|              - _____ minutes (team meetings)                |
|       Total  = _____ available minutes per shift            |
|                                                                |
| ____ minutes available x 60 = _____ seconds per shift         |
|                                                                |
| ____ seconds per shift x 2 shifts = _____ seconds per day     |
|                                                                |
| ____ seconds divided by ____ pcs/day = ____ seconds            |
|                                                                |
|   Takt Time = _____ seconds per piece                         |
```

FIGURE 16.1 Takt time sheet.

```
|                 Calculating Takt Time                          |
|                                                                |
|  8  hours =  480  minutes (based on standard work shift)       |
|             -30   minutes (break time)                         |
|             -10   minutes (wash time)                          |
|             -0    minutes (clean-up)                           |
|             -5    minutes (team meetings)                      |
|      Total  435   available minutes per shift                  |
|                                                                |
|  435  minutes available x 60 =   26,100  seconds per shift     |
| 26,100  seconds per shift x 2 shifts = 52,200 seconds per day  |
| 52,200  seconds divided by  775   pcs/day =    67   Seconds    |
|     Takt Time =   67   seconds per piece                       |
```

FIGURE 16.2 Example takt time calculation.

	Operation 1		Operation 2		Operation 3		
	Machining		Drilling		De-Burring		
	Operator Cycle Time (CT_0)	Machine Cycle Time (CT_m)	Operator Cycle Time (CT_0)	Machine Cycle Time (CT_m)	Operator Cycle Time (CT_0)	Machine Cycle Time (CT_m)	**TCT**
Seconds	100	30	40	10	60	30	270

FIGURE 16.3   Example total cycle time calculation.

Time Observation Sheet. The time observation sheet focuses on manual and walk time elements. The team should fill out a separate sheet for each operator. The time observation sheet has three key steps. The first step is to identify the work elements. Next, the team should determine the observation points. Finally, the team should time each element using a running clock.

The first step in appraising the current process is to time the process. Begin by outlining the process steps. Then, time the existing process for walking, loading, unloading, standard inspection, and machine cycle times. The team should take 10 observations of the process and record them on the time observation form. Figure 16.4 provides the time observation form.

When making the observations, the team can use a running clock. In this case, the team should subtract the times between observations to obtain the time for each step. Then, the team determines the lowest elemental time for each step and adds the lowest elemental times to calculate the time for one cycle. The team should also add the

Process for Observation		TIME OBSERVATION FORM										Part No.		Part Type	
												Part Name		Daily Demand	
No.	Component Task	1	2	3	4	5	6	7	8	9	10	Lowest Elemental Time	Adjustment	Adjusted Elemental Time
	Time for One Cycle													

FIGURE 16.4   Time observation form.

times for individual steps to calculate the time for one cycle. The team can then adjust the steps to make the total of the lowest elemental times equal to the lowest cycle time of the actual observations.

Suppose the total time for one cycle of the actual observations is greater than the takt time for the operator performing machining responsibilities. In that case, the team must improve the process to meet takt time. Figure 16.5 is an example of a completed time observation sheet.

Process for Observation		TIME OBSERVATION FORM									Part No.		Part Type	
											Part Name		Daily Demand	

No.	Component Task	1	2	3	4	5	6	7	8	9	10	Lowest Elemental Time	Adjustment	Adjusted Elemental Time
1	Unload, blow off chips, load, clamp, start	0:33	0:37	0:38	0:43	0:40	0:43	0:56	0:72	0:57	0:52	0:33	0:10	0:43
		0:33	0:37	0:38	0:43	0:40	0:43	0:56	0:72	0:57	0:52			
	Walk	0:10	0:11	0:10	0:10	0:11	0:09	0:19	0:12	0:11	0:15	0:09	0:00	0:09
		0:43	0:48	0:48	0:53	0:51	0:52	1:15	1:24	1:08	1:07			
2	Unclamp, unload, blow off chips, load, clamp, start	0:32	0:38	0:37	0:41	0:30	0:36	0:36	0:33	0:41	0:41	0:30	0:10	0:40
		1:15	1:26	1:25	1:34	1:21	1:28	1:51	1:57	1:49	1:48			
	Walk	0:18	0:16	0:14	0:14	0:17	0:17	0:24	0:19	0:17	0:17	0:14	0:00	0:14
		1:33	1:42	1:39	1:48	1:38	1:45	2:15	2:16	2:06	2:05			
3	Unload, blow off chips, load, start	0:27	0:35	0:32	0:29	0:23	0:29	0:29	0:34	0:40	0:43	0:23	0:05	0:28
		2:00	2:17	2:11	2:17	2:01	2:14	2:44	2:50	2:46	2:48			
	Walk	0:10	0:08	0:07	0:08	0:09	0:09	0:09	0:08	0:11	0:07	0:07	0:00	0:07
		2:10	2:25	2:18	2:25	2:10	2:23	2:53	2:58	2:57	2:55			
4	Unload, blow off chips, load, start	0:24	0:33	0:28	0:28	0:30	0:29	0:35	0:38	0:44	0:43	0:24	0:05	0:29
		2:34	2:58	2:46	2:53	2:40	2:52	3:27	3:36	3:41	3:38			
	Walk	0:08	0:12	0:08	0:11	0:09	0:10	0:12	0:09	0:09	0:09	0:08	0:00	0:08
		2:42	3:10	2:54	3:04	2:49	3:02	3:39	3:45	3:50	3:37			
5	Unload, blow off chips, load, start	0:31	0:30	0:41	0:33	0:32	0:33	0:29	0:33	0:33	0:40	0:29	0:05	0:34
		3:13	3:40	3:35	3:37	3:21	3:35	4:08	4:18	4:26	4:17			
	Inspect	0:13	0:13	0:14	0:13	0:13	0:14	0:13	0:14	0:14	0:13	0:13	0:00	0:13
		3:26	3:53	3:49	3:50	3:34	3:49	4:21	4:32	4:40	4:30			
	Walk	0:08	0:08	0:07	0:08	0:07	0:07	0:08	0:08	0:07	0:07	0:08	0:00	0:08
		3:34	4:01	3:56	3:58	3:41	3:56	4:28	4:40	4:47	4:37			
6	Unload, blow off chips, load, start	0:31	0:30	0:30	0:32	0:33	0:34	0:34	0:36	0:29	0:49	0:29	0:05	0:34
		4:05	4:31	4:26	4:30	4:14	4:30	5:02	5:16	5:16	5:26			
	Inspect	0:16	0:13	0:19	0:14	0:13	0:15	0:13	0:16	0:14	0:14	0:13	0:00	0:13
		4:21	4:44	4:45	4:44	4:27	4:45	5:15	5:32	5:30	5:40			
	Walk	0:03	0:06	0:04	0:04	0:03	0:05	0:03	0:04	0:04	0:03	0:03	0:00	0:03
		4:24	4:50	4:49	4:48	4:30	4:50	5:18	5:36	5:34	5:43			
7	Unload, blow off chips, load, start	0:33	0:29	0:26	0:29	0:30	0:31	0:33	0:35	0:28	0:30	0:28	0:05	0:33
		4:57	5:19	5:15	5:17	5:00	5:21	5:51	6:11	6:02	6:13			
	Inspect	0:08	0:12	0:10	0:09	0:08	0:10	0:09	0:09	0:08	0:09	0:13	0:00	0:13
		5:05	5:31	5:25	5:26	5:08	5:31	6:00	6:20	6:10	6:22			
	Walk	0:12	0:08	0:10	0:08	0:08	0:09	0:08	0:10	0:09	0:09	0:08	0:00	0:08
		5:17	5:39	5:35	5:34	5:16	5:40	6:08	6:30	6:19	6:31			
8	Unload, load, blow off chips, start	0:33	0:20	0:19	0:23	0:20	0:25	0:25	0:27	0:27	0:32	0:19	0:05	0:24
		5:49	5:59	5:54	5:57	5:36	6:05	6:33	6:57	6:46	7:03			
	Walk	0:05	0:05	0:05	0:07	0:07	0:06	0:05	0:06	0:06	0:15	0:05	0:00	0:05
		5:54	6:04	5:59	6:04	5:43	6:11	6:38	7:03	6:52	7:18			
9	Blow off, put gloves on	0:57	0:63	0:67	0:65	0:63	0:65	0:66	0:64	0:65	0:67	0:57	0:00	0:57
		6:51	7:07	7:06	7:09	6:46	7:16	7:44	8:07	7:57	8:25			
	Plug, blow off, remove gloves	0:78	0:85	0:89	0:80	0:79	0:85	0:84	0:86	0:82	0:85	0:78	0:00	0:78
		8:09	8:32	8:35	8:29	8:05	8:41	9:08	9:33	9:19	8:50			
	Walk	0:20	0:13	0:09	0:17	0:22	0:29	0:32	0:28	0:30	0:29	0:09	0:00	0:09
		8:29	8:45	8:44	8:46	8:27	9:10	9:40	10:01	9:49	9:19			
	Time for One Cycle	**8:29**	**8:45**	**8:44**	**8:46**	**8:27**	**9:10**	**9:40**	**10:01**	**9:49**	**9:19**	**7:40**	**:50**	**8:30**

FIGURE 16.5   Example time observation form.

Process Capacity Table. The process capacity table documents the machine capacity per shift. Use one sheet for each cell. The table focuses on the total machine time, including load and unload times. Document only the load, unload, and cycle start when calculating the manual time. The team should also consider tool changes in the calculations. Do not include any abnormalities that are not standard.

The team should perform process capacity calculations for each process step. List each process step's associated manual time, machine time, and walking time. In addition, evaluate tool changes. Then add the manual time, machine time, and walking time to obtain the total time to complete the process step. Finally, divide this time into the available operating time per shift: this calculation results in the processing capacity per shift. Figure 16.6 provides the process capacity table, and Figure 16.7 is an example of a completed process capacity table.

Standard Work Combination Sheet. The next step in outlining the existing process is to fill out the standard work combination sheet. The standard work combination sheet combines manual, automatic machine, and walk elements. Plot these against the takt time. Use one sheet for each operator, and the team should post the sheet at the starting point of each operator sequence. Figure 16.8 shows the standard work combination sheet, and Figure 16.9 provides an example.

Fill out a standard work combination sheet for each operator. Use the same steps to complete this form as the team used when completing the process capacity sheet. Then list the manual, machine, and walking times for their respective process step. Draw the manual time on the combination sheet chart using a straight line. Then add the machine cycle time after the manual time by drawing a dotted line. Finally, draw a curved line from the end of the manual time for the observed length of walking time to the next process step. After the team has determined whether the current process is within takt time, evaluate the process to identify areas for kaizen.

Standard Work Sheet. After documenting the process capacity and time observations, the next step is to draw a standard worksheet to depict the process flow and machine layout of the current process. The standard work sheet is an overhead view of the cell or operations that illustrates the process and work sequence. It documents the standard work-in-process, safety precautions, and quality checks. Again, the team should complete a sheet for each operator and post the standard worksheet at the starting point of each operator sequence. Figure 16.10 shows the standard worksheet, and Figure 16.11 shows an example.

Draw the operation sequence from raw material to finished material. First, draw the machine and assembly stations to illustrate the floor layout. Then add the operator flow to show the steps the machining and assembly operator takes to complete the process. The team should number these steps in sequence for each operator. Then mark each station for quality checks, safety precautions, and work-in-process.

Operator Loading Chart. The final charting of the standard work process is to graph the operator loading chart. The operator loading chart documents the time allocated for all operators in the cell. It also reports how many operators are in the cell. The chart is a bar chart. Figure 16.12 shows an example.

PROCESS CAPACITY FORM

Department Manager		Part No.		Part Type		Operating Time Per Shift in Seconds	
Supervisor		Part Name		Daily Demand			

Step No.	Process Description	Machine No.	Base Time (Seconds)		Tool Change			Time (Seconds)	Processing Capacity	Remarks
			Manual	Machine	# of pcs per change	Replacement Time	Tool change Time	Total Time to Complete		
1										
2										
3										
4										
5										
6										
7										
8										
9										
10										
Total										

FIGURE 16.6 Process capacity table.

PROCESS CAPACITY FORM

Department Manager		Part No.		Part Type		Operating Time Per Shift in Seconds
Supervisor		Part Name		Daily Demand		26,100
						55

Step No.	Process Description	Machine No.	Base Time (Seconds)		Tool Change			Time (Seconds)	Processing Capacity	Remarks
			Manual	Machine	# of pcs per change	Replacement Time	Tool change Time	Total Time to Complete		
1	Machine Z-plane	CNC 1	53	294	800	30	360	347	75	
2	Drill bolt holes	CNC 2	33	414	1500	30	90	447	58	Bottleneck operation
3	Rough drill tube bores	CNC 3	28	349	750	30	90	377	69	
4	Finish drill tube bores	CNC 4	27	196	750	30	90	223	117	
5	Rough and finish drill center bore	CNC 5	32	423	375	30	90	455	57	Bottleneck operation
6	Mill clearance out	CNC 6	34	378	750	30	360	413	63	
7	Drill oil hole	CNC 7	30	343	2500	30	60	373	70	
8	Hand tap	CNC 7	22	229	75	90	0	252	103	
9	Assemble gear housing	Assembly	59	0	0	0	0	59	442	
10										
Total			318	2,626						

FIGURE 16.7 Example process capacity table.

From:		Raw Material				**STANDARD WORK SHEET**			Part No.				
To:		Finished Material							Part Name:				
		Quality Check		Safety		Standard WIP		# Pieces WIP		TAKT Time	Cycle Time		
		◇		+		○							

FIGURE 16.8   Standard work sheet.

From:		Raw Material				**STANDARD WORK SHEET**			Part No.				
To:		Finished Material							Part Name:				

FIGURE 16.9   Example standard work sheet.

This graph depicts the operator versus their respective takt time. It shows if the operators can do their assigned tasks within takt time. If the operator's time exceeds takt time, they will not meet customer demand. However, if the operator time is significantly below takt time, this indicates waste in the process (e.g., the operator or machine is waiting or idle). For example, in Figure 16.12, Operator A has a cycle time of 460 seconds, and Operator B has a cycle time of 458 seconds. The takt time is 474 seconds, indicating that both operators can complete their tasks within the takt time.

STANDARD WORK COMBINATION SHEET

Date Prepared		Quota Per Shift		Manual work	
Dept.		TAKT Time		Machine Work	
				Walking	

Operation Working Time (In Seconds)

| Model | | | | | |
| Work Seq. | | | | | |

Step No.	Description of Operation	Manual	Auto	Walk	25 50 75 100 125 150 175 200 225 250 275 300 325 350 375 400 425 450 475 500
1					
2					
3					
4					
5					
6					
7					
8					
9					
10					
TOTAL					

FIGURE 16.10 Standard work combination sheet.

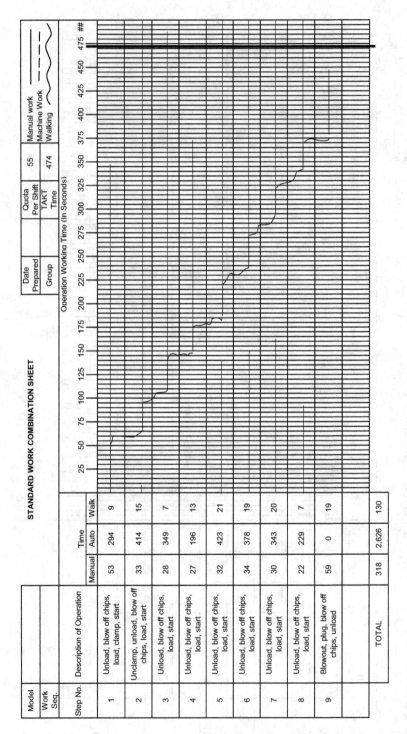

FIGURE 16.11 Example standard work combination sheet.

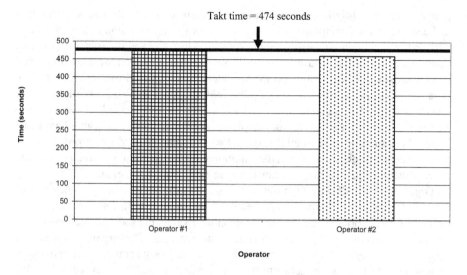

FIGURE 16.12   Operator loading chart.

LEAST OPERATOR CONCEPT

Since the purpose of Lean is to drive continuous improvement, there is a technique within standard work that helps drive continuous improvement. The least operator concept states that the cell should be front-loaded, and the team should allocate all waiting time to the least operator. The least operator should be the last operator in the sequence. The team should fully load the other operators to takt time, which makes the waste (e.g., waiting time) visible. It also exposes the opportunity for improvement at the last operation.

In contrast, natural work has the operator at various loads. The traditional work setup has the operators at equal loads; however, this is usually not at takt time. The front-loaded concept has all the operators except the last operator loaded at takt time.

Teams can calculate resource requirements. The total number of operators required equals the sum of individual operator cycle times divided by the takt time.

INTEGRATING STANDARD WORK AND SUSTAINABILITY

As a tool, organizations can integrate standard work into a Lean Sustainable framework to further achieve the triple bottom line (TBL). In addition, the Shingo model for Lean can support the organization's efforts for Lean Sustainability. Shigeo Shingo stated that the four purposes of improvement were easier, better, faster, and cheaper, in that order. Organizations can implement standard work to make the employee's work more consistent; as a result, products and services are better, faster, and less expensive. These characteristics also relate to TBL. For example, standard work is noted as a means to improve the social and economic pillars of the TBL (Sá et al., 2022). The economics of standard work is evident; however, companies looking to improve their productivity may overlook the social aspects of standard work. Shingo also provides guidance here, highlighting the importance of organizational culture and integration of Lean into company culture (Sá et al., 2022). As a Lean tool, standard work fulfills TBL in both the economic aspect of improved productivity and the social impact as a cultural enabler of Lean Sustainability. Through reduced worker wastage, improved worker satisfaction with improved worker safety, and improved worker environment, organizations can improve the social pillar of TBL (Sá et al., 2022). While Shingo's model is a lens for standard work and Lean Sustainability, standard work is also beneficial regarding the environmental pillar, especially in industries with heavy raw material consumption (Maia et al., 2013). Lean sustainable production promotes the need to reduce or eliminate the seven traditional wastes, particularly overproduction, defects and over-processing, and raw material extraction (Maia et al., 2013).

Organizations will only reap the full value of Lean Sustainability if they have a strategy for capturing the potential benefits of the triple bottom line. While conventional standard work captures the direct economic value, the social value may not be captured indirectly through human-generated measures. The organization should incorporate surveys, interviews, or in general, listening posts among their employees on assessment of social impact from standardizing work, making things easier on the employee, and improving things. Many organizations already have mechanisms for collecting employee feedback, but a team looking to incorporate the social pillar of TBL with standardized work should leverage these systems. Organizations such as OSHA assess improvements in worker safety through regulatory means. However, if a safe worker is productive, then standard work for Lean Sustainability emphasizes both the economic and social pillars. Finally, process standardization can result in a reduction in waste, not only in activity but materially as well. Chapter 10 discusses Lean value and waste analysis that organizations can use when assessing standard work improvements. While all these means of measure and assessment may reside distinctly within the organization, bringing them together for a more holistic approach can result in a Lean Sustainable model.

CONCLUSION

Standard work documents a process so that all operators follow the same method to reduce process variability. A Lean Sustainable approach recognizes how standardized work can impact the triple bottom line if the organization seeks to do so systematically. The next chapter addresses the next step of process standardization: materials movement using Lean tools such as flow, pull, and Kanban.

REFERENCES

Cudney, E., Furterer, S., & Dietrich, D. (2013). *Lean systems: Applications and case studies in manufacturing, service, and healthcare.* New York, NY: CRC Press.
Maia, L., Alves, A., & Leao, C. (2013). Sustainable work environment with Lean production in textile and clothing industry. *International Journal of Industrial Engineering and Management, 4*(3), 183–190.
Sá, J., Reis, M., Dinis-Carvalho, J., Silva, F., Santos, G., Ferreira, L., & Lima, V. (2022). The development of an excellence model integrating the Shingo model and Sustainability. *Sustainability, 14.* https://doi.org/10.3390/su14159472

17 Environmentally Conscious Material Movement throughout the Enterprise

LEAN MATERIAL MOVEMENT OVERVIEW

Lean emphasizes the elimination of waste and the creation of flow within an enterprise. The primary focus of Lean is on the customer, to identify, from a customer perspective, value-added and non-value-added tasks and minimize and eliminate non-value-added tasks. Value-added tasks are the only operations the customer is ready and willing to pay for. On the contrary, non-value-added tasks are processing steps that produce a waste in which the customer would not want to pay to have these activities performed. These non-value-added tasks fall into two main categories: value-added and non-value-added. Value-added activities are necessary to produce a product or service, while non-value-added activities are not necessary to produce a product or service (Cudney, Furterer, & Dietrich, 2013).

The idea for creating flow in Lean is to deliver products and services just-in-time, in the right amounts, and at the right quality levels at the right place. Flow necessitates that organizations only produce products and services when the customer exerts a pull through a signal in the form of a purchase. A well-designed Lean system allows for an immediate and effective response to fluctuating customer demands and requirements (Antony et al., 2022).

LEAN HISTORY AND PROGRESSION

Manufacturing has continued to evolve from traditional manufacturing to Heijunka, and each period had various methods of controlling production: instruction, production control, material, person, machine, and lead time.

Prior to the 1900s, artisans created hand-crafted products one at a time from start to completion. Because of this sequential process, delivery to the customer was typically slow, but the quality was potentially high because the focus was on a singular product. However, there was a wide variation in product and process because a process step from one product to the following product might be several weeks apart. Artisan training lacked consistency as it largely remained an apprenticeship style of learning structure. As a result of this type of customized training, product variation in the form of dimensional control, structural quality, and speed of delivery among different artisans remained erratic. In many cases, the same artisan could not produce the same part repeatability relative to dimensional control and structural characteristics across their products.

Henry Ford's assembly line used batch production. There was one operator at each machine or station and, therefore, a single-task orientation. The machines were high-volume, with a focus on high machine utilization. This style of production resulted in large production lots of sequential steps. Lead times in batch production were long because each product in the batch must wait for the completion of other products in that batch before it could continue to the following process. The following sections describe each manufacturing environment up to current practices.

TRADITIONAL OPERATIONS ENVIRONMENT

Traditional operations consist mainly of verbal production instructions and are entirely reactionary to forecasting and, as a result, often changed by manufacturing planners. Production planners schedule the production of products and services at several locations. Inventory and materials are decentralized and difficult to control often because the material is bought and stored in large non-defined quantities. Management assigns processes to specialized operators. The production aims for maximum capacity and machine utilization, with equipment dedicated to a specific function. Long setup times were often associated with the equipment to justify the sizeable batch-style machine utilization. The lead time to manufacture a product becomes highly variable and difficult to predict.

CONTINUOUS FLOW ENVIRONMENT

Continuous flow is similar to traditional operations in that the orders are mainly verbal. Organizations forecast demand; therefore, the production schedule changes often. Organizations using continuous flow manufacturing produce products at limited locations. Organizations still schedule production in a decentralized manner. The focus of improvements is now on controlling processes, and material has changed from large undefined quantities to limited work-in-process. An operator's responsibilities change from specialized tasks to related tasks within processes. Continuous flow environments arrange equipment according to the process flow rather than grouped by function, with product lead times becoming more predictable with reductions in lead time occurring.

STANDARDIZED WORK ENVIRONMENT

Production instruction in a standardized work environment is similar to continuous flow with verbal instructions, forecasting, and limited production locations. In addition, the organization manufactures products based on customer orders with a defined work-in-process. Standard work environments consist of well-defined processes for the work sequence for the operator, with work instructions clearly defined for a flexible workforce. The idealized state of a standard work environment should be a seamless substitution of workers, regardless of skill level, to perform a specific process function based on the standardized work instructions. In addition to manual labor, the organization synchronizes machines to approximately the same process speed, and the lead time for a product is predictable.

PULL SYSTEMS

A pull system uses a concrete order for the customer's requirements. Production control is visible and disciplined, typically using kanbans (signals for production). Management controls material using kanbans to replenish the system and determine proper inventory levels. Pull systems were developed primarily for economic reasons. However, the impact on material consumption results in alignment with Sustainability. With systems to control inventory, the operator's indirect work becomes more manageable. The lead time now is based on the customer rather than the process. Customer lead time is predictable since each production line only produces products based on specific customer demand. This practice leads to the customer "pulling" the product through the value chain or the sequence of activities that create a product or provide a service.

SMALL LOTS

The method of using small lots is similar to the pull system; however, customer requirements change frequently. Organizations can reduce production to the reduced size of lots. Kaizen is used to improve processes, support operators, and reduce the lead time. Production frequently performs changeovers on equipment for different products. Organizations should use single-minute exchange of dies (SMED) whenever possible to reduce changeovers. With kaizen and SMED, the lead time for an order reduces, reducing material usage and potentially impacting an organization's environmental impact.

HEIJUNKA METHOD FOR LEVEL LOADING

Heijunka is a method focused on leveling production. Production instruction and control are similar to that of the small-lot method. Within this environment, material usage is uniform with a leveled production. The operator workloads, operating equipment efficiency, and machine utilization are uniform. Again, the lead time for production is reduced and predictable, hitting on triple-bottom-line principles of social, economic, and environmental impact.

JUST-IN-TIME

The just-in-time (JIT) production system is a philosophy of providing the right product or service in the correct quantity or amount at precisely the right time based on customer requirements; as such, JIT drives to eliminate waste. The seven forms of waste are overproduction, inventory, transportation, processing, motion, waiting, and defective parts. Organizations should also consider the eighth waste of unused creativity and intellect of people. By implementing JIT concepts to eliminate waste, JIT drives quality, delivery, and cost improvements.

The key to the JIT system is the customer. Customers in the past could only select high quality, good service, or low price. At best, the customer may get two out of three. Organizations must provide for all three to meet or exceed customer requirements. Therefore, the profit equation has changed drastically over time, changing the dynamic perspective of business profitability. The old calculation was to add the cost to the profit desired to determine the selling price, as shown in Equation (17.1). In contrast, the new method calculates the profit by subtracting the cost from the selling price, as shown in Equation (17.2).

$$\text{cost} + \text{profit} = \text{selling price} \qquad (17.1)$$

$$\text{profit} = \text{selling price} - \text{cost} \qquad (17.2)$$

ONE-PIECE FLOW AND CELLULAR LAYOUT

Taiichi Ohno at Toyota developed Lean production in which multiskilled operators run several machines or steps. Lean production may incorporate cellular design, whereas flow production uses customer orders. Other characteristics include one-piece flow and flexible setups.

One-piece flow in a cellular layout has many benefits. It significantly reduces transportation, inventory, and waiting time. At the same time, one-piece flow will significantly improve quality, delivery, and cost. One-piece flow lowers lead times, improves product distribution, and reduces scrap and rework. In addition, one-piece flow makes scheduling easier, uses floor space better, reduces material handling, uses labor better, and increases productivity. Most importantly, one-piece flow exposes problems, which helps drive continuous improvement.

Cellular manufacturing is a group of machines or processes connected by process sequence in a pattern that supports the efficient flow of production. Several elements are characteristic of a good cell design. First, the process will determine the layout. Each step builds quality into the process rather than at a final inspection. Next, the cell is flexible with regard to the number of operators. One operator or multiple combinations of operators could run the cell. Machines are close to each other. The cell is a U-shaped design that flows counterclockwise. The operators are multiskilled.

The cell design should focus on the operator and their multiskilled training. This design aspect employs the philosophy that people appreciate over time, whereas machines depreciate. In other words, people are more valuable than machines.

The team should design the cell around the process. Further, teams can determine product similarities using part/quantity analysis to show model/volume relationships and process route analysis to show process relationships.

There are several different flows, as shown in Figure 17.1. Example A is a small U-shaped layout that provides flexibility and visual management. Example B is the traditional straight-line manufacturing which provides less flexibility than a U-shaped cell. In addition, the straight-line layout hinders communication and visual management since the operators cannot see all the machines easily. Example C is also an example of a U-shaped cell. In Example C, the material enters and leaves the cell at the same point. This layout promotes the most flexibility since one operator up to

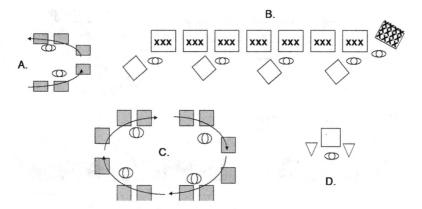

FIGURE 17.1   Types of layouts.

twelve operators can work in the line depending on demand. In addition, the operators can see all machines and easily communicate. Finally, Example D shows a dedicated machine where one operator is at one machine.

The key to determining the proper layout is to be product focused. The team should organize equipment in the process order to promote flow. The machines should be close together to facilitate one-piece flow and reduce non-value-added walking. The U-shaped configuration allows volume flexibility with staffing, reduces non-value-added walking, and improves communication and visual management. It is also critical to be customer-focused. Modules of capacity should match major customer sites, which allows production to match customer needs.

For example, a traditional manufacturing process has one operator per machine, as shown in Figure 17.2. There is inventory before and after each machine. The focus is on the individual machine and labor productivity.

This layout is similar to a transfer line. The flexibility is minimal for labor and change-over, as shown in Figure 17.3. In Figure 17.3, the process currently runs with five operators. If there are only four operators, self-imposed stations make running the process challenging. In addition, the output is the same if the process has five or six operators due to the lack of flexibility. The changeover from one part to another also presents a serious issue. If one station is down for changeover, the entire line is not producing the product. Therefore, the total changeover time is significantly higher than in a U-shaped cell.

Moving from batch and queue processing also significantly reduces the lead time and opportunities for defects. Figure 17.4 presents the difference between a batch and queue process and a one-piece flow. With the batch and queue process, the process batches parts in quantities of ten. Therefore, the parts move to the next step in

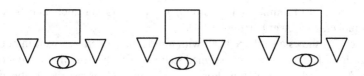

FIGURE 17.2   Traditional manufacturing layout.

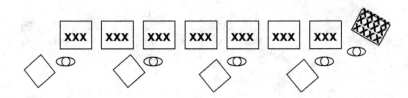

FIGURE 17.3 Transfer line layout.

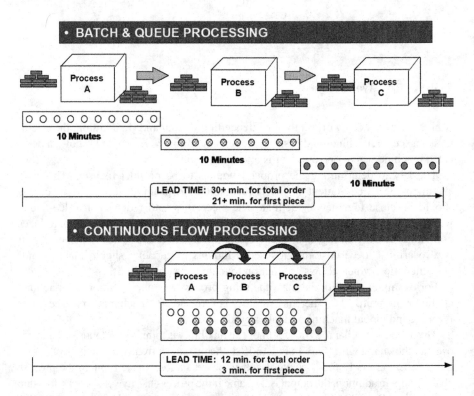

FIGURE 17.4 Batch and queue vs. continuous flow processing.

the process only once all ten parts are complete with each process step. The total lead time for the order is 30 minutes. The first piece is incomplete for 21 minutes. In addition, if a defect occurs, it is only caught at the end of when the batch is complete, and the entire production of thirty pieces is at risk. In continuous flow processing, each part moves to the next step as soon as it is complete. Therefore, the total time for the first piece reduces from 21 to 3 minutes, and the total time to complete the order reduces from 21 to 12 minutes. In addition, the operators can catch defects or quality issues quicker, and fewer parts are at risk.

Figure 17.5 shows a U-shaped cell with multiskilled operators working on a multiprocess line. The operators are assigned stations in such a way that it balances their workload and reduces walking. For example, instead of assigning the operator machines 4, 5, and 6, the operator is assigned machines 4, 7, and 8 to level-load the

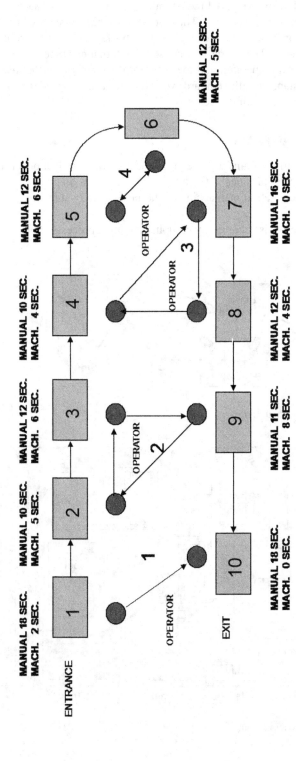

FIGURE 17.5   U-shaped cell with multiskilled operators.

operators and reduce walking. All the operators are inside the U-shaped cell to promote communication and visibility. The layout is flexible to increase or decrease the number of operators depending on the demand. This layout can support one operator or up to ten operators. The operators can use the internal machine time such that the machine waits for the operator, and the operator does not watch the machines run. Ideally, this is balanced with standard work (covered in Chapter 16) to reduce the machine and operator waiting times.

SPAGHETTI DIAGRAMS

Teams use spaghetti diagrams to understand the flow of a product or service. Figure 17.6 provides an example spaghetti diagram. The spaghetti diagram shows the product flow from each station or machine to the next, usually showing an erratic and wasteful flow.

The following flow is achieved by grouping common processes together, as shown in Figure 17.7.

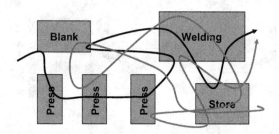

FIGURE 17.6   Spaghetti diagram.

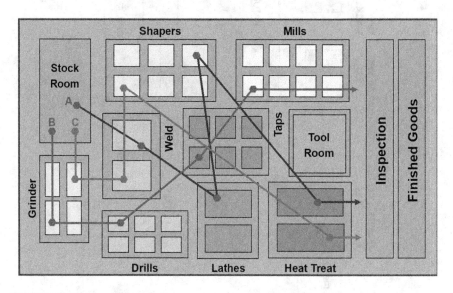

FIGURE 17.7   Process layout.

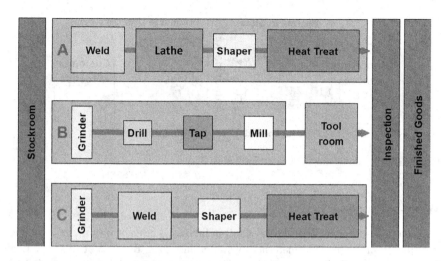

FIGURE 17.8 Process layout based on the product.

Teams can streamline the process using production lines, as shown in Figure 17.8.

PULL SYSTEMS

In a push system, each operation is considered independent. Production departments schedule work schedules for each operation using a forecast. Push systems typically require large, cumbersome computer scheduling systems that generate detailed operation schedules. Expediting is required to identify real priorities. This method also requires looking for and counting actual material versus the computer record balance. Schedules at the upper level seldom agree with schedules at the lower level. Push systems operate under "make all we can just in case we need it." Push systems result in large lots, high inventory, poor product availability, hidden problems, waste, poor communication, and extensive enterprise resource planning software.

A pull system is a customer-controlled system that utilizes signals (kanbans) to authorize material replenishment. It is a method of controlling material flow by replacing the material used in the process. Pull systems operate under "make what we need when we need it." In a pull system, each operation is considered part of the process. The final assembly schedule is the schedule for each operation in the process. The department schedules work based on consumption and only produces a product to replace what the process consumed. Computer systems are much simpler because the focus is on planning systems. In addition, expediting is generally optional because what is required is obvious. Pull systems lead to smaller lots, lower inventory, better product availability, improved visibility of problems, reduced waste, and increased communication.

There are two main kinds of pull systems, as shown in Figure 17.9. A withdrawal pull authorizes the movement of material, while a production pull authorizes the production of the material.

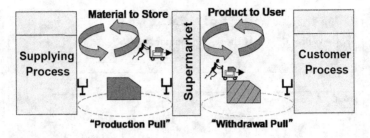

FIGURE 17.9 Production and withdrawal pull.

WORK-IN-PROCESS

High work-in-process (WIP) levels result in increased costs of inventory, scrap, hidden quality problems, and material consumption issues. Because of this, one Lean focus is to keep WIP to a minimum. The most important law governing WIP is Little's Law. Little's Law states that, under steady-state conditions, the average number of items in a queuing system (i.e., WIP) equals the average rate at which items arrive (i.e., throughput (Th)) multiplied by the average time that an item spends in the system (i.e., cycle time (CT)) (Little & Graves, 2008). Equation (17.3) illustrates Little's Law.

$$CT = WIP/Th \qquad (17.3)$$

Research has extensively used this equation to heuristically derive the various equations connecting the simulated production line described below.

$$T_p = \left(\sum_{i=1}^{n} S_i + \sum_{i=1}^{n} P_i + \sum_{i=1}^{n} U_i + \sum_{i=1}^{n} T_i \right) \times S \times OEE \qquad (17.4)$$

$$WT = T_p \times (WIP - 1) \qquad (17.5)$$

$$CT = T_p + WT \qquad (17.6)$$

$$Thb = D \times \left(1 + \sum_{i=1}^{n} Rr_i \right) \qquad (17.7)$$

$$TT = T_a/D \qquad (17.8)$$

$$OEE = \left(1 / \sum_{i=1}^{n} UT_i \right) \times \left(1 + \sum_{i=1}^{n} Rr_i \right) \times P_e \qquad (17.9)$$

Where:

n = number of machines
T_p = total time at the processes
S_i = setup time at machine i
P_i = process time at machine i
U_i = unloading time at machine i
T_i = transport time at machine i
S = safety allowance
UT_i = cumulative uptime percentage (signifies availability efficiency)
Rr_i = rejection rate ratio (signifies quality efficiency)
P_e = performance efficiency
WT = waiting time
WIP = work in progress
CT = cycle time
Th = throughput, the average number of items arriving per unit of time
Thb = throughput at the bottleneck
D = demand rate
TT = takt time
T_a = available time

For simplification, one can assume that only one operator operates the production line and only one process can run at a time. Equation (17.4) states that the total time equals the summation of the setup, process, unloading, and transportation times at all stations, multiplied by a manufacturing line's safety time factor and overall equipment effectiveness (OEE). Equation (17.5) states that the waiting time is the product of the total time and number of products waiting in the queue (here, WIP is −1 as the operator can only work on one product at a time). Equation (17.6) states that the cycle time is the addition of the total time and waiting time. Equation (17.7) limits the throughput rate at the bottleneck to the addition of demand and rejected products. Equation (17.8) (Nicholas & Soni, 2005) states that the takt time should equal the ratio of available time to the demand rate. Equation (17.9) (Braglia, Frosolini, & Zammori, 2009; Reyes et al., 2010) states that OEE is the product of availability, quality, and performance efficiency.

Organizations can use the mathematical model to calculate the number of kanban cards (Equation (17.10)) (Mukhopadhyay & Shanker, 2005). The number of kanban cards depends on the order package, which includes information such as the demand rate, available time, and safety time. The container size depends upon the size and process constraints of the product.

$$n = \frac{D \times (T_a + S_f)}{N} \qquad (17.10)$$

Where:

n = number of kanban cards
D = demand rate or number of orders rate

T_a = manufacturing lead time or time available
S_f = safety time
N = container size
These concepts give a broad understanding of how to implement Lean.

KANBAN

The term *kanban* originates from a Japanese word meaning "card" or "visible record" that refers to cards used to control production flow through a factory. Kanban acts as a signaling method to produce a specific amount of product to be consumed downstream in the process. In a simplified system, kanbans take the physical shape of simple cards or the container itself. In a more complex signaling system, kanbans may be electronic signals programmed into production planning software. When adjusting a production line or setting up a new one, the team may need to determine the number of kanban cards needed to manage the production signaling. Organizations can use Equation (17.11) to determine the appropriate amount of kanban containers needed, n_k. They can also use Equation (17.12) to calculate the percent of safety stock, s.

$$n_k = \frac{\left[\left(D_{Units} \times t_l\right) + s\right]}{c} \tag{17.11}$$

$$s = p\left(D_{Units} \times t_l\right) \tag{17.12}$$

where D_{Units}, is the average unit demanded over a given period of time; t_l is the lead time it takes to restock an order; s is the percentage of safety stock during demand lead time; p is the specified management buffer percentage; and c is the container size.

For example, an industrial engineer can determine the number of kanban containers necessary for a new production line as a U-shaped production cell. The cell is required to produce 100 parts per hour. Each container has a single kanban card attached to it, and the maximum number of parts a container can contain is 15. Management has determined that there must be a safety stock of 10% at all times. It takes about 15 minutes to forklift new parts from the previous workstation. The industrial engineer can determine the number of kanbans needed as follows:

$$D_{Units} = 100 \text{ parts per hour}$$

$$T_l = 15 \text{ minutes} = \left(15/60\right) = 0.25 \text{ hour}$$

$$p = 10\%$$

$$c = 15 \text{ parts}$$

$$s = 0.10\left(100 \times 0.25\right) = 2.5 \text{ parts}$$

$$n_k = 1.833 \text{ or } 2 \text{ kanban cards needed}$$

KAIZEN

Kaizen is the philosophy in which one seeks to improve continuously. It is a state of mind never to accept the status quo. *Kai* means change, and *zen* means for the good. Kaizen is a constant process. What a team implements today to improve should be done tomorrow as second nature. It drives us to improve.

The improvement cycle begins with exposing and quantifying problems. The next step is determining the root cause. After uncovering the root cause, a continuous improvement team should implement solutions. After implementation, the focus is on standardization and adherence. Because this is a cycle, the process continues for further improvements.

INTEGRATING SUSTAINABILITY INTO MATERIAL MOVEMENT

Organizations can incorporate the principles of the circular economy and several of the 5 Rs to enhance Sustainability aspects related to materials and material movement. Designing production systems with efficient material movement by incorporating cells, kanban, pull systems, just-in-time, and continuous and one-piece flow reduce wasted movement and use of materials, energy, equipment, and people. These tools can reduce the use of extra materials, shine a light on the quality of products and therefore reduce defects, and reduce unnecessary energy use by reducing cycle times. There is a natural alignment between Lean and Sustainability within material movement in a Lean environment. By better planning the purchase of materials for more timely use, waste, rework, and scrap are also reduced.

CONCLUSION

Flow, pull, and kanban are powerful tools for improving organizational responsiveness and flexibility. The focus on material movement in this chapter extends Lean concepts into the realm of the triple bottom line (TBL), where the goals of material reduction via Lean techniques may be understood as a reduction of material consumption, impacting environmental concerns. Finally, the use of sequence, standardized work, kaizen, and kanban has an operator focus, improving the firm's social impact. Chapter 18 discusses how to integrate Sustainability practices throughout the supply chain.

REFERENCES

Antony, J., Swarnakar, V., Cudney, E., & Pepper, M. (2022). A meta-analytic investigation of lean practices and their impact on organizational performance. *Total Quality Management & Business Excellence*, *33*(15–16), 1799–1825.

Braglia, M., Frosolini, M., & Zammori, F. (2009). Uncertainty in value stream mapping analysis. *International Journal of Logistics: Research and Applications*, *12*(6), 435–453.

Cudney, E., Furterer, S., & Dietrich, D. (2013). *Lean systems: Applications and case studies in manufacturing, service, and healthcare*. New York, NY: CRC Press.

Little, J. D., & Graves, S. C. (2008). Little's law. *Building intuition: insights from basic operations management models and principles*, 81–100.

Mukhopadhyay, S. K., & Shanker, S. (2005). Kanban implementation at a tyre manufacturing plant: a case study. *Production Planning & Control*, *16*(5), 488–499.

Nicholas, J., & Soni, A. (2005). *The portal to lean production: Principles and practices for doing more with less*. CRC Press.

Reyes, J., Eldridge, S., Barber, K. D., & Soriano-Meier, H. (2010). Overall equipment effectiveness (OEE) and process capability (PC) measures: A relationship analysis. *International Journal of Quality & Reliability Management*, *27*(1), 48–62.

18 Creating a Green Supply Chain

OVERVIEW OF GREEN SUPPLY CHAIN

Organizations can tremendously impact the environment by implementing Sustainable practices internally. The next step then is to apply these principles to supply chain practices. Supply chain emissions account for approximately 92% of an organization's greenhouse gas (GHG) emissions (CDP, 2021). Further, supply chain emissions average over 11 times more than operational emissions. Therefore, organizations must extend their Sustainability initiatives throughout the supply chain.

Multiple studies investigated Green supply chain practices. Simpson and Power (2005) investigated how having a trustworthy and close relationship with suppliers is critical for a company to ensure environmental Sustainability. However, the authors also highlight that rising transaction costs due to environmental standards to the purchasing criteria, added to the difficulty of appropriately managing it effectively, are critical barriers to Green supply chains. A study by Venkat and Wakeland (2006) analyzed the environmental performance of Lean supply chains using CO2 emissions as a key performance indicator. Supply chain emissions depend on the frequency and mode of transportation used and the type and volume of inventory held at each point in the chain. The authors concluded that Lean supply chains are not necessarily Green. The synergies between Lean and Sustainability will depend on whether integration is enabled or hampered by the characteristics of the relations between the organizational actors involved in the knowledge transfer (Larsson & Finkelstein, 1999). Azevedo et al. (2013) proposed Green and resilient supply chain practices for the automotive industries. Suppliers and customers act as middlemen and enable the emergence of synergies (Campos & Vazquez-Brust, 2016).

BENEFITS OF GREEN SUPPLY CHAIN

The benefits of a Green supply chain are clear in terms of environmental performance. Reducing energy consumption results in using fewer materials, consuming less water, and fewer emissions (Corbett & Klassen, 2006). Researchers generally agree that integrating Lean and Green fosters the impact on supply chain Sustainability (Mason et al., 2008). The synergy between Lean and Green is complementary as both focus on waste reduction (e.g., solid waste, greenhouse gas emissions, intangible waste such as lost efficiency, and underutilization of resources) (Dues et al., 2013). Green Supply Chain Management practices reduce negative environmental impact without compromising quality, productivity, and operating costs (Azevedo et al., 2011).

Multiple factors encourage firms to benefit from and pursue Green supply chain practices, specifically global environmental standards such as ISO 14000 (Miles & Russell, 1997), the impact of environmental performance on firms' global reputation, cost reduction, and pressure from stakeholders (Zhu et al., 2005).

INTEGRATING GREEN INTO A LEAN SUPPLY CHAIN

Lean supply chain practices are related to supplier feedback, just-in-time (JIT) delivery by suppliers, supplier development, operations (e.g., pull system, employee involvement), and customer relationships (e.g., risk sharing, user-friendly design) (Anand & Kodali, 2008; Cudney & Kestle, 2010; Cudney & Elrod, 2011; Hundal et al., 2022). Green supply chain practices include increased collaboration with suppliers to implement recycling initiatives, managing by-products of supplied inputs such as packaging, and using environmental criteria in risk sharing and evaluating buyer performance (Govindan et al., 2015; Zokaei et al., 2013). Integrating Lean and Green in the supply chain creates synergies fostering improvements in information frequency, integration level, production lead time, and transportation lead time (Carvalho et al., 2011). However, the divergences are capacity surplus, replenishment frequency, and inventory level. A study by Dües et al. (2013) suggested that Lean supply chain practices are a catalyst for greening the supply chain.

The critical commonality between Lean and Green supply chain practices, as highlighted in Figure 18.1, is waste reduction. However, Lean and Green supply chain practices define waste differently. For instance, Lean supply chain practices consider the seven wastes of manufacturing, all non-value-adding activities, as defined by Ohno (Nicholas, 1998; Vonderembse et al., 2006; Mollenkopf et al., 2010; Grantham & Cudney, 2011). However, Green supply chain practices target environmental wastes in the form of inefficient resource use, excess products, and by-products (e.g., scrap, emissions) (Carvalho & Cruz-Machado, 2011; Mollenkopf et al., 2010). Although the two paradigms have different objectives for waste elimination, they target almost the same type of waste: inventory, transportation, and the production of by-products or non-product output. Just-in-time (JIT) and higher replenishment frequency are divergent practices compared to Green (Venkat and Wakeland. 2006; Dües et al., 2013). Higher replenishments to optimize inventory demands more frequent transportation, resulting in increased CO_2 emissions. Using an efficient mode of transportation and sharing truckloads with mixed product lines are strategies for greening a Lean supply chain (Venkat & Wakeland, 2006). Lean and Green supply chains consider broader adoption and development of Sustainability. Therefore, the Sustainability of the supply chain considers a product from the initial processing of raw materials to customer delivery and also integrates issues, specifically product design, manufacturing by-products, product life extension, and recovery processes (Linton, Klassen & Jayaraman, 2007).

Life cycle assessment is a Green supply chain practice used (Kärnä & Heiskanen, 1998) to design a usable product minimizing environmental impact. An extended supply chain includes reducing and eliminating by-products using Lean tools and cleaner technologies (Zink, 2007; King & Lenox, 2001). By-products include

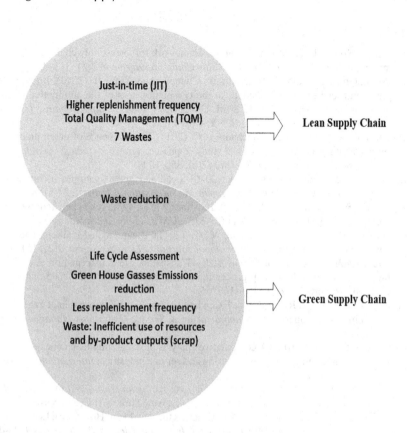

FIGURE 18.1 Lean and Green supply chain practices (Dües et al., 2013).

wasted heat for conditioning space or food waste for producing new food products (Frosch & Gallopoulos, 1989). The product design has a crucial influence on whether it can be reused, remanufactured, refurbished, recycled, or incinerated. Therefore, adopting a life cycle design and analysis approach could encourage design for Sustainability.

CONCLUSION

While organizations can impact the environment through the internal implementation of Sustainability principles, the most significant impact stems from extending these practices throughout the supply chain. In addition, Green supply chain management practices reduce the environmental impact without affecting quality, productivity, or operating costs. The key to implementing Sustainability practices is partnering with suppliers and customers to implement recycling initiatives and manage by-products. Lean and Green supply chain practices are complementary in reducing waste. The next chapter discusses Hoshin Kanri, which is a method for integrating Sustainability into the overall objectives of the organizations and driving the Green metrics throughout all levels of the organization.

REFERENCES

Anand, G., & Kodali, R. (2008). A conceptual framework for lean supply chain and its implementation. *International Journal of Value Chain Management*, *2*(3), 313–357.

Azevedo, S., Cruz Machado, V., Hofstetter, J., Cudney, E., & Yihui, T. (2013). Importance of green and resilient SCM practices to the competitiveness of the automotive industry: A multinational perspective. In S. M. Gupta (Ed.), *Reverse supply chains: Issues and analysis* (pp. 229–252). New York, NY: CRC Press.

Azevedo, S. G., Carvalho, H., & Machado, V. C. (2011). The influence of green practices on supply chain performance: A case study approach. *Transportation Research Part E: Logistics and Transportation Review*, *47*(6), 850–871.

Campos, L. M., & Vazquez-Brust, D. A. (2016). Lean and green synergies in supply chain management. *Supply Chain Management: An International Journal*, *21*(5), 627–641.

Carvalho, H., & Cruz-Machado, V. (2011). Integrating lean, agile, resilience and green paradigms in supply chain management (LARG_SCM). *Supply Chain Management*, (April).

Carvalho, H., Duarte, S., & Machado, V. C. (2011). Lean, agile, resilient and green: Divergencies and synergies. *International Journal of Lean Six Sigma*, *2*(2), 151–179.

CDP (2021). Global Supply Chain Report 2020 – Transparency to transformation: A chain reaction. https://cdn.cdp.net/cdp-production/cms/reports/documents/000/005/554/original/CDP_SC_Report_2020.pdf?1614160765

Corbett, C. J., & Klassen, R. D. (2006). Extending the horizons: Environmental excellence as key to improving operations. *Manufacturing & Service Operations Management*, *8*(1), 5–22.

Cudney, E., & Elrod, C. (2011). A comparative analysis of integrating lean concepts into supply chain management in manufacturing and service industries. *International Journal of Lean Six Sigma*, *2*(1), 5–22.

Cudney, E., & Kestle, R. (2010). *Implementing lean six sigma throughout the supply chain: The comprehensive and transparent case study*. New York, NY: CRC Press.

Dües, C. M., Tan, K. H., & Lim, M. (2013). Green as the new Lean: How to use Lean practices as a catalyst to greening your supply chain. *Journal of Cleaner Production*, *40*, 93–100.

Frosch, R. A., & Gallopoulos, N. E. (1989). Strategies for manufacturing. *Scientific American*, *261*(3), 144–153.

Govindan, K., Azevedo, S. G., Carvalho, H., & Cruz-Machado, V. (2015). Lean, green and resilient practices influence supply chain performance: Interpretive structural modeling approach. *International Journal of Environmental Science and Technology*, *12*(1), 15–34.

Grantham, K., & Cudney, E. (2011). Leaning and greening the supply chain. *Industry & Higher Education*, *25*(1), 53–58.

Hundal, G., Thiyagarajan, S., Alduraibi, M., Laux, C., Furterer, S., Cudney, E., & Antony, J. (2022). The impact of Lean Six Sigma practices on supply chain resilience during COVID-19 disruption: A conceptual framework. *Total Quality Management & Business Excellence*, *33*(15–16), 1913–1931.

Kärnä, A., & Heiskanen, E. (1998). The challenge of product chain thinking for product development and design-the example of electrical and electronic products. *Journal of Sustainable Product Design*, (4).

King, A. A., & Lenox, M. J. (2001). Lean and green? An empirical examination of the relationship between lean production and environmental performance. *Production and Operations Management*, *10*(3), 244–256.

Larsson, R., & Finkelstein, S. (1999). Integrating strategic, organizational, and human resource perspectives on mergers and acquisitions: A case survey of synergy realization. *Organization Science*, *10*(1), 1–26.

Linton, J. D., Klassen, R., & Jayaraman, V. (2007). Sustainable supply chains: An introduction. *Journal of Operations Management, 25*(6), 1075–1082.

Mason, R., Nieuwenhuis, P., & Simons, D. (2008). Lean and green supply chain mapping: adapting a lean management tool to the needs of industrial ecology. *Progress in Industrial Ecology, An International Journal, 5*(4), 302–324.

Miles, M. P., & Russell, G. R. (1997). ISO 14000 total quality environmental management: The integration of environmental marketing, total quality management, and corporate environmental policy. *Journal of Quality Management, 2*(1), 151–168.

Mollenkopf, D., Stolze, H., Tate, W. L., & Ueltschy, M. (2010). Green, lean, and global supply chains. *International Journal of Physical Distribution & Logistics Management, 40*(2), 14–41.

Nicholas, J. M. (1998). *Competitive manufacturing management: continuous improvement, lean production, customer-focused quality.* New York, NY: McGraw-Hill.

Simpson, D. F., & Power, D. J. (2005). Use the supply relationship to develop lean and green suppliers. *Supply Chain Management: An International Journal, 10*(1), 60–68.

Venkat, K., & Wakeland, W. (2006, June). Is lean necessarily green? Proceedings of the 50th Annual Meeting of the ISSS-2006, Sonoma, CA, USA.

Vonderembse, M. A., Uppal, M., Huang, S. H., & Dismukes, J. P. (2006). Designing supply chains: Towards theory development. *International Journal of Production Economics, 100*(2), 223–238.

Zhu, Q., Sarkis, J., & Geng, Y. (2005). Green supply chain management in China: Pressures, practices, and performance. *International Journal of Operations & Production Management, 25*(5), 449–468.

Zink, K. J. (2007). From total quality management to corporate Sustainability based on stakeholder management. *Journal of Management History, 13*(4), 394–401.

Zokaei, K., Lovins, H., Wood, A., & Hines, P. (2013). *Creating a Lean and Green business system: Techniques for improving profits and Sustainability.* New York, NY: CRC Press.

19 Integrating Sustainability into the Organization's Strategic Goals using Hoshin Kanri

LEAN AND STRATEGIC THINKING

Quality thinking traces back to before 1645 in Japan. Miyamoto Musashi, a Japanese swordsman, wrote *A Book of Five Rings* to guide samurai warriors on strategy, tactics, and philosophy. Musashi was legendary for his duels and distinctive style of swordsmanship (Cudney, 2016a). In his book, Musashi states, "If leadership are thoroughly conversant with strategy, leadership will recognize the enemy's intentions and have opportunities to win."

Leadership should include the corporation's strategic plan in the organization's macro-level value stream map to identify optimal improvement opportunities and promote strategic thinking. Often organizations identify improvement activities with silo thinking. However, continuous improvement teams need to consider the impact of changes on other systems or processes within the organization. Improvements in one area can harm another business area.

Therefore, an organization-wide strategy is necessary. Senior leadership should use Hoshin Kanri to develop long-term strategic objectives. Mid-level managers should then use macro-level value stream mapping to identify opportunities for improvement to achieve strategic goals. Finally, department-based teams conduct continuous improvement projects to drive local process improvement.

The senior leadership of a corporation should first determine the vision for the organization to start strategic thinking. Then leadership needs to identify the business's value streams linked to key processes. Next, leadership should perform a gap analysis between the organization's current state and the vision. Understanding the gap leads to a strategic approach to continuous improvement.

To become a Lean enterprise, leadership must integrate Lean throughout all levels of the organization. Leadership must break down the silos between departments and take a global perspective to process improvement. What leadership needs is a holistic approach to continuous improvement throughout the corporation. A holistic approach enables the corporation to make improvements that impact the entire organization rather than small, siloed improvements. Lean promotes working across units or departments and encourages an holistic approach to continuous improvement that links to the corporation's long-term goals.

DOI: 10.1201/9780429506192-19

HISTORY OF HOSHIN KANRI

Hoshin Kanri began in Japan as statistical process control (SPC) in the early 1960s. SPC later became total quality control (TQC). Organizations often refer to Hoshin Kanri as Policy Deployment (PD). "Hoshin" means shining metal, a compass, or pointing in a direction. "Kanri" means management or control.

Hoshin Kanri is a systems approach to managing change in critical business processes. Hoshin Kanri is also a Lean methodology to improve the performance of critical business processes and achieve strategic objectives (Case & Cudney, 2015). Hoshin Kanri links the overall business goals to the entire organization. Therefore, Hoshin Kanri improves the focus of continuous improvement activities, links improvements to strategic goals, increases accountability of strategic goals, increases buy-in to ongoing improvement initiatives, increases communication throughout the organizations, and enhances employee involvement in improvement projects. Communicating common business goals promotes breakthrough thinking and encourages a focus on processes rather than tasks. Hoshin Kanri is also a disciplined process that starts with the organization's vision to develop a three- to five-year business plan and then drives down to one-year objectives that business units deploy for implementation and regular process review.

Hoshin Kanri is a business management system that sits at the top of the Toyota Production System (TPS), as shown in Figure 19.1. Hoshin Kanri cascades the organization's goal of achieving world-class customer satisfaction excellence. The TPS begins

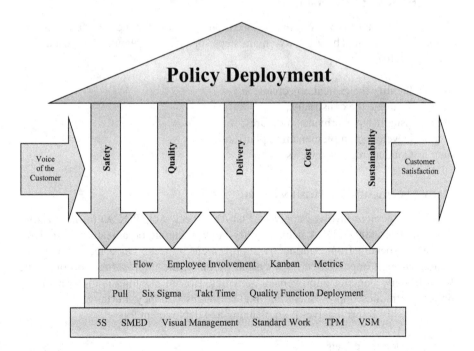

FIGURE 19.1 Strategic business system.

with the voice of the customer and continuously strives to improve safety, quality, delivery, and cost throughout every aspect of the organization. Lean tools support the TPS to achieve specific business objectives through the involvement of all employees.

As shown in Figure 19.1, leadership should take the voice of the customer to drive business targets. Then, using Hoshin Kanri as the management strategy, leadership should drive down this strategy throughout all levels of the business to enhance safety, quality, delivery, cost, and Sustainability. Individual business units may then use foundational Lean tools such as value stream mapping (VSM), 5S, standard work, single-minute exchange of dies (SMED), and total productive maintenance (TPM) to drive continuous improvement. Implementing Lean tools leads to improved customer satisfaction, further enhancing sales growth for the organization.

TWO LEVELS OF HOSHIN KANRI

Hoshin Kanri is a methodology to capture strategic goals and integrate these goals with the entire organization's daily activities. The two levels of Hoshin Kanri include (Cudney, Furterer, & Dietrich, 2013) the following:

(1) management or strategic planning, and
(2) daily management.

PLANNING FOR HOSHIN KANRI

Effective planning throughout the organization is critical for the long-term success of the organization. There are five main steps for effective planning (Agustiady & Cudney, 2016):

Step 1: Identify the critical objectives,
Step 2: Evaluate the constraints,
Step 3: Establish performance measures,
Step 4: Develop an implementation plan, and
Step 5: Conduct regular reviews.

DAILY MANAGEMENT OF HOSHIN KANRI

Daily management involves applying Plan-Do-Check-Act (PDCA) to daily activities (Cudney, 2009). PDCA helps identify broad systemic organizational problems that would benefit from continuous improvement projects. Once leadership gains a breakthrough improvement in a system problem, the improvement becomes the focus of daily ongoing improvement activities. Hoshin planning is the system that drives continuous improvement and breakthroughs (Cudney, Furterer, & Dietrich, 2013). Hoshin Kanri involves both planning and deployment to:

• develop the targets,
• develop action plans to achieve the targets, and
• deploy both.

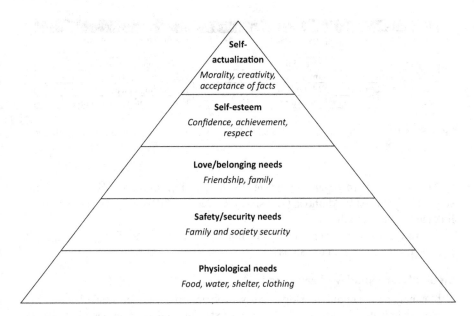

FIGURE 19.2 Maslow's hierarchy of needs.

Maslow introduced the concept of the hierarchy of needs, which outlines the basic needs people require before moving on to a higher need. Figure 19.2 illustrates Maslow's hierarchy of needs.

In concurrence with the individual hierarchy of needs, there are five levels of organizational needs:

Level 1: Core vision,
Level 2: Alignment,
Level 3: Self-diagnosis,
Level 4: Process management, and
Level 5: Target focus.

Figure 19.3 illustrates the five levels of organizational needs.

FIGURE 19.3 Levels of organizational needs.

Organizational needs	Hoshin planning steps	Hoshin methods
Core vision	5-year vision 1-year plan	Hoshin strategic plan summary
Alignment	Deployment	Hoshin plan summary
Self-diagnosis	Implementation	Hoshin action plan
Process management	Monthly reviews	Hoshin implementation plan
Target focus	Annual review	Hoshin implementation review

FIGURE 19.4 Linkage of organizational needs, Hoshin planning steps, and Hoshin methods.

The five levels of organizational needs directly link to the six Hoshin Planning steps and five Hoshin Methods (Agustiady & Cudney, 2016). Figure 19.4 shows the linkage between the three.

There are six main steps to the Hoshin Planning process. The following paragraphs discuss each of these steps.

Step 1: Develop a Five-Year Vision

Top management should develop a five-year vision to define the strategic objectives of the organization based on the internal, external, and environmental challenges the organization faces. The five-year vision is the future target for the organization. Leadership determines the five-year vision using the organization's goals, capabilities, and culture. It is a statement of where the organization wants to be in five years. Senior leadership should use the organization's vision as a communication tool to relate the ideal future for the organization. For example, an organization could state they want to reduce resource extraction by using at least 40% recycled materials in their products. Neste Corporation, an oil refinery in Finland, is committed to investing in biofuels and developing half of its total revenue stream by 2050. Prologis is a real estate investment trust that focuses on sustainable developments and buildings. In addition to encouraging their suppliers to go Green, 82% of their buildings have energy-efficient light, and 40% have cool roofs. Finally, GlaxoSmithKline committed to reducing waste and emissions by 25% by 2030, which results in 60% of its revenue being clean.

Step 2: Develop a One-Year Plan

Based on the five-year vision, leadership should develop a one-year plan to outline continuous improvement activities that enable an organization to achieve its long-term strategy. The one-year plan takes an incremental step and defines key targets to attain that step. This step aims to focus the activities throughout all levels of the organization on addressing external issues and improving internal problems. As part of this step, leadership should analyze external factors, including competition and the economy. In addition, leadership should analyze past problems so the organization can avoid repeating them. Top management must prioritize the objectives based on safety, quality, delivery, cost, and Sustainability. Developing the one-year plan solidifies the company's path to achieving its five-year vision.

Step 3: Deploy the One-Year Plan

The next step is to deploy the one-year plan to all departments within the organization. Deploying the one-year plan is where leadership begins to set measurable goals for each department. This planning step determines specific improvement opportunities within each department. At this point, each department develops a strategy to achieve the path set by the one-year plan, which leads to step 4 and implementation.

Step 4: Implement Continuous Improvement Activities

Each department must drive continuous improvement activities aligned with the one-year plan and five-year vision. This step is where the improvement process planning begins. Steps 1–3 involved planning for improvement. Now leadership must support the improvement activities. For example, a team could focus on reducing scrap in a production cell. The improvement activities in step 4 must link directly to the one-year plan. These improvement activities involve developing a master plan with appropriate measures and goals.

Step 5: Conduct Monthly Reviews

Leadership should track the progress of the continuous improvement activities using quantitative metrics that each team presents to senior leadership (CEO and Directors) in a monthly review. The monthly reviews should link directly to the deployment of the 1-year plan. Leadership should monitor the actual improvements against the planned improvements as a monthly self-diagnosis to ensure the sustainment of corrective actions. During the formal monthly review for management, each department presents a problem analysis: (a) how they addressed the problem and (b) what results were achieved. As Hoshin Kanri becomes more engrained into the organization, the organization may shorten the monthly reviews to highlight or overview the problems and corrective actions.

Step 6: Perform an Annual Review

Finally, leadership should conduct an annual review to monitor the progress and capture the organization's results. The yearly review helps ensure the implemented projects will enable the organization to attain its one-year plan and five-year vision. The annual review checks how the implementation affected the organizational metrics set out in the five-year vision. Based on the previous year's results and the effectiveness of the implementations, each team develops a new one-year plan to set the targets and goals for the upcoming year. In addition, the organization may redevelop its five-year vision based on the current business environment.

The strategic planning process is critical as it lays the foundation for when leadership cascades the organization's strategic goals throughout the organization. The Hoshin Methods align with the phases to accomplish the six Hoshin phases, including (Cudney, 2013):

1. Hoshin strategic plan summary,
2. Hoshin action plan,
3. Hoshin implementation plan, and
4. Hoshin implementation review.

HOSHIN STRATEGIC PLAN SUMMARY

Effective planning is critical for leadership to create an appropriate organizational strategy and vision. Leadership's next step is to cascade the strategic vision and goals to all levels of the organization. The first step in Hoshin Kanri is to develop the strategic plan summary. The Hoshin Strategic Plan Summary links the organization's strategic vision with measurable goals for each unit or department (Cudney, 2016b). The Hoshin Strategic Plan Summary highlights the relationship between the organization's strategic goals, core objectives, and metrics while indicating ownership, as shown in Figure 19.5. A value stream map gives leadership a picture of all the activities required to produce a product. The Hoshin Strategic Plan Summary provides the overall organizational strategy that cascades throughout the organization. The linkage must be clear between the metric for each strategic goal and who is ultimately responsible.

Creating a Hoshin Strategic Plan Summary for the Organization

Several key steps are required for leaders to develop their own Hoshin Strategic Plan Summary.

List the Strategic Goals

In Figure 19.5, leadership should list the strategic goals vertically on the left-hand side of the matrix under the heading "Strategic Goals." These are the organization's broad strategic goals for the next five to ten years. The strategic objectives should be what the organization needs to do to ensure long-term success.

List the Core Objectives

The next step is to drive down a level to get more specific measurable goals. Leadership should list the specific, measurable long-term goals (for the next three to five years) horizontally under the heading "Core Objectives," as shown in Figure 19.5.

Make Sure the Core Objectives Link to the Strategic Goals

In the plan summary, leadership must ensure a linkage between these goals and the overall strategic objectives (in Figure 19.5). A coding system indicates the relationship's strength. A filled-in circle (●) indicates a strong relationship between the strategic goal and the core objective. An open circle (O) represents a weak relationship, which means the core objective is not likely a key driver for the strategic goal. Understanding the relationships in the strategic plan is essential to ensure that leadership adequately addresses the organization's strategic goals through the core objectives. In addition, this is a check that leadership appropriately measures them using the appropriate metrics.

Identify Who Is Responsible: Identify the Metrics

Leadership must ensure proper ownership to drive the necessary improvements. Leadership needs to assign each improvement activity to a specific person for accountability.

HOSHIN STRATEGIC PLAN SUMMARY

Measures / Strategic Goals	Improve financial returns by 5% by 2027	Grow sales by $3M by 2028	Reduce greenhouse gas emissions by 20% by 2028
Director of Finance	O		
Director of Quality			O
Director of Engineering		O	●
Director of Marketing	●	●	
Director of New Business	●	●	
Director of Operations	●		●
New sales projects of $2M for 2023	O	●	
New sales growth to $1M by 2023	O	●	
Labor and overhead productivity to 10%	●		
100% kaizen participation	O		O
Kaizen event savings of $1.2M	●		O
Reduce supply chain emissions by 15%	●	O	●
Internal quality to 4.1 σ	O	O	
External quality to 4.9 σ	O	O	
Reduce cost of poor quality (COPQ) by $5.67	●	O	
Measures			
Core Objectives			
Implement kaizen projects	●		●
Implement cost reduction projects	●	O	O
Implement Sustainability initiatives		O	●
Develop world class new business	●	●	
Strategic Goals			

FIGURE 19.5 Hoshin strategic plan summary.

Determine How Leadership Will Measure Improvements for Meeting Each Goal

Now, leadership cascades the overall objectives into how leadership will manage the business and measure the progress of the process improvement activities. In this step, leadership needs to determine the metrics and short-term goals for the next one to two years. These metrics drive how leadership manages the business and prioritizes process improvement activities. List the metrics vertically on the right side of the matrix, as shown in Figure 19.5.

Make sure leadership ties the metrics to the core objectives. These metrics must meet several criteria to ensure the organization will meet the measurable core objectives. First, the metric must be measurable. In other words, it should be quantitative rather than qualitative. These metrics assess the effectiveness of the process improvement initiatives. Each department should also have a baseline for each metric to show the current performance or benchmark against the competitors or the industry's standards. In addition, these metrics must be achievable. When the metrics are unachievable (e.g., zero internal defects), the employees will become discouraged, and the system will fail. In contrast, if leadership sets realistic goals (e.g., zero external defects), the employees will team together to ensure success. Next, leadership should use the same coding scheme. A filled-in circle (●) indicates a strong relationship between the strategic goal and the core objective. An open circle (O) represents a weak relationship.

Identify Who Is Responsible for Meeting the Core Objectives: Assign Ownership

The strategic plan summary's final step is assigning ownership of each core objective. The ownership at this level falls on the organization's executive leadership because they are ultimately responsible for developing and communicating the strategic vision and driving it down through the organization. Executive leadership lists the leadership team vertically on the far right of the matrix, as shown in Figure 19.5. The matrix uses the same coding scheme to illustrate ownership. A filled-in circle (●) indicates ownership of the core objective. While an open circle (O) indicates cursory responsibility. The matrix will likely show some core objectives with several owners because of the linkage to the organization's strategic goals. For example, one of the strategic goals would be to implement Sustainability initiatives. Sustainability initiatives would likely involve Operations and Engineering, as well as potentially others. Therefore, in this example, Operations and Engineering could have primary ownership.

HOSHIN PLAN SUMMARY

The Hoshin Plan Summary outlines the strategic goals, which are then cascaded down to the department level. While the Hoshin Strategic Plan Summary is at the highest organizational level, the Hoshin Plan Summary is the tactical plan for each department. Now leadership needs to drive the strategy down to each department. Figure 19.6 illustrates the Hoshin Plan Summary.

HOSHIN PLAN SUMMARY

| Strategic Goals | Mgt. Owner | Goals | | Implementation | Improvement Focus | | | | |
		Short Term	Long Term	Strategies	Safety	Quality	Delivery	Cost	Sustainability
Develop world class new business	Director of New Business	$1M by 2025	$3M by 2027	Grow sales				●	
Implement Sustainability initiatives	Director of Operations	8% for 2025	20% for 2028	Green supply chain	○	○	○	○	●
Implement cost reduction projects	Director of Operations	$1.2M annual savings	$4M annual savings	Improve financial returns	○	●	●	●	○
Implement kaizen projects	Director of Operations	100% participation	100% participation	Achieve world class supplier status	●	●	○	●	○

FIGURE 19.6 Hoshin plan summary.

The first column in Figure 19.6 should correspond to the strategic goals listed in the Hoshin Strategic Plan Summary (Figure 19.5). Now that strategic goals are moving down to the department level, the management owner becomes the department manager. Each department will create its own Hoshin Plan Summary. In some cases, depending on the organization's management structure, the management owner will be the same as the core objective owner in the Hoshin Strategic Plan Summary.

The following two columns are for the short-term and long-term goals. Long-term goals may correspond to the strategic objectives from the left side of the Hoshin Strategic Plan Summary. However, the goals should correspond to the metrics leadership outlined in the Hoshin Strategic Plan Summary. This relationship ensures that leadership aligns the proper activities with the overall strategic vision. Based on the metrics leadership previously outlined, leadership should have already developed the short-term and long-term goals. These goals may be different for each department.

For example, look at greenhouse gas emissions. Distribution's short-term and long-term goals should be very aggressive since considerable emissions stem from transporting products and supplies throughout the supply chain. However, operations should also focus on reducing scrap and energy consumption to reduce GHG emissions. Therefore, the operation's short-term and long-term goals for reducing GHG emissions will be less aggressive. Also, the organization must be aligned and managed by the senior leadership team to ensure each department works together. The combined efforts will provide the overall necessary reduction in GHG emissions that the organization seeks. This alignment encourages multiple departments to work together to achieve a common goal, eliminating silos.

In addition, for the goals, several metrics may relate to a core objective. As noted in Figure 19.6, leadership may need to list a core objective in multiple rows because it is associated with several appropriate metrics. Further, each metric for a core objective may call for a different implementation strategy. For example, the team can measure a core objective of improving product quality with internal and external Parts Per Million (PPM). Continuous improvement teams can address internal PPM by implementing a poka-yoke. On the other hand, the team may conduct a Six Sigma project to reduce external PPM. Therefore, leadership would want to list these in two rows to highlight that they are different metrics with varying implementation strategies.

IMPLEMENTATION STRATEGIES FOR THE HOSHIN PLAN SUMMARY

The next step in developing the Hoshin Plan Summary is to develop the implementation strategies. This step is critical in how the organization makes process improvements appropriately, using the most efficient and effective technique. Each department must develop a plan for achieving its short-term and long-term goals. The team members should use their current state map(s) to understand all the activities involved. This approach will enable them to select the most effective technique (e.g., VSM, 5S, standard work, SMED, TPM).

DECIDE WHERE LEADERSHIP WANTS TO FOCUS THE IMPROVEMENT EFFORTS

The final step in completing the Hoshin Plan Summary is determining the improvement focus. Most organizations focus on improving safety, quality, delivery, cost, and Sustainability. Here, again, leadership should use the same coding scheme. A filled-in circle (●) indicates a strong relationship between the implementation strategy and a focus area (e.g., safety, quality, delivery, cost, and Sustainability). An open circle (O) shows cursory relationships.

The purpose of showing the relationships in the Hoshin Plan Summary (Figure 19.6) is slightly different. Here, the leadership team wants to balance the improvement efforts. Leadership must ensure a clear linkage between the implementation strategies and core objectives. Further, leadership also wants to make sure that the implementation strategies leadership will have an impact on the improvement focus areas. For example, suppose leadership develops an implementation strategy that only impacts one focus area, such as quality. The implementation strategy does not affect safety, delivery, or cost. In that case, that may signal that it is not the most effective strategy. Leadership may want an implementation strategy that affects multiple focus areas to increase the impact. Sometimes though, there must be a balance. If leadership has a critical safety issue, it should take precedence even though it may not impact any other improvement focus areas. However, in general, because leadership will be expending time and money on process improvement, leadership would want to impact multiple focus areas.

HOSHIN ACTION PLAN

Next, leadership should develop the Hoshin Action Plan. This further drives the core objectives into the organization's daily activities and accountability for process improvement by creating a detailed action plan. Leadership should present this action plan to the senior leadership at a predetermined frequency (typically a weekly walk-through or monthly management review).

The top of the Hoshin Action Plan shows the linkage between the action plan and each strategic core objective. The following information is required: core objective, management owner, department, team, date, and next review. Figure 19.7 illustrates the Hoshin Action Plan for implementing Sustainability initiatives.

The following section provides a situation summary, which is the current status of the problem. This problem statement should make a case for the continuous improvement initiative and provide specific, measurable, achievable, relevant, and time-bounded (SMART) goals. The following is a situation summary example.

Sustainability is a key market driver in our industry. We currently average using only 9.8% recycled materials in our paper-based products for the past 12 months, while EPA rates for recycling approach 66% (EPA, 2022). As a result, our customers do not view our products as sustainable or Green.

Next, define the overall objective. This objective should relate to one of the core objectives. Therefore, the objective statement could be to increase the use of recycled materials to 20% in the short term and 50% over the next five years.

Hoshin Action Plan		
Core objective: Implement Sustainability initiatives		**Team:** Brian, Caroline, Josh, Winnie
Management owner: Riley		**Date:** 9/14
Department: Supply chain management		**Next review:** 10/15
Situation summary: Sustainability is a key market driver in our industry. We currently average using only 9.8% recycle materials in our paper-based products for the past 12 months while EPA rates for recycling approach 66% (EPA, 2022). As a result, our customers do not view our products as sustainable or Green.		
Objective: Increase use of recycled materials to 20%.		
Short-term goal: Increase use of recycled materials to 20%. **Long-term goal:** Increase use of recycled materials to 50%.	**Strategy:** Evaluate recycled material specifications	**Targets and milestones:** Conduct material strength analysis by 9/21 Conduct failure modes and effects analysis by 10/2

FIGURE 19.7   Hoshin action plan.

The team should then complete the short-term and long-term goals using the metrics leadership previously detailed in the Hoshin Strategic Plan Summary (shown in Figure 19.5). Leadership should identify the short-term goals for the next three to six months, and the long-term goal should focus on improvements for the next 12 months.

Next, the team should discuss the implementation strategy. The implementation strategy should flow from the Hoshin Plan Summary (Figure 19.6). At this point, however, they should have a very detailed Hoshin Plan Summary. For example, suppose the core objective is to increase the percentage use of recycled materials. In that case, the implementation strategy in the Hoshin Plan Summary might be to evaluate the recycled material specifications. In the Hoshin Action Plan, leadership would clarify with additional detail. For example, leadership might explain this as a product redesign based on material specifications, specifically the allowable percent of recycled material.

The final step for the team is to outline the targets and milestones of the strategy in the Hoshin Action Plan. Continuing with the recycled material example, the targets include conducting material strength analysis and a failure modes and effects analysis. The team would provide a milestone, which is the anticipated completion date.

HOSHIN IMPLEMENTATION PLAN

Now leadership should develop the Hoshin Implementation Plan, which records the progress and lists the implementation activities. Figure 19.8 is a template leadership can use for this. The implementation plan compares the current status of milestones to the initial projections. Teams typically use a Gantt chart format for their implementation plan.

			Schedule and Milestones											
Hoshin Implementation Plan														
Core objective: Implement Sustainability initiatives														
Management owner: Riley														
Date: 9/14														
Strategy	Performance		Jan	Feb	Mar	Apr	May	June	July	Aug	Sept	Oct	Nov	Dec
Evaluate recycled materials specifications	Target	20%	9.0%	10.0%	11.0%	12.0%	13.0%	14.0%	15.0%	16.0%	17.0%	18.0%	19.0%	20.0%
	Actual	16.5%	9.8%	10.2%	10.5%	12.1%	13.3%	13.8%	15.7%	16.5%				
Kaizen participation	Target	100%	10%	20%	30%	40%	50%	60%	70%	80%	90%	100%	100%	100%
	Actual	82%	12%	23%	31%	42%	55%	58%	74%	82%				

FIGURE 19.8 Hoshin implementation plan.

Review the Hoshin Implementation Plan with the organization's senior leadership monthly. Each department outlines its expected improvement gains by month in the review schedule.

The top of the Hoshin Implementation Plan provides each core objective, who owns each core objective, and the date leadership is targeting to achieve that objective. The core objectives of the Hoshin Implementation Plan should link directly to the high-level Hoshin Strategy Summary Plan (shown in Figure 19.5). Further, the management owner should link to the Hoshin Plan Summary (Figure 19.6).

The first column in Figure 19.8 lists the implementation strategies determined by each department. Then, the department should have a Hoshin Action Plan for each implementation strategy.

The next column of Figure 19.8 defines each implementation strategy's target and actual performance. The performance should be measured using the metrics defined in the Hoshin Strategic Plan Summary (Figure 19.6). The team should track their performance by month to monitor their performance improvement trend for the year. It is also helpful to visually show which metrics are on track by month by color-coding. The team can color the background green for months on track (i.e., meet the performance target), while months that did not meet the target performance can have a red background. Areas of concern can have a yellow background. Color-coding makes it easy for leadership to see which implementation strategies are not meeting their target performance.

HOSHIN IMPLEMENTATION REVIEW

Finally, leadership should conduct a Hoshin Implementation Review, which records the progress of the performance. Figure 19.9 provides a blank template. The Hoshin Implementation Review also records the company's performance relative to the

Hoshin Implementation Review	
Core objective: Strategy owner: Date:	
Performance status	Implementation issues

FIGURE 19.9   Hoshin implementation review.

industry's overall performance. The implementation plan also lists the highest-priority implementation issues.

During the presentation to senior leadership, teams should use the Hoshin Action Plans as backup information to show what targets and milestones leadership has met and recovery plans to get performance back on track.

The following sections describe the five critical steps for implementing the Hoshin Kanri strategy.

STEP 1: MEASURE THE ORGANIZATION'S SYSTEM PERFORMANCE

In measuring the organization's system performance, developing a plan to manage the strategic change objectives is critical. The initial plan should be adaptable to respond to business changes. In addition, regular assessments of planning and implementation are necessary.

STEP 2: SET THE CORE BUSINESS OBJECTIVES

The "catchball" method incorporates group dialogue into how leadership determines and sets core business objectives. The concept of catchball is equivalent to tossing an idea around. This method enables leadership to determine the most appropriate goals for the overall business system (Wilson, Cudney, & Marley, 2022).

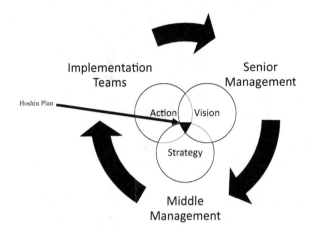

FIGURE 19.10 Hoshin plan alignment.

STEP 3: EVALUATE THE BUSINESS ENVIRONMENT

Leadership must evaluate the business environment to understand the needs of the organization's customers. These customers include stockholders, employees, external customers, etc. The environmental analysis consists of the business's technical, economic, social, and political aspects. The purpose is to answer the question – How does the company perform relative to its competitors?

STEP 4: PROVIDE THE NECESSARY RESOURCES

For successful strategic alignment throughout the organization, management must provide the necessary resources to lead the strategic objectives and daily management efforts. Remember – the purpose of Hoshin is to align the system to strategic change initiatives. Hoshin Kanri requires resource commitment.

STEP 5: DEFINE THE VALUE SYSTEM AND PROCESSES

Another critical aspect is to define the Value System and related processes. Hoshin Kanri enables consensus planning across all departments and levels of the organization, which aids in the execution of continuous improvement projects, as shown in Figure 19.10. The Hoshin Plan aligns with the organization's strategic vision, strategy, and actions. All levels of the organization must align around the common Hoshin Plan. The following section discusses the three main tools of Hoshin Kanri for gaining consensus.

THREE MAIN TOOLS OF HOSHIN KANRI

Hoshin Kanri is one of the pillars of Total Quality Management (TQM). Deming's Plan-Do-Check-Act (PDCA) cycle is the foundation of TQM (Mittal et al., 2023). The three main tools of Hoshin Kanri include the PDCA cycle, cross-functional management, and catchball.

FIGURE 19.11 Deming's plan-do-check-act cycle.

The following sections will look at each in more detail to show how leadership should use these three tools to drive consensus planning and project execution.

DEMING'S PLAN-DO-CHECK-ACT CYCLE

Deming developed the Plan-Do-Check-Act cycle, shown in Figure 19.11, as an iterative four-step problem-solving process. The plan step establishes objectives and processes to achieve specific results. The do step involves implementing the processes. The team monitors and evaluates processes against the specifications in the check step. In the final step, Act, the team implements changes to improve the outcome to meet or exceed the specifications.

One of the critical differences between PDCA and Hoshin Kanri is that Hoshin Kanri begins with the check step, Step 3 of Deming's cycle (Cudney, Furterer, & Dietrich, 2013). Therefore, the cycle is CAPD – check-act-plan-do, which propels the Hoshin process. Leadership starts by checking the current status. Each company-wide check begins with deploying a new target and action plan for continuous improvement.

CROSS-FUNCTIONAL MANAGEMENT

Cross-functional management (CFM) is critical for continuous improvement. CFM helps break down silos. Hoshin plans should include feedback from a cross-functional group. Using a cross-functional group enables the diverse group to address the needs of all the shareholders (e.g., internal customers, external customers, stockholders) in the Hoshin Plan. Leadership can ensure a balanced representation of customer needs by involving a cross-functional group.

CATCHBALL

Catchball involves continuous communication, which is essential for CFM to develop targets and action plans. Catchball is also crucial for deployment throughout the organization. Leadership must create feedback systems to allow bottom-up, top-down, horizontal, and multidirectional communication. There must be a commitment to total employee involvement.

CONCLUSION

Lean is a philosophy that an organization must fully embrace to reap its full potential truly. Unless leadership ties Lean to the organization's strategic vision, the employees may view it as merely a "flavor-of-the-month" strategy. Employees will refrain from embracing, implementing, or buying into continuous improvement activities. Employees want to see a clear linkage between where they focus their time and how it drives their organizations' growth. Therefore, Lean projects that significantly impact the organization will have the most effective results and have the most buy-in from employees.

Leadership must ensure that the strategic vision cascades throughout the organization into everyone's daily activities. This clear linkage enables an organization to focus on common goals. Hoshin Kanri enables the organization's strategic vision to cascade down throughout the organization.

When employees understand the organization's direction, continuous improvement initiatives align with the organization's strategic vision, which enables the long-term success. Using strategic vision, the organization can employ Lean and Green techniques to eliminate waste and improve flow. As leadership targets improvement opportunities, leadership will be able to see how they impact the organization's overall strategic vision. The alignment within the organization will also become apparent.

The next chapter addresses how organizations can sustain their Sustainability efforts to continue their Lean and Green journey.

REFERENCES

Agustiady, T., & Cudney, E. (2016). *Total productive maintenance: Strategies and implementation guide*. Boca Raton, FL: CRC Press.

Case, K., & Cudney, E. (2015). Using Hoshin Kanri to address ISO 9001:2015 requirements. Proceedings of the European Organization for Quality (EOQ) Congress, Athens, Greece.

Cudney, E. (2009). *Using Hoshin Kanri to improve the value stream*. Boca Raton, FL: CRC Press.

Cudney, E.A. (2016a). Development of Strategic Quality Metrics for Organizations Using Hoshin Kanri. In P. Sampaio, & P. Saraiva (Eds), *Quality in the 21st Century*. Cham: Springer.

Cudney, E., Furterer, S., & Dietrich, D. (2013). *Lean systems: Applications and case studies in manufacturing, service, and healthcare*. Boca Raton, FL: CRC Press.

Cudney, E. (2013). Value stream mapping: Hoshin planning at Carjo manufacturing. In D. Kudernatsch (Ed.), *Hoshin kanri: Enterprise strategy implementation of lean management tools* (pp. 197–210). Stuttgart, Germany: Schäffer-Poeschl.

Cudney, E. (2016b). Development of strategic quality metrics for organizations using hoshin kanri. In P. Sampaio, & P. Saraiva (Eds.), *Quality in the 21st century – Perspectives from ASQ Feigenbaum medal winners* (pp. 57–68). New York, NY: Springer.

EPA. (2022). National Overview: Facts and Figures on Materials, Wastes, and Recycling. https://www.epa.gov/facts-and-figures-about-materials-waste-and-recycling/national-overview-facts-and-figures-materials

Mittal, A., Gupta, P., Kumar, V., Antony, J., Cudney, E., & Furterer, S. (2023). TQM practices and their impact on organizational performance: The case of India's Deming Award industries. *Total Quality Management & Business Excellence*. DOI: 10.1080/147833.2023.2177148

Wilson, R., Cudney, E., & Marley, R. (2022). Current status of Hoshin Kanri. *The TQM Journal*. DOI: 10.1108/TQM-07-2022-0216

20 Sustaining Lean Sustainability as a Strategic Initiative

INTRODUCTION

While organizations often need help launching continuous improvement initiatives, more organizations need help sustaining them. When organizations do not maintain their Lean initiatives, it undermines the value that implementing Lean can continue to bring to the organization. Therefore, it is vital to understand the common reasons continuous improvement initiatives fail in organizations. By understanding these challenges, organizations can proactively address these risks. This chapter discusses these critical Sustainability challenges and a few strategies to help managers overcome them toward sustaining Lean.

In most organizations, regardless of industry, implementing a continuous improvement program starts with considerable attention and excitement. However, typically after a few cycles of training and projects, the initiative begins to lose momentum. Sustaining improvements over time becomes difficult. There are several reasons why sustaining project improvements becomes challenging. If the focus is the short-term quick wins through the execution of projects, then the organization will not sustain its continuous improvement program. Organizations must consider how to embed the principles of Lean Sustainability into their culture for this initiative to sustain. Lean should be a catalyst to change the attitudes and behaviors of the workforce (Antony et al., 2019). It is crucial to sustaining Lean efforts to maintain the organization's returns on investment from the Lean program and prevent staff from losing interest in continuous improvement. When sustained over a longer time, Lean Sustainability offers several benefits, including employee learning and satisfaction, customer satisfaction and loyalty, a culture of continuous improvement, and, most importantly, a competitive edge for the company (Agustiady & Cudney, 2022). Therefore, sustaining Lean is essential and should be part of the leadership agenda.

LEAN SUSTAINABILITY CHALLENGES

There are several challenges to sustaining a Lean initiative and maintaining the gains from process improvement efforts. Womack and Jones (1997) cautioned that if "Lean is seen as a means of quickly cutting costs to meet budget deficits, organizations fail to achieve the real benefits." This failure is typically true when organizations focus on short-term successes or quick wins and need to realize that Lean is a journey. Therefore, the organization fails to sustain its Lean initiative over the long run. The challenges relate to a need for top management support, a systems perspective,

 DOI: 10.1201/9780429506192-20

alignment to strategic goals, and resources. Challenges also stem from employee turnover and ownership. In addition, organizations face challenges because they need to tailor their Lean initiatives to their type of organization or to meet their internal culture.

TOP MANAGEMENT SUPPORT

Top management commitment is critical to the success of a Lean initiative. It is not only a factor for successful implementation but also essential to sustaining the initiative. Often top management will be actively involved during the rollout and implementation of the initiative. However, top management's involvement may fade over time. Management must consistently provide uncompromising support by actively identifying, prioritizing, and overseeing projects (Antony et al., 2019). Organizational leaders play a significant role in sustaining Lean. For example, Jack Welch was known for his leadership at General Electric. However, the program underwent significant changes after his exit from the company. When leadership changes at the top, sustaining Lean becomes challenging. Top management involvement should begin with selecting the project through project completion. It is important to choose projects with full support and commitment from top management as this gives a strong signal to the entire organization about the project's priority.

SYSTEMS VIEW

Lean practitioners may also need more understanding of a systems perspective. When leadership or a team views a Lean project from a narrow perspective, it tends to focus on a metric improvement. The focus on a chosen metric is essential. It is equally important to see the big picture of the overall system at times (Cudney, 2016). A narrow focus on a metric could negatively influence another metric within the same process. Unlike project managers, business leaders do not see individual Lean projects. Instead, they see how the overall system and associated metrics perform together. When business leaders perceive Lean to be a narrow focus on a metric and lose sight of the overall systemic view of the process, they may not sponsor the initiative over the long run, which leads to Sustainability issues.

ALIGNMENT TO THE ORGANIZATION'S STRATEGIC GOALS

From a project-level perspective, another critical challenge to sustaining Lean is when the continuous improvement projects do not align with the organization's strategic objectives (Cudney, 2009). Only a few projects may show results. However, the Lean program will die naturally over the long run due to a lack of direction. Most projects fall behind schedule or fail due to a poor linkage between the project and the organization's strategic business goals (Bryce, 2002). Projects also fail because of their broad scope. Organizations often refer to these projects as attempting to "boil the ocean" or "save the planet." Proper project scoping with the right team members and frequent project reviews can target some of the scoping issues, particularly at the early stages of the project (Antony et al., 2022b).

RESOURCES

Leadership must also provide sufficient time for teams to work on the project. One of the significant challenges for many people after continuous improvement training is the need for more time to complete their projects due to other priorities in the organization. Therefore, organizations should use a project champion to ensure teams have sufficient time and resources. It is also critical to select the right people to execute the project. Selecting appropriate team members is essential to the project's success (Barclay et al., 2022). Team members should include employees who are highly capable of managing organizational change and are eager to learn and implement new ideas.

Lean Sustainability projects should also have sufficient available data to understand the problem. Senior management should confirm data availability during project selection (see Chapter 7 on project selection). Projects with medium to high availability of data should be selected.

It is also essential to consider the optimal team size and composition. The continuous improvement team should have four to six members. When the team size increases, finding mutually agreeable meeting times and reaching a group consensus becomes more difficult. More importantly, the composition of a project team is a critical element. Teams must include adequate representation from relevant functional units. Diversity in a team is a much-needed feature. Team members should also take time to understand each other's personalities for better team cohesion (Gupta et al., 2019).

EMPLOYEE TURNOVER

Lean improves team members' skills, knowledge levels, and abilities during their involvement in the initiative. Employee learning through problem-solving is a positive effect of Lean. This learning among the participating team members improves their marketability in the market. Several practitioner-based surveys indicate that individuals trained in Lean have higher salaries than others. Therefore, retaining Lean-trained staff members becomes challenging when an organization loses a trained team member to its competitors or other markets. The knowledge (tacit knowledge) gets diffused to outside organizations, which hinders the rate of maturity of Lean leading to issues in its Sustainability.

OWNERSHIP

The previous challenges have discussed more organizational-level challenges. However, it is also important to discuss sustaining individual Lean improvements at the project level ownership of sustaining the project (Cudney, Furterer, & Dietrich, 2013). It is essential to sustain improvements after the completion of a project. Once a team completes its project, they typically transfer to a new one. During this transition, it will be difficult to sustain the improvements if there is a lack of ownership or buy-in for the improvements (Alexander et al., 2021). The process will revert to its old habits. Therefore, ownership is essential to sustaining the results achieved from the project.

STANDARD LEAN APPROACH

Many practitioners often employ similar strategies to deploy Lean with little or no changes to address the sectoral context of its application. For example, Lean implementation in services is significantly different from that in manufacturing due to the inherent and distinct characteristics of the service industry (Manickam et al., 2021). More specifically, even within services, a contextual distinction exists between pure services and product-based services. Realizing the contextual differences unique to every sector alleviates the challenges in sustaining Lean journeys.

UNDERSTANDING LEAN

Organizations and teams can also choose the wrong improvement methodology for the problem they are trying to solve. There is not a single methodology that addresses all the business problems in any organization. The team must choose a suitable methodology based on the nature of the problem they are trying to solve.

FLAVOR OF THE MONTH

Another big challenge in sustaining Lean is understanding its true purpose and position as Lean relates to other technologies. When a new technology comes to the market, a few organizational leaders incorrectly assume that the new technology could replace Lean. The true purpose of Lean is to create a culture of continuous improvement. Lean is a strategic resource for the organization. Any new technology can only supplement or complement this culture and should not replace or compete with Lean (Agustiady & Cudney, 2022). For example, Industry 4.0 enhances Lean tools with process automation and machine learning technologies. However, automating a process with waste and variation is meaningless. Therefore, Lean should be an enabler for engaging new technologies. Top management needs to understand the Lean philosophy and how it relates to new technologies. Otherwise, there will be challenges in sustaining the initiative.

REWARDS AND RECOGNITION

Senior management should also address appropriate rewards and recognition within the organization's culture. Introducing appropriate rewards and recognition programs can motivate people to participate and become more involved in continuous improvement projects. An incentive or reward system can foster a sense of achievement, and company recognition can generate stronger employee motivation and commitment to future improvement projects (Ho, Chang, & Wang, 2008).

PROJECT MANAGEMENT

It is also essential to consider how continuous improvement teams monitor and control projects using project management techniques. Project management is vital for setting the pace of continuous improvement projects by the team leader and project champion. Monitoring systems should track the on-time progression of a project. A monitoring system report can disseminate each project's status using visual management tools (see Chapter 12) throughout the organization to create awareness.

CULTURE

Management needs to address any resistance to change. Implementing a continuous improvement program involves changing the existing culture and accepting a new culture for top management and everyone else in the organization (Rodgers, Antony, & Cudney, 2022). Therefore, management should identify potential causes of employee resistance to change and take appropriate action by developing strategies and sustaining a positive culture (see Chapter 5).

STRATEGIES TO SUSTAIN LEAN

There are several strategies that organizations can adopt to sustain their Lean initiative. These strategies help ensure that the organization consistently maintains the initiative and sustains the improvements. First, a consistent management commitment, leadership, accountability, and participation culture is essential (Antony et al., 2022a). For a Lean initiative to be successful, leadership must realize the organizational benefit of Lean. Most importantly, their actions should reflect their support. Leadership must create a sense of urgency in purpose so that Lean is not an attraction factor but a hygiene factor in their organization.

Lean must be linked to the business strategy and periodically updated to reflect environmental changes and organizational maturity. Organizations should schedule and address these periodic revisions.

The organization should create an effective reward and recognition program that attracts, develops, and retains motivated team members. Senior leadership should promote total employee participation, agility, and customer-centricity in Lean project management. Leadership should ensure robust governance in project identification, prioritization, execution, and ownership of the results during and after completing a continuous improvement project. Leadership must also invest in creating an attractive, appropriate organizational infrastructure for Lean. The infrastructure should include project management, communication, market, research, and ideation platform training.

Leadership must also ensure knowledge management of Lean projects. Teams must document the Lean knowledge that emerges from a team member's participation and experience.

Organizations generally focus on sustaining the gains after implementing a Lean improvement. Instead, organizations should focus on sustaining improvement gains during the implementation. Otherwise, improvements are unlikely to last. To drive Sustainability from the start, organizations should implement project management systems.

Finally, organizations must institutionalize Lean, which is essential for Sustainability. Once a Lean program becomes part of the organizational culture, the organization can sustain the financial impact, which leads to pervasive Lean culture for transformations.

CONCLUSION

Sustaining Lean involves significant change management and naturally involves addressing several challenges. This chapter presented frequently occurring challenges and associated strategies to overcome them. The next chapter will discuss how Lean contributes to the shift from a linear to a circular economy.

REFERENCES

Agustiady, T., & Cudney, E. (2022). *Building a sustainable Lean culture: An implementation guide*. New York, NY: CRC Press.

Alexander, P., Antony, J., & Cudney, E. (2021). A novel and practical conceptual framework to support Lean Six Sigma deployment in SMEs. *Total Quality Management & Business Excellence, 33*(11–12), 1233–1263.

Antony, J., Laux, C., Cudney, E., & Sundar, V. (2019). *Ten commandments of LSS: A practical guide for senior executives and business leaders*. Bingley, UK: Emerald Publishing.

Antony, J., Swarnakar, V., Cudney, E., & Pepper, M. (2022a). A meta-analytic investigation of lean practices and their impact on organizational performance. *Total Quality Management & Business Excellence, 33*(15–16), 1799–1825.

Antony, J., Swarnakar, V., Gupta, N., Kaur, J., Jayaraman, R., Tortorella, G., & Cudney, E. (2022b). Critical success factors for operational excellence initiatives in manufacturing: A meta-analysis. *Total Quality Management & Business Excellence*, DOI: 10.1080/14783363.2022.2157714

Barclay, R., Cudney, E., Shetty, S., & Antony, J. (2022). Determining critical success factors for lean implementation. *Total Quality Management & Business Excellence, 33*(7–8), 818–832.

Cudney, E. (2009). *Using Hoshin Kanri to improve the value stream*. New York, NY: CRC Press.

Cudney, E. (2016). Development of strategic quality metrics for organizations using Hoshin Kanri. In P. Sampaio, & P. Saraiva (Eds.), *Quality in the 21st century – Perspectives from ASQ Feigenbaum medal winners* (pp. 57–68). New York, NY: Springer.

Cudney, E., Furterer, S., & Dietrich, D. (2013). *Lean systems: Applications and case studies in manufacturing, service, and healthcare*. New York, NY: CRC Press.

Gupta, S. K., Gunasekaran, A., Antony, J., Gupta, S., Bag, S., & Roubaud, D. (2019). Systematic literature review of project failures: Current trends and scope for future research. *Computers & Industrial Engineering, 127*, 274–285.

Ho, Y. C., Chang, O. C., & Wang, W. B. (2008). An empirical study of key success factors for Six Sigma Green Belt projects at an Asian MRO company. *Journal of Air Transport Management, 14*(5), 263–269.

Manickam, B.K., Parameshwaran, R., Antony, J., & Cudney, E. (2021). Framework for lean implementation through fuzzy AHP-COPRAS integrated approach. *IEEE Transactions on Engineering Management*, DOI: 10.1109/TEM.2021.3089691

Rodgers, B., Antony, J., & Cudney, E. (2022). A critical evaluation of organizational readiness for continuous improvement within a UK public utility company. *Public Money & Management, 42*(8), 584–592.

Womack, J. P., & Jones, D. T. (1997). Lean thinking—banish waste and create wealth in your corporation. *Journal of the Operational Research Society, 48*(11), 1148–1148.

21 Shifting from a Linear to a Circular Economy

INTRODUCTION

The basic concept of a linear economy is to take-make-dispose products. The production cycle for the linear economy starts with taking the resources needed, making the goods, and disposing of everything, including a product, at the end of its life cycle (Sariatli, 2017). According to the Ellen MacArthur Foundation (2013), several current trends based on the depletion of non-renewable resources, market volatility, and commodity prices inflation extrapolated the detrimental impact of a continued linear economy model. A study by MacArthur and Eurostat (2011) highlighted that the volume of material input to the European economy was 65 billion tons in 2010, out of which Europe dumped 2.7 billion tons as waste, and merely 40% was used again (i.e., recycled, reused, or composted). The challenges of a linear economy are the problems of waste, waste landfills, and environmental hazards, and it is not sustainable (Luttenberger, 2020). A linear economy does not regain value from the end-cycle of the product. Therefore, due to the unsustainable impacts of a linear economy, organizations must transition to a circular economy (Rodríguez-Antón & Alonso-Almeida, 2019). However, most sustainable management systems do not detail how to adopt circular economy methods in an organization (Nascimento et al., 2019). According to the European Commission, circular economy systems keep the added value in products for as long as possible and eliminate waste.

CIRCULAR ECONOMY AND SUSTAINABILITY

From the Sustainability perspective, a circular economy is a regenerative system in which resource input, waste, emissions, and energy leakage are minimized by slowing, closing, and narrowing material and energy loops (Geissdoerfer et al., 2017). According to Stahel (2016), "A circular economy system would turn goods that are at the end of their service life into resources." A study conducted by Sariatli (2017) highlighted the benefits of a circular economy fostering Sustainability. The closed-loop processes in the circular economy reduce the material input needed, reducing the material cost and minimizing resource dependence. Due to the closed loop and recycling of input material, this leads to less growth in raw material price fluctuation, resulting in more efficient use of resources (Sariatli, 2017).

The Ellen MacArthur Foundation (2013) estimated that the European Union might save US$400–600 billion annually in material costs by following a circular economy. Implementing circular economy principles into the early product design lifecycle of research and development results in innovative designs with progress in material science and the developing of high-quality and durable products Bonviu

216 DOI: 10.1201/9780429506192-21

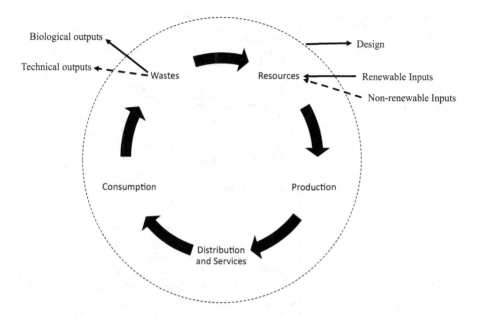

FIGURE 21.1   Circular economy model (Suárez-Eiroa et al., 2019).

(2014). With benefits come the challenges for implementing circular economy principles, which are predominantly model-based and lack a standard framework. No internationally recognized standards and guidelines exist for implementing a circular economy (Circular Academy, 2017). A study conducted by Suárez-Eiroa et al. (2019) defined and proposed an elements-based model for a circular economy based on monitoring input resources, production, distribution and services, consumption, outputs waste management, and design. Figure 21.1 highlights the circular economy model proposed by Suárez-Eiroa et al. (2019), which is a closed-loop system with design elements connected with all other system elements. Organizations must minimize non-renewable inputs and technical outputs; therefore, Figure 21.1 illustrates these with broken arrows.

The model also describes practical strategies for implementing a circular economy through the elements described in Figure 21.2.

There is a need to educate on how to implement the circular economy principles, as described in Figure 21.2. According to Kirchher et al. (2017), a circular economy is "an economic system that is based on business models which replace the 'end-of-life' concept with reducing, alternatively reusing, recycling and recovering materials in production, distribution and consumption processes with the aim to accomplish sustainable development." Therefore, the circular economy overlaps with Sustainability.

TRANSITION FROM A LINEAR ECONOMY TO A CIRCULAR ECONOMY

The European Commission highlighted transiting from a linear to a circular economy as "the transition to a more circular economy, where the value of products, materials, and resources is maintained in the economy for as long as possible, and the

Elements of circular economy	Strategies
Input resources	• Renewable substitutes for non-renewable inputs • Renewable inputs with low regeneration rates substituted with higher regeneration rates • Aligning taxes and subsidies of technology, products, and materials based on resource regeneration rates
Production	• Developing processes that produce technical outputs by those which produce biological outputs • Aligning taxes and subsidies of technology, products, and materials based on waste generation rates • Developing more eco-efficient production processes
Distribution and services	• Promoting green procurement (e.g., local products, seasonal products) • Expanding consumer information and responsibility (e.g., eco-labeling) • Promoting functional service economy and sharing economy (e.g., redistributing second-hand goods)
Consumption	• Adjusting consumption to production • Promoting consumer responsibility for recycling
Waste	• Improving recycling and upcycling of wastes
Design	• Designing for reproducible and scalable products • Designing for consumer preferences and customization • Designing new methodologies for continuous improvement and Sustainability

FIGURE 21.2 Elements of a circular economy and strategies for implementation (Suárez-Eiroa et al., 2019).

generation of waste is minimized." A circular economy fosters a sustainable, low-carbon, resource-efficient, and competitive economy (Jones & Comfort, 2017). The circular economy is considered a possible solution to problems from a linear economy, specifically increasing global demand for resources, price volatility for raw materials, and growing global population and consumption worldwide (Alonso & Rodriguez, 2019). Managing growth in a circular approach requires a different perspective of production, adding the element of Sustainability to meet global emissions reduction goals. To achieve this, products and services need to be engineered with a product life cycle approach, or more recently stated, life cycle engineering (Chen et al., 2022). Life cycle engineering (LCE) may be defined as Sustainability-oriented product development and manufacturing within an organizational scope without exceeding biosphere limitations (Chen et al., 2022). Organizations define the focus of linear economies by efficiency. Efficiency is a traditional focus of engineering and production, aiming to maximize output or value creation while minimizing input or costs. For LCE, from an environmental performance perspective, efficiency may be determined as energy efficiency, resource efficiency, or a broader eco-efficiency of the activity, product, or service (Hauschild et al., 2020). This perspective addresses a significant barrier to the circular adoption of measurement and assessment for economic improvement. Hauschild et al. (2020) propose that eco-efficiency is the ratio between the product's created value or fulfilled function divided by resource use or impact, as noted in Equation (21.1) (Hauschild et al., 2020).

$$\text{Eco - efficiency} = \frac{\text{Value created or functionality provided}}{\text{Environmental impact caused}} \qquad (21.1)$$

Organizations can assess the environmental impact of manufacturing using life cycle assessment (LCA) from the cradle to the grave. The focus on increasing energy efficiency or eco-efficiency promotes the development of products that offer more functionality than that caused by environmental impact or resource use to support a more circular economic approach (Hauschild et al., 2020). Regardless of the specific approach, environmental indicators should be incorporated into production economics for a sustainable approach.

Businesses might face multiple challenges, namely workforce management, financial management, stakeholder management, and handling issues with consumer acceptance (Stewart & Niero, 2018; Sharma et al., 2021). Therefore, businesses must consider value creation and transfer to successfully transition to a circular economy (Centobelli et al., 2020).

CONCLUSION

This chapter illustrated the difference between a linear and circular economy and described the value of moving to a circular economy to enhance Sustainability. The next chapter discusses the future and challenges of integrating Lean and Sustainability.

REFERENCES

Bonviu, F. (2014). The European economy: From a linear to a circular economy. *Romanian Journal of European Affairs*, *14*, 78.

Centobelli, P., Cerchione, R., Chiaroni, D., Del Vecchio, P., & Urbinati, A. (2020). Designing business models in circular economy: A systematic literature review and research agenda. *Business Strategy and the Environment*, *29*(4), 1734–1749.

Chen, W., Hauschild, M., Huang, B., Kara, S., Sutherland, J., & Umeda, Y. (2022). Life cycle engineering and sustainable manufacturing for net-zero targets and environmental Sustainability. *Resources, Conservation and Recycling*, *186*. https://doi.org/10.1016/j.resconrec.2022.106480

Circular Academy. (2017). Circular economy: critics and challenges – How can we bridge the circularity gap? [Online]. Retrieved on February 21, 2017. Available at: http://www.circular.academy/circular-economy-critics-and-challenges/

Geissdoerfer, M., Savaget, P., Bocken, N. M., & Hultink, E. J. (2017). The circular economy – A new Sustainability paradigm? *Journal of Cleaner Production*, *143*, 757–768.

Hauschild, M., Kara, S., & Røpke, I. (2020). Absolute Sustainability: Challenges to life cycle engineering. *CIRP Annals*, *69*(2), 533–553. https://doi.org/10.1016/j.cirp.2020.05.004

Jones, P., & Comfort, D. (2017). Towards the circular economy: A commentary on corporate approaches and challenges. *Journal of Public Affairs*, *17*(4), e1680.

Kirchherr, J., Reike, D., & Hekkert, M. (2017). Conceptualizing the circular economy: An analysis of 114 definitions. *Resources, Conservation and Recycling*, *127*, 221–232.

Luttenberger, L. R. (2020). Waste management challenges in transition to circular economy– case of Croatia. *Journal of Cleaner Production*, *256*, 120495.

MacArthur, E. (2013). Towards the circular economy. *Journal of Industrial Ecology*, *2*(1), 23–44.

Nascimento, D. L. M., Alencastro, V., Quelhas, O. L. G., Caiado, R. G. G., Garza-Reyes, J. A., Rocha-Lona, L., & Tortorella, G. (2019). Exploring Industry 4.0 technologies to enable circular economy practices in a manufacturing context: A business model proposal. *Journal of Manufacturing Technology Management*, *30*(3), 607–627.

Rodríguez-Antón, J. M., & Alonso-Almeida, M. D. M. (2019). The circular economy strategy in hospitality: A multicase approach. *Sustainability*, *11*(20), 5665.

Rodriguez-Anton, J. M., Rubio-Andrada, L., Celemín-Pedroche, M. S., & Alonso-Almeida, M. D. M. (2019). Analysis of the relations between circular economy and sustainable development goals. *International Journal of Sustainable Development & World Ecology*, *26*(8), 708–720.

Sariatli, F. (2017). Linear economy versus circular economy: a comparative and analyzer study for optimization of economy for Sustainability. *Visegrad Journal on Bioeconomy and Sustainable Development*, *6*(1), 31–34.

Sharma, N. K., Govindan, K., Lai, K. K., Chen, W. K., & Kumar, V. (2021). The transition from linear economy to circular economy for Sustainability among SMEs: A study on prospects, impediments, and prerequisites. *Business Strategy and the Environment*, *30*(4), 1803–1822.

Suárez-Eiroa, B., Fernández, E., Méndez-Martínez, G., & Soto-Oñate, D. (2019). Operational principles of circular economy for sustainable development: Linking theory and practice. *Journal of cleaner production*, *214*, 952–961.

Stahel, W. R. (2016). The circular economy. *Nature*, *531*(7595), 435–438.

Stewart, R., & Niero, M. (2018). Circular economy in corporate Sustainability strategies: A review of corporate Sustainability reports in the fast-moving consumer goods sector. *Business Strategy and the Environment*, *27*(7), 1005–1022.

22 Future and Challenges of Lean Green Sustainability

INTRODUCTION

In this book, we integrated Lean with Green Sustainability from a principle, tool, and application perspective. We demonstrated the natural alignment and synergy between Lean's focus on reducing and eliminating waste from production and service processes and the desire to reduce, reuse, and recycle from the Green Sustainability perspective. We will now discuss the challenges of implementing the tightly coupled, integrated systemic Lean Green Sustainability framework (LGSF) that we developed and discussed in Chapter 6, the important factors to making this happen, and the future of Lean Green Sustainability.

CHALLENGES TO IMPLEMENTATION

Chapter 6 introduced our Lean Green Sustainability framework (LGSF), shown again in Figure 22.1. The framework integrates the Lean and Sustainability principles, tools, and methodology that can help adoption. We integrated the Plan-Do-Check-Act Total Quality Management continuous improvement methodology with the 5Rs of recycle, refuse, reflect, reduce, and reuse.

Several recent systematic literature reviews have investigated the state of the literature regarding Lean Sustainability. Ciarniene and Vienazindiene (2014) identified people-related and organization-based challenges that impact implementing both Lean and Sustainability in organizations. The people-related challenges include the employees' attitudes toward Sustainability, employee resistance to change, the lack of awareness and knowledge of Lean and Sustainability, and poor communication. These factors are common for any large program where change is necessary, including Lean independently or with Six Sigma or Sustainability. It can take quite some time for organizations to mature to a level where they are used to implementing and embracing large organizational change programs. Lean Sustainability is not unique in this respect. The organizational barriers include culture (discussed in Chapter 5), lack of resources for providing implementation, weak alignment between improvement programs and the defined strategy, scarce data collection and performance measures, and the tendency to return to the old ways of working. These organizational challenges are quite familiar to anyone implementing continuous improvement, digital transformations, Lean, information systems, or large, complex people, process, and technology-oriented programs. Other challenges identified in the literature

DOI: 10.1201/9780429506192-22

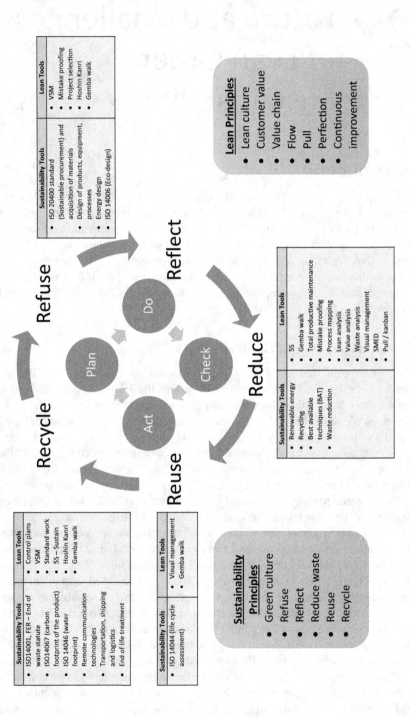

FIGURE 22.1 Lean Green Sustainability framework.

include the lack of environmental performance (EP) measures and measurement, the lack of research on developing measurement methods or models, social performance (SP) being the least studied area of the Triple Bottom Line (i.e., economic, environmental, and social), and the lack of a framework and empirical research to support its impact (Henao, Sarache, & Gomez, 2019). The good news is that these are known and common barriers. The challenge is that they still remain complex challenges to overcome, regardless of awareness.

Data, metrics, and technology challenges are also prevalent when integrating Lean Sustainability. There have been many recent research articles regarding the value and challenges of the Internet of Things (IoT) helping to integrate Lean with Sustainability, including the studies by Rejeb, Suhaiza, Rejeb, Seuring, and Treiblmaier (2022):

- Scalable connectivity, where organizations find it difficult to achieve the scale needed for big data, networking, 5G, and the cyber security elements of IoT.
- Seamless interoperability of services across software, platforms, networks, and equipment.
- High trustworthy value chains that exhibit low complexity and cost.

IMPORTANT FACTORS

Gaikwad and Sunnapwar (2020) performed a systematic literature review to identify success factors and directions for future research in integrated Lean, Green, and Six Sigma strategies. Many of these factors align with the authors' experiences as challenges of implementing Lean Green Sustainability. They also provided their framework, which still needs to be validated for its impact on implementing Lean Sustainability. The important factors to enhance the success of implementing an integrated Lean Sustainability program, are illustrated in Figure 22.2. Leadership and culture provide the critical foundation for implementing Lean Sustainability. As in any other organizational transformational program, leadership must set the direction and communicate this constantly to the organization, the press, in their annual report, on social media, and many other internal and external communication avenues. This leadership must extend to the organization's customers, suppliers, partners, and employees. Organizations incorporating Lean Sustainability strategies into their strategic plan must fund and resource initiatives aligned with their other strategic initiatives. In other words, leadership must genuinely care about Lean Green Sustainability.

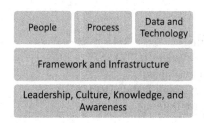

FIGURE 22.2   Important factors of Lean Green Sustainability.

Knowledge, awareness, and training are critical to Lean Sustainability implementation. Those involved in implementation must understand the value of Lean Sustainability, the principles, and how to use the tools and methodologies to make change happen. Organizations must utilize experienced change agents to help the organization and its employees overcome their resistance to change and migrate to the circular economy.

A validated framework and the related infrastructure are essential elements of the Lean Sustainability program. The framework should include principles, methodology, and tools to support the program. Lastly, the people, processes, and technology are ultimately the who (people), how (processes), and what (technology) that gets implemented in the organization's Lean Sustainability program.

FUTURE OF LEAN GREEN SUSTAINABILITY

The future of Lean Green Sustainability is wide open. There still needs to be more research performed in this area. There are few, if any, validated frameworks and extensive opportunities for incorporating technology into the mix to develop much-needed data, metrics, dashboards, scorecards, and integration across the value streams. We encourage study, research, and application in the following areas:

- Development and validation of integrated Lean Green Sustainable frameworks, including principles, tools, and methodologies.
- Incorporation of big data, integrated analysis, collection, visualization, and continuous improvement with dashboards and scorecards with viable and valuable metrics and key performance indicators (KPIs) for sustaining operations excellence.
- Strategies to move the needle on people and cultural barriers, to remove resistance to change and Sustainability of the Lean Green Sustainability program.
- Advancing knowledge and awareness of Lean and Sustainability.
- Advanced leadership and cultural transformations around Lean Green Sustainability.
- The ability to advance IoT to integrate value chains incorporating the leading technologies of IoT (Rejeb, Suhaiza, Rejeb, Seuring, & Treiblmaier, 2022):
  - Artificial intelligence and machine learning
  - Augmented reality for training
  - Big data
  - Blockchain
  - Cloud computing
  - Cyber-physical systems (CPS)
  - IoT connected machines
  - Radio frequency identification (RFID)
  - Virtual reality for training
  - 3D printing
  - 5G networking

Other future implications of Lean Green Sustainability might be exploring the idea of Industry 5.0, a term coined for the fifth industrial revolution. Industry 5.0 humanizes the concept of Industry 4.0, which adds human productivity with process efficiencies that organizations may improve through digital technologies, another social impact area. Another region to explore is how Lean Green Sustainability practices and IoT technologies might improve human productivity and safety. How Lean Green Sustainability practices integrated with cutting-edge IoT-based technologies may make the human experiences with technology productive, secure, and effective not only an exciting area to explore but a humane one. Moreover, IoT devices have a carbon footprint, and their increase from 50 billion (2020) to 80 (2030) billion need cost and energy-efficient design solutions for IoT-based systems (Anand et al., 2020). Therefore, how organizations implement Lean and Sustainable practices to design secure and sustainable IoT-based cyber-physical systems might be an interesting question to explore.

CONCLUSION

The future and challenges of Lean Green Sustainability is an incredibly rich area for study, research, and application to leverage both Lean and Green Sustainability to help create sustainable efforts to save our environment and truly achieve a circular economy. This chapter describes the challenges of implementing an integrated Lean Green Sustainable program, the essential factors, and the future of this fascinating and critically important area. The following four chapters include real-world case studies incorporating Lean Sustainability principles, tools, and methods in a university's recycling program, farming, airport refueling, and a hospital's surgical sterile instrument processes.

REFERENCES

Anand, P., Singh, Y., Selwal, A., Alazab, M., Tanwar, S., & Kumar, N. (2020). IoT vulnerability assessment for sustainable computing: threats, current solutions, and open challenges. *IEEE Access, 8,* 168825–168853.

Ciarniene, R., & Vienazindiene, M. (2014). How to facilitate implementation of lean concept? *Mediterranean Journal of Social Sciences, 5,* 177e183. https://doi.org/10.5901/mjss.2014.v5n13p177

Gaikwad, L., & Sunnapwar, V. (2020). An integrated Lean, Green and Six Sigma strategies: A systematic literature review and directions for future research. *The TQM Journal, 32*(2), 201–225.

Henao, R., Sarache, W., & Gomez, I. (2019). Lean manufacturing and sustainable performance: Trends and future challenges. *Journal of Cleaner Production, 208,* 99–116.

Rejeb, A., Suhaiza, Z., Rejeb, K., Seuring, S., & Treiblmaier, H. (2022). The Internet of Things and the circular economy: A systematic literature review and research agenda. *The Journal of Cleaner Production, 350,* 131–439.

23 Developing a University Sustainability Recycling Process*

OVERVIEW

This chapter provides a case study for developing a university's Sustainability recycling process and its associated metrics. A student team at the university applied Lean and Sustainability principles and tools to understand the current recycling process for the dorms and define improvements to the process and metrics for improving recycling.

PROJECT METHOD

The University's Director of Sustainability reached out to the instructor teaching the Lean Six Sigma course to request a project to improve recycling on campus. The director discussed the overall goals of the campus' Sustainability program to incorporate better processes and metrics to enhance Sustainability across campus. This effort included the dorms, classroom buildings, administration buildings, and when students move into and out of campus, contributing to significant amounts of waste and potentially recyclable material ending up in the local landfills. Figure 23.1 provides the value stream map for the overall Sustainability program. This project's focus was to improve the dorm recycling process, collect the voice of the customer (VoC) data to understand student attitudes towards recycling, and build better metrics to encourage and assess recycling levels. The value stream activities include

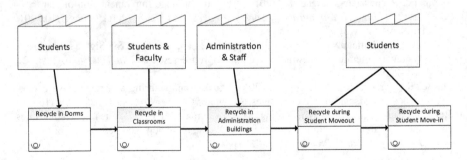

FIGURE 23.1 University Sustainability recycling value stream map.

* Contributing Authors: Sandra Furterer, Katie Dong, Ben Steitz, Matt Murin, and Breanne Smith.

     DOI: 10.1201/9780429506192-23

recycling in dorms, classrooms, and administration buildings, during student move-out and student move-in.

The team developed the project overview, charter, and goals.

Project Overview: At the university, there is a significant amount of waste in recycled bins and a tremendous amount of recycled material in the waste bins on campus.

Problem Statement: The diversion/contamination of recycling and waste has consistently been a problem at the university that still needs to be solved. The lack of recycling impacts the greater community because the campus does not recycle a lot of material, and waste is put in the recycling bin when it is not recyclable.

Goals: This project aims to increase the diversion and decrease the contamination rates by creating a process and metrics for dorm recycling.

STAKEHOLDER ANALYSIS

The team performed a stakeholder analysis to identify each stakeholder's internal and external customer roles and potential impacts/concerns, as shown in Figure 23.2.

Students: The university's students are a primary stakeholder in this project because they are responsible for most of the waste collected in the residential and academic buildings. Without the students, this project would not be measurable and possible. They may have yet to be very receptive at first, but once the project gets going, the team expects to receive moderate support from them.

Facilities (including waste management vendor and environmental services staff): The Facilities Department is a primary stakeholder in this project because after students throw away their trash and recycling, the Facilities Department will collect and dispose of the waste/recycling. This process makes the waste audit more manageable since they are the primary collectors. They need to be highly supportive of the process by the end of it.

Director of Sustainability: The Director of Sustainability is a primary stakeholder in this project because they manage the waste and recycling process at the university. This project benefits her because it helps her manage the Sustainability that is occurring at the university. They will be a prominent supporter of the process, and the team wants to ensure her support throughout it and at the end.

Local Community: The local community outside of the university is a secondary stakeholder in this project because after Facilities collect the waste and recycling, it is their responsibility to handle the waste and recycle and dispose of it in the local landfills. They would benefit from this because local communities are constantly looking for ways to be more sustainable and reduce waste, and the university is a heavy contributor to this. The university has multiple Sustainability clubs, programs, financial endeavors, and initiatives to become more sustainable and green in which the local community is involved.

University Administration: The university is a secondary stakeholder in this project because the waste and recycling impact the university, and the school creates a vast amount of waste in general. The university would benefit from this project because it makes them more sustainable. In addition, the university can implement the project university-wide after the semester project ends. The team believes the university will initially strongly support the project and in the future.

Stakeholder Analysis

Identify the internal and external customer roles and concerns to ensure their expectations are addressed. Define roles, impacts, concerns, and receptivity.

Stakeholder	Type	Primary Role	Potential Impacts/ Concerns	Initial Receptivity	Future Receptivity
Students	Primary	The students who are mostly responsible for the majority of the waste collected in residential and academic buildings	Overall waste reduction, reducing recycling contamination	Neutral	Moderate Support
Facilities	Primary	Are responsible for the process of collecting and disposing of the recycling and waste	Making the overall process easier, easier ways to audit waste	Moderate Support	Strongly Support
Director of Sustainability	Primary	Manages the recycling and waste process	Benefit Director in managing the Sustainability program	Strongly Support	Strongly Support
Local Community	Secondary	Is responsible for taking on the trash created by the University and has to dispose of it in their local landfills	Looking to cut down on landfill waste especially that contributed from the University	Strongly Support	Strongly Support
University Administration	Secondary	Creates a large amount of waste from it's residential, academic and facilities buildings	Helping reduce waste to help community, reducing waste	Strongly Support	Strongly Support

FIGURE 23.2   Stakeholder analysis.

Project Risk Analysis

Brainstorm the potential risks to a successful project, identify the likelihood that each will occur, the potential impact, and develop a mitigation strategy.

Potential Risk to Successful Project	Occurrence of Risk	Impact of Risk	Risk Mitigation Strategy
Insufficient staff	Moderate	Moderate	Gain more members or reallot resources
Return home order (Pandemic)	Moderate	Very High	Stress good health and safety practices
Resistance from employees and students	Low	High	Make sure employees and students are on board and have the correct information about the project and its benefits
Change in waste and recycle collectors	Very Low	High	Make sure that this plan or setup is in the contract

FIGURE 23.3 Project risk analysis.

Project Risk Analysis

The team used project risk analysis to identify the potential risks to a successful project. The middle columns in Figure 23.3 provide the occurrence and impact of the risk. The strategy for how the team would handle the risk if it occurred is also included in the last column and would occur during the improvement phase.

Supplier-Input-Process-Output-Customer Diagram

The supplier-input-process-output-customer (SIPOC) diagram explains the customer/supplier relationship in the process. The SIPOC includes where the process begins and ends, and the activities included within the scope need improvement. Figure 23.4 illustrates the SIPOC.

Critical to Satisfaction Criteria

Continuous improvement teams use a project's Critical to Satisfaction (CTS) section to determine the elements that will significantly improve the process, systematically satisfy the customer's needs, and control the process. The team identified six CTS criteria for this project. The first criterion is the throughput rate at which the waste can be processed and recorded. Next is ensuring the process prevents too much work or strain on one individual or group. The third criterion is measuring the number of recyclable items. Another criterion is satisfaction with the recycling program. In addition, there is a criterion for standardizing the recycling program. The final criterion is providing incentives for recycling. Figure 23.5 highlights the CTS criteria.

Potential Project Benefits

One benefit of this project is that it reduces employees' work at the recycling and waste plants. It also increases the university's Sustainability goal and helps the earth with the amount of waste produced and put into landfills. Another benefit is that

SIPOC

Explain the Customer / Supplier relationship in the process. Identify where the process begins and where it ends, and the activities included within the scope of the process to be improved.

Suppliers	Inputs	Process	Outputs	Customers
Students causing waste and contamination, University administration	Contaminated waste	**Inform them of changes in process**	Lower contaminated waste in recycling collection bins	University Administration
University Administration Director of Sustainability	High amounts of waste and contaminated waste from residential, academic and facilities buildings	**Promote change in the process of waste collection**	Lower contaminated waste in recycling collection bins which will lower overall waste from university	Director of Sustainability
Director of Sustainability Community	Trying to monitor waste and contaminated recycling	**Facilitate and monitor changes in the Sustainability process**	More aware students/ university, and less waste	Community
Community	Large amounts of waste and contaminated recycling from the University	**Understanding and helping with changes to process**	Less waste needed to be collected from University, Less waste in landfills	Community

FIGURE 23.4 SIPOC for the recycling process.

Critical to Satisfaction (CTS)

CTS' are basic elements that can be used in driving process measurement, improvement, and control. They are elements of a process that significantly affect the output of the process. What are the characteristics of the process are critical as perceived by the customer?

	Title	Description
1	Throughput	The rate at which the waste can be processed and recorded.
2	No Excess Strain	Making sure that the process isn't putting too much work or strain onto one individual or group.
3	Condition	We are measuring only the actual recyclable items and not counting some items which almost meet the requirement. Would need to know what disqualifies a recyclable item (i.e. caps on bottles, grease, etc.) and the regulations on common recyclable items.
4	Satisfaction	This would include anyone directly or indirectly involved with recycling system. We want to make sure that most are happy with the implementation or if there are any areas in need of improvement. To do this, we will need to be given feedback in the form of surveys and will be transparent with our sponsors about the received feedback so they are aware of the sentiment as well.
5	Standardization	We want to make sure that process we implement in one building is the same for all the other buildings as it creates less work for the students, volunteers, and faculty.

FIGURE 23.5 Critical to satisfaction criteria.

future projects can take the data and expand upon it to increase the university's Sustainability further and to give a better understanding of where the university sits on the Sustainability level. It also prevents the things that can be recycled and reused from going into landfills and oceans.

DATA COLLECTION PLAN

The first critical to satisfaction was the Rates. The operational definition is the data from the audits to determine the percentage of contamination of landfill waste found in recycling bins to determine the plan's effectiveness. The data collection source is waste audits, and the analysis mechanisms used are statistical and at a monthly frequency. Reporting and collecting the data involves regular audits by knowledge-able individuals or groups to determine the amount of waste in recycling bins. The team developed no excess strain metric based on surveys done with Sustainability employees. The operational definition for this metric was regular surveys or meetings done with environmental services and other Sustainability employees to shed light on how the process has affected their job performance and function. The data collection source involved surveys of the students and faculty. In this case, the approach to col-lect data was regular "check-in" surveys, which the team analyzed to gauge the imple-mentation of processes. The frequency of these surveys was a monthly survey for the employees involved in the audits of specific buildings. The condition affects the types and quantities of items that students can recycle. The process to collect and report on this is first checking in with the company responsible for exporting the recyclables to acknowledge and implement the acceptable items into the audits. The frequency of this measure was monthly and excluded event days that may cause a fluctuation in the data. The analysis mechanism was audits of waste and was statistically analyzed. For satisfaction, the metric was the rate approval. The team collected and reported data using monthly surveys to check in and gauge the satisfaction of the project and the processes implemented. The analysis mechanism for this was statistical analysis. The team used set methods for the standardization of user satisfaction. The team distrib-uted and analyzed the check-in surveys bi-weekly. Lastly, the team developed incen-tives critical to satisfaction to gauge the initial and final satisfaction of the waste and recycling processes among the users, faculty, and students. The sampling plan for this metric was two surveys before and after implementing the strategies, which the team statistically analyzed. Figure 23.6 illustrates the data collection plan.

VALUE STREAM MAP

The team developed a more detailed value stream map for recycling activities. Figure 23.7 provides the value stream map for the recycling process.

PROCESS MAP

The team developed a more detailed process map of the student dorm recycling pro-cess, shown in Figure 23.8.

Data Collection Plan

Identify metrics to measure and assess improvement that relate to the CTS's from the Define Phase.

Critical to Satisfaction (CTS)	Metric (short title)	Operational Definition (metric description)	Data Collection Source	Analysis Mechanism	Sampling Plan (size, frequency)	Process to Collect and Report
Rates	Percent of contamination in recycling	We will be using the data from the audits to measure the throughout. We will find the percentage of contamination or landfill items that end up in the recycling bins in order to know how effective our plan is.	Reports from audits	Audits of waste	Once a month on days with no events to give false numbers.	Regular audits of chosen building to see if contaminated waste has decreased
No excess strain	Surveys with Sustainability employees	Regular surveys/meetings with Environmental Services employees to see how new process affects their job/strain.	Students and faculty	Surveys	A survey through email sent out once a month after an audit to the building that the audit was performed at.	Regular surveys to check in with workers
Condition	Percent of materials that can actually be recycled vs overall waste	The number of items that the recycling company actually is able to recycle.	Reports from waste audits	Audits of waste	Once a month on days with no events to give false numbers.	Check in with recycle company to see if anything changed and with audits
Satisfaction	Rate of approval	The measurement of happiness of those involved with for the process we implement.	Students and faculty	Surveys	Once a month a survey will be sent out through their emails to provide honest feedback about their satisfaction or happiness with the project. Will be sent out in conjunction with the no excess strain survey.	Regular surveys to check in with the University
Standardization for method	Set method with user satisfaction	Helping to implement concrete methods to collect data while taking into account employee satisfaction with new data collection process.	Environmental Services	Surveys	Bi-weekly for 1-2 months after process is implemented to collect data using visual audits.	Regular surveys to check in with employees
Incentives	Surveys	Surveys of the initial and final satisfaction of the recycling/waste process.	Users, faculty, and students	Surveys	Survey before and after implementation to compare satisfaction.	Two surveys before and after implementation of process

FIGURE 23.6 Data collection plan.

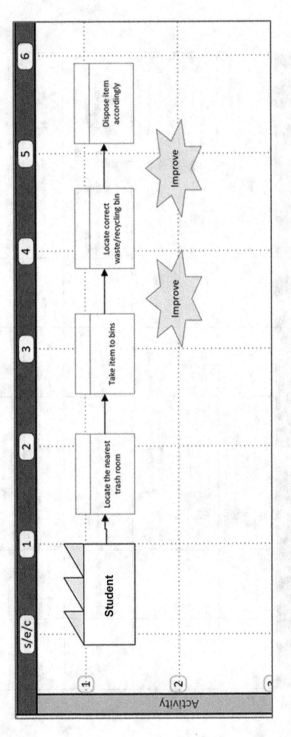

FIGURE 23.7   Value stream map of the recycling process.

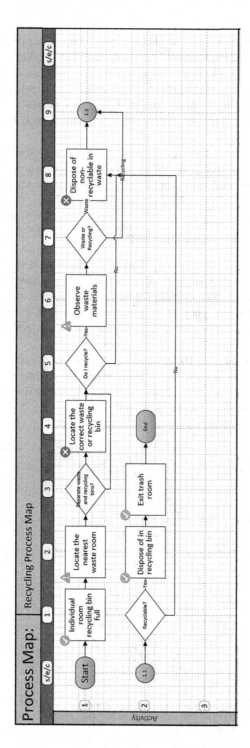

FIGURE 23.8 Process map of recycling.

CHECK SHEET

Continuous improvement teams use check sheets to track the defective parts in a system and other critical information, such as the day they found the defects and the location of the defect. Check sheets enable teams to see the primary defects and how often they occur so continuous improvement teams can implement process improvements to reduce them. Check sheets are simple, yet they provide so much information by collecting data and identifying reasons for mistakes, such as cause and effect diagrams and Pareto charts.

The purpose of the check sheet for this project is to determine why students do not recycle and then correspond to where they live. This analysis will help the team understand which halls need more work than the others and the main issues they face with recycling. Figure 23.9 provides the check sheet.

BAR GRAPH OF RECYCLED MATERIALS AND PARETO CHART

A bar graph shows a comparison among discrete categories. One axis shows the categories, the other shows the measured values, while a Pareto chart puts the categories in order from highest to lowest count. Continuous improvement teams use Pareto charts to determine the frequency and the majority or 80% of the problem within a data set. The Pareto chart is an essential depiction of what students throw away. The team can later use this to further the project goals.

The bar graph in Figure 23.10 represents the common materials people recycle and their count. This data can help us determine where the students' thinking or recycling process needs to be corrected. It also gives us reliable information and data, as many students think they can recycle pizza boxes.

Reason Types	Residence							Total
	Dorm 1	Dorm 2	Dorm 3	Dorm 4	Dorm 5	Dorm 6	Other	
No bin in areas								
Lack of information								
Too much separation required								
Inconvenient								
Take too much time								
Too messy								
Limits on types accepted								
Believe materials end up in landfill instead of recycling								
Lack of support from housemates								
Recycle bins already full								
Bins are not clearly defined								
Other								
Total								

FIGURE 23.9 Check sheet of reasons for not recycling.

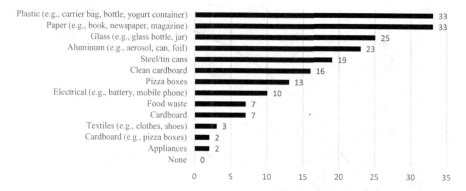

FIGURE 23.10   Bar graph of survey responses.

The Pareto chart in Figure 23.11 shows what common materials people tend to throw in the recycling bin. The team used the data from this in the future to meet the project goals. For example, the team could take the top 80% and have trash cans dedicated to them.

HISTOGRAMS OF RECYCLING CONTAMINATION

Continuous improvement teams use histograms to show data sets and if the data forms a normal distribution and to have a visual to assist in establishing the data trends. The histogram in Figure 23.12 shows how often a student throws a recyclable item in the trash bin in a given week. The histogram provides essential information because the team wants to target the highest section to bring the contamination rate down and the diversion rate up. The team can use the data in conjunction with the other data in this report to determine why so many students throw away so many recyclable items in a given week.

In the last bar graph in Figure 23.13, the team is trying to determine if there is a relationship between someone's standing at the university and how often they recycle. The bar chart can help us determine who and where to focus resources and efforts.

LINE GRAPH AND PIE CHART OF INFORMATION DISBURSEMENT

The line graph's purpose shown in Figure 23.14 is to see if there is a correlation between the students' happiness with campus recycling and their understanding of recycling rules. The team chose this to determine if those who said they were unhappy with the university's recycling program were unhappy. After all, they found it difficult to know what should be recycled and not for some other reason.

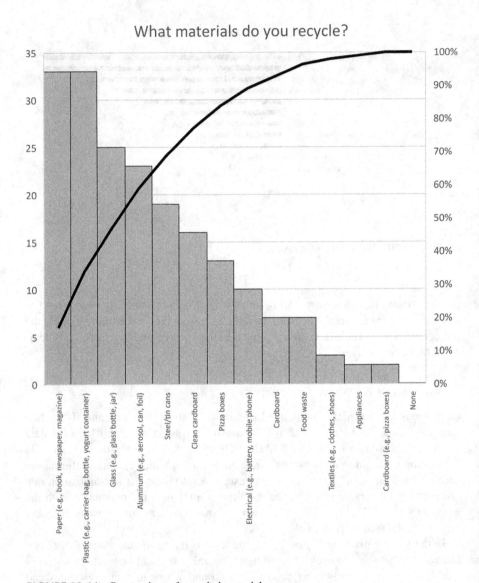

FIGURE 23.11   Pareto chart of recycled materials survey.

Continuous improvement teams use pie charts to show how teams can split data into different-sized chunks to represent the whole data range. Pie charts only show the categories that have been collected or have data and exclude the zero-value categories.

The pie chart in Figure 23.15 visually represents the percentage of students who preferred a method of communication based on the type that the university can provide. Most of the students surveyed (95.3%) would like to receive information about recycling on campus, with the top mode of communication being via email (38.1%).

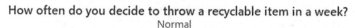

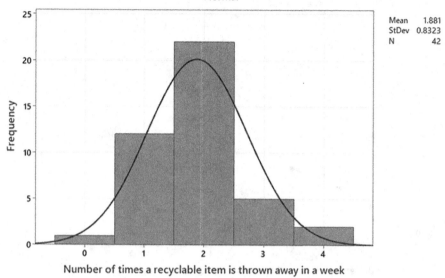

FIGURE 23.12 Histogram of frequency of recyclable items.

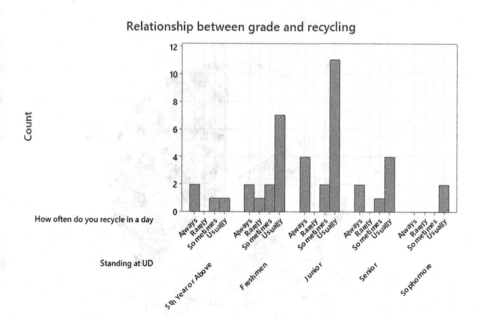

FIGURE 23.13 Chart of the relationship between grade and recycling.

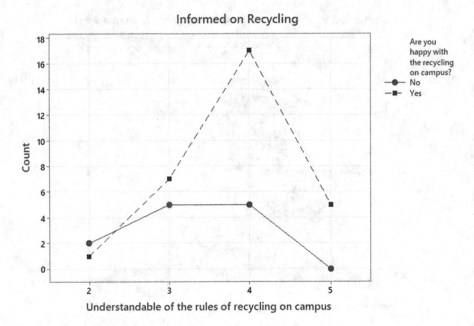

FIGURE 23.14   Line chart of informed on recycling.

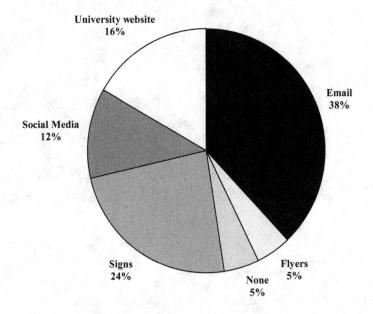

FIGURE 23.15   Pie chart of information on recycling.

ATTRIBUTE AGREEMENT ANALYSIS

Continuous improvement teams use attribute agreement analysis to test how close or correct the appraisers or workers are to the standard of the company or project. It lets us know how well the workers did and what items were a common struggle. The team used three members in the attribute agreement analysis shown in Figure 23.16. The team gave the member 15 items to identify whether they belonged in the recycling or landfill bin. The project sponsor gave the team the standard used to determine that they would accurately know the current bins of the items. The team did this to test the knowledge of what students think can be recycled and not recycled and identify everyday items that need to be labeled. The team found that item 2, a plastic hanger, was the most miss-labeled item as it is recyclable. The team also found that most believe they can throw away plastic utensils, which is untrue, as anything with food contaminants, like a pizza box, cannot be recycled. Overall, students can correctly identify recyclable items about 70% of the time.

VALUE ANALYSIS

In the value analysis, the team used the three categories of value-added, limited-value-added, and non-value-added. For the process, the team observed the process of a student disposing of materials in a dorm. The value-added section is anything that aids the process in any way. Limited value-added activities do not add or assist the process in any way. Non-value-added steps impact the process negatively and possibly hurt the process.

Value-added activities include disposing of items in a recycling bin. Limited-value consists of having an individual room's recycling bin being full. Non-value-added includes locating the nearest recycling bin, locating the correct bin, and observing waste materials to determine what is recyclable.

WASTE ANALYSIS

The team analyzed the following non-value activities for which of the eight wastes are occurring.

Locating the nearest recycling bin

- Motion
- Processing waste

Locating the Correct Bin

- Delay
- Processing

Observe Waste materials and determine the recyclability

- Delay
- Processing

Attribute Agreement Analysis for Results
Summary Report

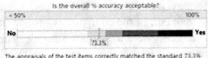

Is the overall % accuracy acceptable?

The appraisals of the test items correctly matched the standard 73.3% of the time.

Misclassification Rates

Overall error rate	26.7%
Recyclable rated Landfill	14.3%
Landfill rated Recyclable	37.5%
Mixed ratings (same item rated both ways)	13.3%

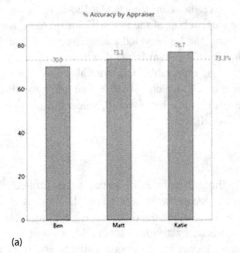

% Accuracy by Appraiser

Comments

Consider the following when assessing how the measurement system can be improved:
• Low Accuracy Rates: Low rates for some appraisers may indicate a need for additional training for those appraisers. Low rates for all appraisers may indicate more systematic problems, such as poor operating definitions, poor training, or incorrect standards.
• High Misclassification Rates: May indicate that either too many Recyclable items are being rejected, or too many Landfill items are being passed on to the consumer (or both).
• High Percentage of Mixed Ratings: May indicate items in the study were borderline cases between Recyclable and Landfill, thus very difficult to assess.

(a)

Attribute Agreement Analysis for Results
Accuracy Report

All graphs show 95% confidence intervals for accuracy rates.
Intervals that do not overlap are likely to be different.

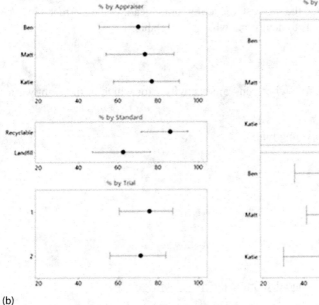

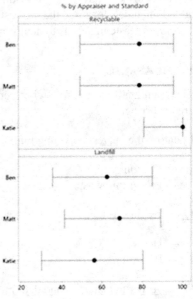

(b)

FIGURE 23.16   Attribute agreement analysis results.

WHY-WHY DIAGRAM

The Why-Why Diagram is a simple diagram to find the root cause of system problems. The team started with the stated problem and then asked why repeatedly, ideally five times, until determining the root cause. The root causes are sometimes fixable, but other times the teams cannot change them due to the lack of resources or ability. Using the Why-Why diagram, the team found repeating root cause factors affecting the process. Figures 23.17 through 23.20 provide the Why-Why diagrams.

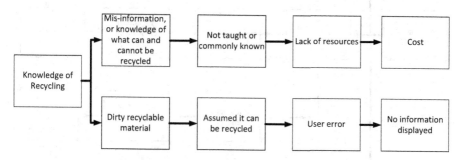

FIGURE 23.17   Why-Why diagram for knowledge of recycling.

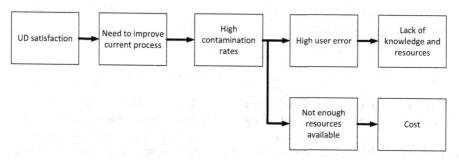

FIGURE 23.18   Why-Why diagram for satisfaction.

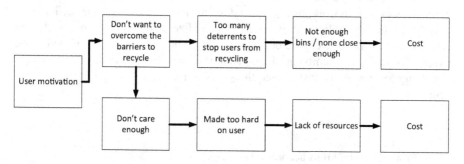

FIGURE 23.19   Why-Why diagram for user motivation.

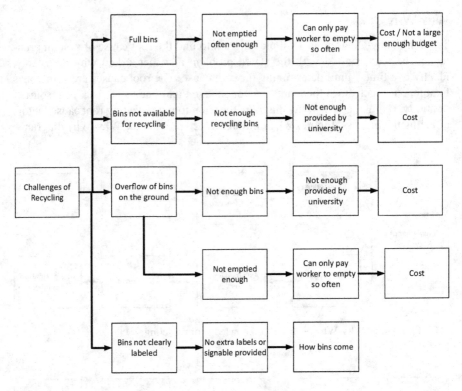

FIGURE 23.20   Why-Why diagram for recycling challenges.

5S

The 5S is a process used to understand where there are opportunities for improvement throughout the system and the root causes of problems. This system helps standardize the process, so it is done orderly and is a way to increase productivity and profitability. 5S consists of sort/simplify, straighten, shine/scrub, standardize/stabilize, and sustain.

Sorting identifies what items are necessary and unnecessary by an arrangement. Systemize ensures that there is a clear place for everything and clear organization. Shine creates a clean workplace to understand the root causes of problems. This step clearly shows the problematic situations. Standardize/Stabilize develops a system or a procedure in which everyone can agree. Sustain helps keep discipline within the system for sorting, systemizing, shining, and standardizing. The team developed the following 5S strategy to ensure everything can be put in place and organize the system well.

Sort

- Properly sort all bins accordingly.
- Clearly distinguish and label between waste bins versus recycling bins.

Systemize

- Ensure all waste bins are the same size, have the same labels, are in the same location in the waste room, and are in the same orientation in the waste room.
- Create the same waste process with all students.

Shine/Scrub

- Have clear and concise labeling.
- Ensure facilities pick up the waste daily or a few times a week.

Standardize/Stabilize

- Create a standard location across campus in each building (all waste rooms are to the right of the women's restrooms).
- Standardize the same type of bins.

Sustain

- Keep track of all waste and recycling.

RECOMMENDATIONS FOR IMPROVEMENT

Figure 23.21 aligns the CTS to improvement ideas to eliminate root causes and problems for each CTS. From the root causes and their associated improvement

Recommendations for Improvement

Identify Improvements that eliminate root causes, wastes, limited and non-value added activities. Use your Lean Analysis, FMEA, Why-Whys, current state process maps, value stream maps.

Improvement Ideas	Improvement Description	Root Causes	CTS	Category	Priority
Increase the number of recycling bins across campus	Provide more recycling bins across campus to increase the availability of bins	Not enough bins currently leading to more recycling being thrown in trash	Incentives	Motivation	1
Increase the number of times bins will be collected to prevent overflow	Instead of once a day or once every other day, increase collection to twice a day to prevent overflowing of bins	Already limited recycling bins being full and causing overflow	Condition	Clarity	2
Post flyers with recycling information to help improve knowledge and newsletters	Flyers with detailed yet simplistic information of what can and cannot be recycled above bins	Lack of knowledge by users of what can and cannot be recycled	Satisfaction	Information	3
Show on the trash or map where the next nearest recycle bin can be found	Provide information of where next nearest bin is, if the current bin is full and already overflowing	Bins being full and users not knowing where the next closest bin is located	No Excess Strain	Satisfaction	7
Pizza box bin	Have a separate bin for pizza boxes	Pizza boxes being put into the recycle bin as students see the cardboard and think it can be recycled	Rates	Clarity	4
Separation of waste room	Separate the recycling and waste bin with a physical barrier to prevent mixing of waste	Bins are not clearly labeled and close together leading to mixing of waste from user error and overflow	Standardization for method	Satisfaction	5
More defined waste bin labels	Noticeable colors and signage that clearly defines bins	Bins not being clearly define leading to mixture of trash	Standardization for method	Clarity	6

FIGURE 23.21   Recommendations for improvement.

ideas, the team prioritized each to establish what the team should do first. The number of recycling bins should be increased across campus to increase the likelihood that someone will use them. Facilities should collect the recycling from the bins more frequently to ensure they are not full, which may discourage students from recycling. Posting flyers around campus and especially in the dorms can increase proper recycling use. If the closest recycling bin is full, show a sign on the bin where the next nearest recycling bin is so that the student will be encouraged to recycle. Incorporate a separate pizza box bin to separate them from the recycling and trash. Separate the waste room from recycling to prevent students from using the wrong bin. Implement more colorful signage that can help students know what to recycle.

QUALITY FUNCTION DEPLOYMENT

A Quality Function Deployment chart is a visual tool used to help establish a ranking of the proposed improvements the team could implement in the process. It uses a ranking system of importance (1–10) for each CTS, which the team multiplies by the suggested improvements rankings that the team determines appropriate (ranked against each CTS on a scale of 1–10). This step produces an absolute number, which can then be converted into a relative weight, showing us the most important topics. For us, the most critical improvement to implement first would be to have more defined waste bin labels and increase the number of recycling bins around campus. Figure 23.22 illustrates the QFD house of quality.

SCORECARD

The team created a scorecard, shown in Figure 23.23, to provide a comprehensive and cumulative report to ascertain the composition recycling percentage of a room, dorm, or building. The team can use the scorecard at a glance to let the Sustainability team (or anyone interested in the data) know how the recycle bin(s) are doing on a specific date. The scorecard also allows the team to take notes if the data has an outlier, such as the university hosting an event that day, which might skew the data. There is also room for adding items or transforming the material section into floor numbers and even building names. Using the data from the scorecard, the team made an I-MR Chart to see the data visually, as shown in Figure 23.24. The chart shows outliers and the limits, so the team determined what day(s) the contamination was high and the average contamination percentage.

TRAINING PLAN

The training plan shown in Figure 23.25 is how the team intends to train the main stakeholders to implement the improvement plan through the various improvements to the process listed above and training the respected individuals listed in their necessary roles and responsibilities.

Quality Functional Deployment (QFD) or House of Quality

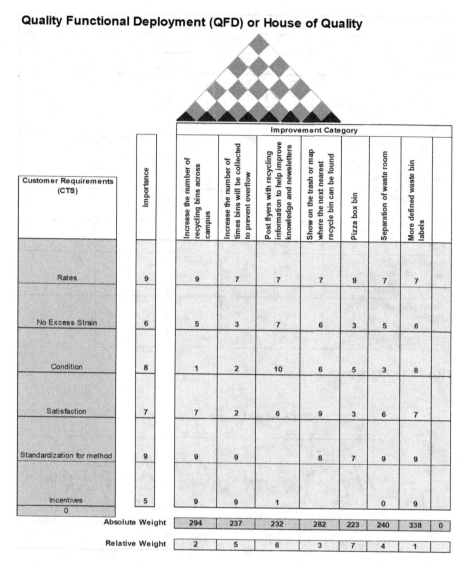

FIGURE 23.22 Quality function deployment house of quality.

Impact-Effort Matrix

An impact-effort matrix is an advanced root cause analysis tool that helps prioritize improvement ideas for the team. It lets us know which improvements are of a higher priority or impact. The team plots all ideas based on the level of the impact-effort matrix. From the grid, the team noticed that ideas 3, 4, and 6 are all high-impact, indicating where to focus time and resources. The team also noticed that idea three takes the least effort, making it the optimal solution. This selection is because it requires little resources (time, labor, money, etc.) to make it happen, yet it makes the same impact as ideas 4 or 6.

Operator:					
Location:					
Time and Date:					
Material	Material State	Fullness Level (%)	Amount	Composition (Amount/Total)	Notes
Glass (food and beverage containers)					
Plastics (food and beverage containers w/out caps or lids)					
Plastic tubs with lids					
Metal cans (steel, aluminum, and tin)					
Aseptic (milk cartons, juice boxes)					
Paper (newspaper, clean cardboard, magazines, junk mail)					
Plastic bags (shopping or grocery)					
Foam cups or containers					

FIGURE 23.23   Scorecard.

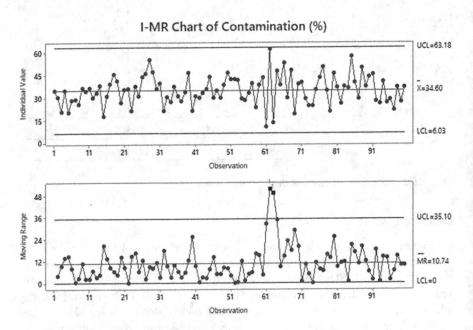

FIGURE 23.24   Example I-MR chart.

Training Plan

Training Objectives and Outcomes:	Change the behaviors of users by spreading information and refining obstacles in
Training Audience and Resources:	Students
Instructional Strategies	
Exercise and case studies:	None
Assessments and exams:	Survey what people know about what to recycle
Homework assignments:	None
Team and individual work:	Individual
Project work:	None
Presentations:	Posters
Training mode:	- Flyers/Posters of information of recyclable material closest to be placed in the recycling bin - Telling where more defined bins to tell what can be placed in each bin.
Training schedule and syllabus:	One time posting of flyers/ handouts at CBMs
Training location:	Waste rooms

FIGURE 23.25   Training plan.

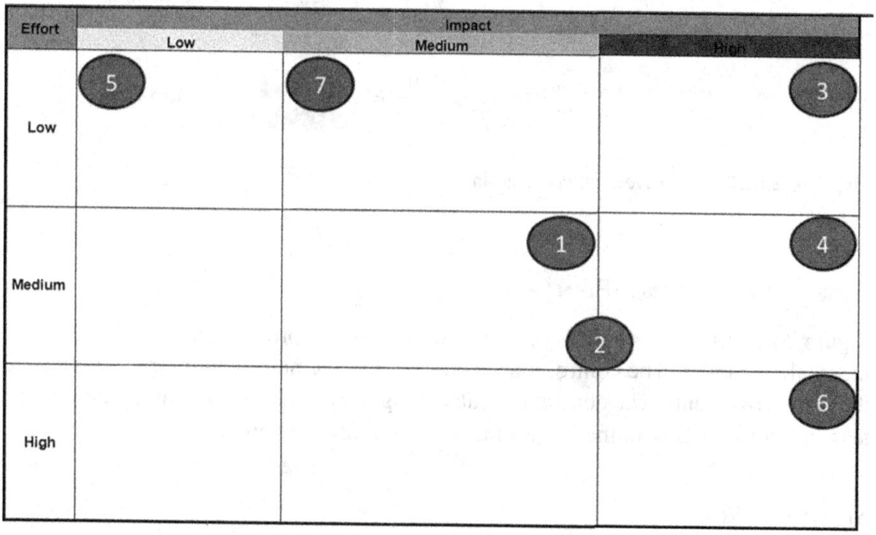

FIGURE 23.26   Impact-effort matrix.

IMPROVEMENT IDEAS

The team developed several ideas to improve campus recycling. The first idea is to increase the number of recycling bins across the campus. In addition, the team recommends increasing the frequency of recycling collection to prevent overflow. Posting flyers and including information in newsletters with recycling bin information will help improve knowledge. The team suggests showing where students can find the next nearest recycle bin on campus and building maps. Separate bins for pizza boxes will also reduce confusion. Finally, the team recommends better signage on waste bin labels.

Improvement Control Plan

The control plan is a detailed assessment and guide for maintaining all of the positive changes that you have implemented.

Process Steps	Control Mechanism	Measure/Metric	Criticality (H M L)	Action Taken if Problems Occur	Owner
Individual room bin full	Offer more recycling bins and regularly empty cans	Diversion rate of recycling from visual audits	M	Assign cause	User
Locate the nearest waste room/bin	Door signage	Diversion rate of recycling from visual audits	M	Process improvement	User
Locate the correct recycling / trash bin	Different color / labeled bins	Diversion rate of recycling from visual audits	H	Process improvement	User
Observe material and determine what can be recycled and what can be thrown in the trash	Clearly label above the waste bins for the acceptable items for each bin	Diversion rate of recycling from visual audits	M	Assign cause	User
Dispose of waste in proper bin	Different color / labeled bins	Diversion rate of recycling from visual audits	H	Process improvement	User

FIGURE 23.27   Improvement control plan.

IMPROVEMENT CONTROL PLAN

Figure 23.27 illustrates how to control and monitor the process once the team implements the changes. The control plan includes improvements and metrics to measure those improvements. The control plan also assigns ownership to monitor changes and take corrective action in the event of a conflict in the new process.

STANDARD WORK

Figure 23.28 shows the standard work sheet for the recycling process. The first step is when a student realizes an individual bin room is full. No time is associated with this step as it varies from room to room and how often the people are there. The next step is to locate the nearest waste room/bin, which could take 5 to 45 seconds, depending on the room's location. The team wants to keep the time low, though, as students may be less willing to travel far when the time increases to find a recycle bin. The student then locates the correct recycling/waste bin, which takes approximately 2 seconds since the bins should be clearly labeled and distinguishable. Students should be able to put the waste in quickly and leave. Next, the student observes the material and determines what can be recycled or should go in the trash. This step takes 10 seconds on average. The team also wants the material to be easily identifiable. The final step is for the student to dispose of waste in the proper trash bin, which should take approximately 5 seconds.

Activity	Time	Notes
Individual room bin full	N/A	
Locate the nearest waste Room/bin	Variable	
Locate the correct recycling/trash bin	2s	
Observe material and determine what can be recycled and what can be thrown in the trash	10s	
Dispose of waste in proper bin	5s	

FIGURE 23.28 Standard work instruction sheet.

CONCLUSIONS

The University Sustainability recycling project demonstrates how organizations can use Lean and Sustainability to develop, improve, and assess recycling programs to enhance a university's recycling program.

24 Implementing Lean Sustainability Practices in Agriculture*

INTRODUCTION

Manufacturing is the most common setting for applying Lean manufacturing principles. However, any application area with a process in place can be understood and analyzed from the perspective of eliminating waste and improving efficiency while reducing the utilization of resources, including material, workforce, machines, and time. As such, small businesses benefit from applying Lean principles in process improvement, particularly when constrained by the availability of resources.

One such application is in the field of agriculture. There is an increased awareness of food safety on farms. Many farmers audit their food safety policies through the Good Agricultural Practices (GAP) certification program of the US Department of Agriculture (USDA). The USDA implemented GAP in 2002 to allow the fruit and vegetable industry to verify their operations' efforts to minimize the risk of contamination of fresh produce by microbial pathogens (USDA, 2020). Many US retailers, such as supermarket chains, school systems, and restaurants, require third-party GAP audits.

Small- and mid-sized farmers agree on the importance of food safety from a liability perspective and as an incentive to attract and retain buyers. However, they feel overburdened by recordkeeping requirements associated with food traceability. Documentation for traceability is critical in the event of recall due to contamination. Once the source of contamination is known, farmers should be able to use their records to identify every customer potentially affected and recall all contaminated products. Most farmers use solutions such as clipboards with paper logs and handwritten checklists for recordkeeping purposes, requiring a considerable time to collect and record data. These inexpensive solutions offer value but are prone to errors, are easily lost, and only provide benefits when a farmer has time to transfer the information into a more usable digital format.

This chapter describes a case study of a GAP-certified vegetable farm in Iowa called Grow: Johnson County. The farm earlier used a paper-based system to manage its recordkeeping required per the GAP guidelines. The team identified Lean wastes in the farm's paper-based recordkeeping system. Poka-yoke, a Lean technique to reduce waste and the occurrence of errors in a process, was used through the development of

* Contributing Author: Anuj Mittal.

DOI: 10.1201/9780429506192-24

a low-cost and open-source tool called FarmTabs. The chapter also discusses the positive impact of Lean implementation at the farm on promoting overall social, economic, and environmental Sustainability.

CASE STUDY – GROW: JOHNSON COUNTY FARM

Grow: Johnson County (hereinafter referred to as Grow), a GAP-certified farm, grows vegetables on four acres of land at the Johnson County Historic Poor Farm in Iowa City, Iowa. The farm donates 100% of the food grown to various local hunger relief agencies. Many governmental, private, and non-profit organizations support its operations. The total farmland consists of 16 fields, each further divided into beds. Each field can have up to seven beds, depending on the size of the area. Figure 24.1 shows the map of the Grow farm, with each field indicated by a rectangle and a zoomed view of Field B and its seven beds.

GAP audit requires farmers to be able to perform a mock recall in case of contamination. Depending upon the sources of contamination, there are three instances for a possible recall. The first type is a field-related recall, which is due to contamination in soil or water. The second type is a harvest, pack, or pickup-related recall due to contaminated containers or water used for washing or an uncleaned vehicle. Finally, a crew-related recall is due to a sick crewmember handling the produce.

It is crucial to be able to trace the source of contamination and subsequently identify the lot of produce that a farm must recall from specific customers. This traceability allows the farm to manage these and other situations of recalls. Grow farm initially performed the food safety recordkeeping required per the GAP guidelines by manually writing information on the printed-paper logs. Each time they harvested a crop, they recorded information on three separate logs, including the harvest, pickup, and vehicle clean and inspection logs.

The harvest log included transcribing the date of harvest, crop name, lot number (comprising of the field and bed name), any specific notes related to harvesting (e.g.,

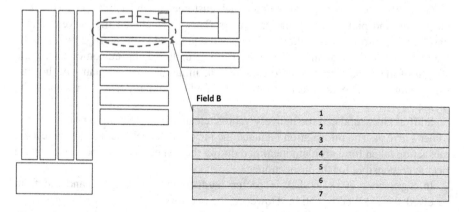

FIGURE 24.1 Map of Grow: Johnson County farm shows 16 fields, and Field B consists of seven beds.

Daily Harvest Log
This log is to be completed on a daily basis.

Date: ____11/13/2020_____

Crop	Lot #	Preharvest Inspection Notes	Weight of Harvested Crop (lb.)	Initials
Ace, Bell Peppers	Field F Bed 1	None	20 lbs.	RS
Cobra, Onion	Field H Bed 2	None	30 lbs.	RS
Provider, Bean Bush	Field A Bed 1	None	40 lbs.	RS
Sora, Radish	Field B Bed 2	Washing needed	20 lbs.	RS

Total amount harvested: ____110 lbs._____

FIGURE 24.2 Snapshot of a harvest log used in the recordkeeping process at the Grow farm before Lean implementation.

deer activity observed in the field), the weight of the harvested crop, and initials of the person responsible for the harvest. Grow used the harvest log to write a handwritten note card detailing crop name, harvest date, lot number (e.g., field and bed number), and weight of the harvested crop for each container where the harvested crop is stored. Figure 24.2 shows a snapshot of a paper-based harvest log used in the recordkeeping process at the Grow farm.

Grow filled out a new pickup log for each customer when each crop was ready to be packed and picked up by the customers. This log included the harvest details based on the information written in the notecard attached to the storage bin or in the harvest log. Additional information on the log included the customer name, the weight of the packed crop, pack/pickup date in Julian day format, name of the customer, name of the person responsible for the pickup, and any other notes about the pickup.

Staff at Grow updated the delivery vehicle clean and inspection log on each customer's arrival. The information included the pickup date, vehicle inspection results, any action taken for a problem identified during the inspection, and the initials of the person responsible for the inspection.

In September 2018, USDA inspectors audited the Grow farm, and the farm received the GAP certification. However, the auditors observed several issues surrounding traceability records in the paper-based recordkeeping process. In addition, manually entering repeated data at multiple steps in the process was time-consuming, cumbersome, and prone to human errors.

LEAN WASTES IN THE GROW: JOHNSON COUNTY FARM RECORDKEEPING PROCESS

In a manufacturing setting, one of the first steps to Lean implementation is to remove the waste or "muda" so that it does not overburden or "muri" people. Irregularities or "mura" in the process cause waste and overburden. These three m's are the Japanese terms used by Taiichi Ohno, who developed the seven wastes as part of the famous Toyota Production System between 1948 and 1975. Lean practitioners often call these seven wastes (plus the waste of talent) by acronyms such as TIMWOOD+T, DOWNTIME, and TIMWOODS, among others, each letter representing a type of waste. For the recordkeeping process, Grow farm used the TIMWOODS acronym to identify the wastes.

Transportation. Transportation wastes involve repetitive and unnecessary movement of material, tools, or equipment in a process. Different logs were printed in an office in the recordkeeping process at Grow farm and brought to the farm. After that, these paper logs were physically moved around the farm and from person to person to manually fill and transfer the data between the logs, contributing to transportation waste.

Inventory. Excessive raw materials and supplies and a considerable stock of work-in-progress inventories in a process contribute to this waste. Grow farm stored all the paperwork in files; therefore, there was no real-time visibility of the produce in stock. This practice required a manual inventory count every time there was an update in the harvest or pickup log. Lack of real-time inventory data resulted in produce forgotten about in the warehouse that ultimately went bad, resulting in food wastage. Another way inventory waste occurred in the process was due to the need for paper trails to be stored for at least one year at a physical location due to the GAP audit requirements. This practice required a lot of floor/file cabinet storage for the paper to sit.

Motion. This waste is defined as a repetitive and unnecessary movement of people and equipment, resulting in non-value-adding activities in a process. At Grow farm, an example of motion waste includes looking for a specific paper log to fill another log, for example, finding the appropriate harvest log to fill the pickup log at customer arrival. Another example is manual inventory checks at the warehouse on customer arrival for pickup.

Waiting. When people or equipment are not performing work in a process, this is waiting waste. Waiting for printed templates of various logs at the farm from an office location contributed to waiting waste. In addition, since Grow required a manual inventory check upon a customer's arrival, it resulted in a wait time to enter the pickup log.

Over-processing. This waste involves performing the same task(s) multiple times or performing a non-value-adding task(s). Writing the same information multiple times on the paper logs is an example of over-processing waste.

Overproduction. Producing faster and more than required contributes to overproduction waste. Since there was no visibility of real-time crop inventory, Grow farm often picked produce directly from the fields, occasionally resulting in an abundance of produce in the warehouse and already harvested food spoiling.

Defect. This waste leads to over-processing due to the rework or repair of defects within a process and occurs primarily due to poor process control. Transcribing incorrect data caused defects in the recordkeeping process, thus leading to an inefficient recall process. Adopting inconsistent naming conventions for the same crop, forgetting to write things down, or switching the order of information in the lot numbers (e.g., writing the field name in place of the bed number) all contributed to defects in the process. The process was also prone to errors due to legibility issues. Frequently, dirt and moisture on the farm also spoiled the paper logs, leading to data loss.

Skills underutilized. This waste exists if there is poor utilization of skills and talents of the existing workforce. Collecting and recording data using clipboards with printed logs and handwritten checklists required considerable time to collect and record data. Since there were no standard work instructions on filling out the paper logs, it increased the learning curve for new volunteers in the recordkeeping process.

This paper-based recordkeeping process was inexpensive but prone to error and only offered benefits once Grow transferred the handwritten information into a more usable digital format. The Lean wastes identified above were primarily attributable to data management in a paper-based format and errors caused by significant manual work. There was a need to adopt a more robust and real-time recordkeeping solution that enabled the storage of data digitally and minimized the chances of human error. Therefore, Grow farm implemented Lean implementation to improve the recordkeeping process.

IMPLEMENTATION OF LEAN PRINCIPLES AT THE GROW: JOHNSON COUNTY FARM

Poka-yoke, a Japanese term for mistake proofing, is one of the most commonly used Lean methods to minimize human errors. The objective of adopting a poka-yoke method is to prevent the defect. Since one human error could lead to another error in the system, resulting in a domino effect, addressing these issues at the origin and making the process leaner and more standardized is essential. By adopting a digital format to eliminate paper logs, Grow used various poka-yoke mechanisms to avoid human errors in the recordkeeping process at Grow farm. These methods help prevent errors due to forgetfulness, misunderstanding, lack of experience, clear identification, absentmindedness, and lack of suitable work instructions (Cudney, Furterer, & Dietrich, 2013).

The data management for recordkeeping at Grow farm was transferred from a paper-based system to a digital one via a Microsoft Excel-based tool, further automated using Visual Basic for Applications. The tool, formally named FarmTabs, is a customizable decision support tool that tracks produce inventory and allows farmers to use data to improve food safety, crop planning, and overall farm operations. FarmTabs aims to eliminate or minimize the Lean wastes in the Grow farm recordkeeping process, as previously described.

FarmTabs includes a centralized database that allows the input of standard data such as crop names, field and bed names, customer names and details, and staff initials, among others. An update at this location is reflected automatically in the entire tool. FarmTabs uses drop-down menus across the tool to allow users to choose the data entered into the central database. This feature allowed for avoiding manual typing in many instances, thus, reducing waste due to defects in the process through transcribing errors and those caused due to legibility issues. Through FarmTabs, additional steps are introduced in the new recordkeeping process to comprehensively track the food from farm to fork. Upon crop harvesting, Grow records information in the following digital logs in FarmTabs.

The harvest log assigns a new Harvest ID for every new harvest-related entry. This ID is unique to a combination of harvest date, crop, field, bed, the weight of crop harvested, any specific notes related to the harvest, and the personnel involved in the harvest. FarmTabs saves this data, available for later reference using the unique Harvest ID generated. Once FarmTabs saves this data, harvest labels for the storage bins can be auto-generated by entering the required number for a particular harvest entry. Figure 24.3 provides a snapshot of the digitalized harvest log in FarmTabs, with an example of a drop-down menu for selecting a crop name.

FarmTabs introduced a new pack log between harvest and pickup log to enable the recall of contaminated produce caused due to packing operations. As the date of pack and pickup can differ, it is necessary to record the information related to these two operations separately to trace back produce in case of contamination related to the packing process. The system creates a new pack ID every time a Grow packs harvested produce. Grow can access the harvest data via the harvest ID drop-down menu, and all the details related to the harvest automatically appear in the "Crop Details" field. This feature eliminated a lot of transportation waste by avoiding the need to physically move the harvest paper logs from one farm area to another (e.g., packing) area. Also, it helped reduced motion waste by avoiding looking at multiple attributes of one log to fill another one.

Further, FarmTabs eliminated over-processing waste by preventing the entry of repeated data from the harvest log into the pack log. FarmTabs generates pack labels, which go to the customers, once it saves data in the pack log by entering the required number and weight for each pack entry. Figure 24.4 shows a snapshot of the pack log in FarmTabs.

Grow completes the pickup log when a customer comes for a pickup. The entries made in the pack log in the previous step are visible in the pickup log (e.g., crop details and weight of packed crop). Further, with each order, a unique order ID is created. Grow farm lost points in the 2018 GAP audit for not properly documenting they cleaned and checked the functionality of the delivery vehicle before generating a pickup order. Therefore, in FarmTabs, a dialogue box is generated asking for confirmation regarding delivery vehicle cleanliness and functionality from the farm manager and entering the initials of the delivery driver before confirming the pickup order. This step also eliminated the need for a separate delivery vehicle cleaning and inspection log as used in the previous process. Figure 24.5 shows a snapshot of the pickup log in FarmTabs.

FarmTabs also allows for real-time visibility of available inventory in the warehouse. The pack log (as shown in Figure 24.4) records the quantity of the crop that was packed, sold, and remaining in the warehouse. Once a customer picks up a

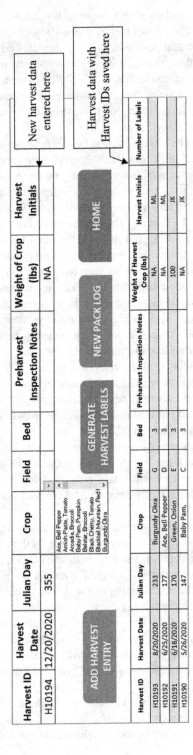

FIGURE 24.3   Snapshot of a digitalized harvest log created in FarmTabs.

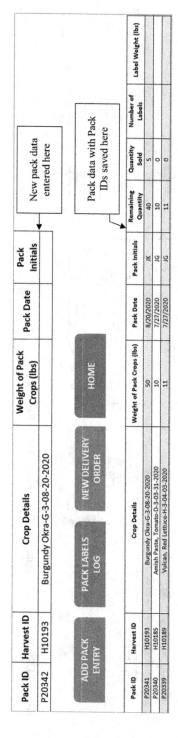

Pack ID	Harvest ID	Crop Details	Weight of Pack Crops (lbs)	Pack Date	Pack Initials
P20342	H10193	Burgundy Okra-G-3-08-20-2020			

New pack data entered here

ADD PACK ENTRY   PACK LABELS LOG   NEW DELIVERY ORDER   HOME

Pack data with Pack IDs saved here

Pack ID	Harvest ID	Crop Details	Weight of Pack Crops (lbs)	Pack Date	Pack Initials	Remaining Quantity	Quantity Sold	Number of Labels	Label Weight (lbs)
P20341	H10193	Burgundy Okra-G-3-08-20-2020	50	8/20/2020	JK	40	5		
P20340	H10185	Amish Paste, Tomato-D-3-03-31-2020	10	7/27/2020	JG	10	0		
P20339	H10189	Vulcan, Red Lettuce-H-3-04-03-2020	11	7/27/2020	JG	11	0		

FIGURE 24.4 Snapshot of a digitalized pack log created in FarmTabs.

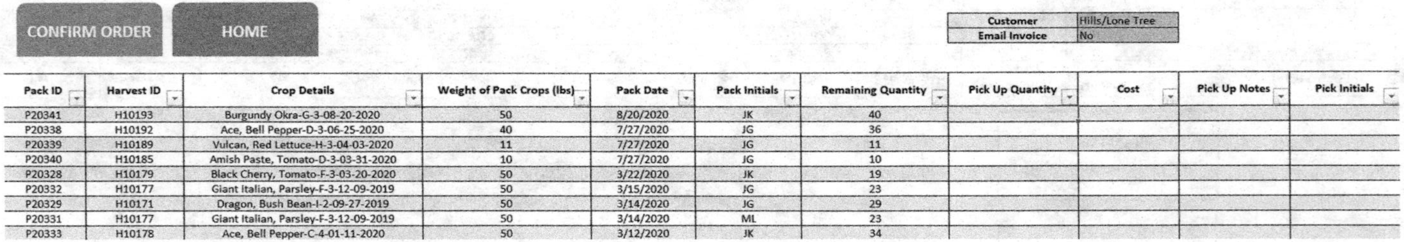

Pack ID	Harvest ID	Crop Details	Weight of Pack Crops (lbs)	Pack Date	Pack Initials	Remaining Quantity	Pick Up Quantity	Cost	Pick Up Notes	Pick Initials
P20341	H10193	Burgundy Okra-G-3-08-20-2020	50	8/20/2020	JK	40				
P20338	H10192	Ace, Bell Pepper-D-3-06-25-2020	40	7/27/2020	JG	36				
P20339	H10189	Vulcan, Red Lettuce-H-3-04-03-2020	11	7/27/2020	JG	11				
P20340	H10185	Amish Paste, Tomato-D-3-03-31-2020	10	7/27/2020	JG	10				
P20328	H10179	Black Cherry, Tomato-F-3-03-20-2020	50	3/22/2020	JK	19				
P20332	H10177	Giant Italian, Parsley-F-3-12-09-2019	50	3/15/2020	JG	23				
P20329	H10171	Oragon, Bush Bean-I-2-09-27-2019	50	3/14/2020	JG	29				
P20331	H10177	Giant Italian, Parsley-F-3-12-09-2019	50	3/14/2020	ML	23				
P20333	H10178	Ace, Bell Pepper-C-4-01-11-2020	50	3/12/2020	JK	34				

Customer: Hills/Lone Tree
Email Invoice: No

CONFIRM ORDER   HOME

FIGURE 24.5 Snapshot of a digitalized pickup log created in FarmTabs.

particular amount of a crop and Grow enters information in the pickup log, it automatically updates the sold and remaining quantity in the pack log. The next time a new customer arrives, the pickup log shows the updated quantity of crops available in the warehouse, thus preventing overselling. Allowing real-time inventory data tracking significantly improved the digital recordkeeping process over the previous paper-based system. Digital recordkeeping also minimized waste due to waiting by avoiding manual checks of available inventory, motion by avoiding staff moving around the warehouse to verify inventory levels, and inventory and overproduction waste by using the available inventory to be sold first before harvesting new crops.

The adoption of FarmTabs eliminated the need to bring printed paper logs from the office location to the farm, further reducing transportation and waiting waste. Eliminating the need for paper logs also reduced the inventory waste of maintaining trails of papers stored in multiple files. FarmTabs also reduced the skills and talent waste. In the old process, the learning curve involved in recordkeeping was much more significant due to the inconsistent data written on multiple paper logs. The improvements included enabling prompts to ensure required data fields are not left blank, adding drop-down menus for entering data, providing prefilled fields to reduce typing, and eliminating the entering of redundant data across the logs. These improvements helped reduce training time for the new volunteers in the recordkeeping process.

Although the number of steps has increased in the new process, the overall cycle time of entering the data decreased significantly. For example, it took around 41 minutes to do 25 entries for the crops using the paper-based harvest, pickup, and delivery vehicle cleaning and inspection logs, as well as writing harvest labels for the storage bins using notecards. This time does not include time involved in printing and transporting paper logs to the farm, movement of paper logs across various farm areas, and several hours each week on manual inventory checks at the farm upon a customer's arrival. The new recordkeeping process adopted using FarmTabs takes 29 minutes to make the same 25 entries in the digital harvest, pack, pickup logs, generate harvest labels for the storage bins, and pack labels for the customers.

To summarize, Grow farm adopted several of the following poka-yoke mechanisms to minimize Lean wastes and avoid errors in the old recordkeeping process at the Grow farm. The first poka-yoke is an alert due to incomplete information. Whenever the data entry is incomplete in any log, the system generates a prompt notifying the user to provide complete information before proceeding, thus eliminating errors due to forgetfulness and absentmindedness. The second poka-yoke eliminated human intervention by automating the label generation in the harvest and pack logs in place of handwritten labels on the notecard and prefilling multiple fields in all the logs eliminates possibilities of errors due to misunderstanding, lack of experience, clear identification, and lack of suitable work instructions. The third poka-yoke restricted choices by using drop-down menus for entering data, which prevented errors due to entering wrong information in a particular field. This feature further reduced errors due to absentmindedness, misunderstanding, lack of experience, and clear identification.

Data entry errors can still occur in the system, but FarmTabs reduces the number of opportunities for those errors. Standardized content and formatting of data saves time, improves the ease of training of new employees, and provides digital access to the data for later analysis and future decision-making. As FarmTabs was starting to be used across the farm more consistently, the employees began to see the value in the tool as it made their tasks more manageable and increased their overall available time during the day. FarmTabs was implemented at the Grow farm in 2019 and has been used for two consecutive growing seasons to record food safety-related data.

IMPACT OF LEAN PRINCIPLES IMPLEMENTATION ON THE THREE PILLARS OF SUSTAINABILITY

Lean implementation, as demonstrated in the above case study, created significant positive impacts on farm operations as well as on the three pillars of Sustainability. First, with respect to social Sustainability, food contamination can have severe repercussions for consumers' health as well as farmers' operations on a long-term basis. Enabling faster recall of contaminated food can avoid the spread of illness among people, reduce stress on farmers, and improve trust in farm operations. Reducing the time to investigate the cause of contamination can help faster repair the problem, thus enabling continued operations on the farm with fewer disruptions. Digital tools like FarmTabs can also allow for effective farm decision-making. For example, using FarmTabs, the Grow farm staff can easily access and evaluate distribution records to ensure equitable food distribution to multiple hunger relief agencies throughout the season. Staff can check that each local food shelf receives some of the pumpkin harvest, which only happens once per year.

With respect to economic Sustainability, low-cost digital recordkeeping methods based on familiar tools such as Microsoft Excel help farmers meet GAP requirements without additional financial burden. GAP certification can increase sales and provide better prices to farmers through access to more markets. With more income, farmers are less likely to sell their farmland, thus preserving the original landscape of the region and promoting other related economic activities such as agritourism and recreation. The additional income within the region would allow farmers, other workers, and businesses to invest in better and more efficient business practices. Streamlining food safety records reduced time and labor costs enabling farmers to spend more time in the fields growing crops and on better farm planning. Accessing the historical data stored by FarmTabs, farmers can see production information, such as the quantity of each crop produced for the year or selling price comparisons for each crop, and make more effective decisions for their farm business going forward.

Finally, with respect to environmental Sustainability, digital recordkeeping drastically reduced the amount of paper required. Further, such simple solutions do not require the production of more electronics as they can run on existing computers. In addition, food waste is a major problem and is a significant contributor to greenhouse gas emissions. Produce may be wasted in a warehouse without appropriate inventory tracking mechanisms in place due to food safety concerns. For example, using FarmTabs, the Grow farm can help reduce food waste by keeping track of its inventory stock and distributing items to its partners promptly to avoid food spoilage. Analyzing historical data also gives insight into the loss of each crop due to spoilage, and farmers could reduce the production of crops with high post-harvest loss rates.

CONCLUSION

This chapter discusses the application of Lean manufacturing principles in agriculture. As described in this chapter, farmers need tools such as FarmTabs to improve their overall farming operations. Collaboration between academic institutions, nonprofits, and the local agricultural community could effectively serve these needs. Improving efficiency and performance helps the overall well-being of the community and farmers.

REFERENCES

Cudney, E. A., Furterer, S., & Dietrich, D. (2013). *Lean systems: Applications and case studies in manufacturing, service, and healthcare*. Boca Raton, Florida: CRC Press.
USDA. (2020, December 18). From USDA Agricultural Marketing Service: https://www.ams.usda.gov/services/auditing/gap-ghp/audit

25 Applying Lean Sustainability Principles to Aviation Fuel Testing*

INTRODUCTION

A national airport in the Midwest has a process for replenishing aviation fuel reserves as mandated by the Federal Aviation Administration (FAA). This process has considerable regulations and specific requirements due to the potential safety hazards associated with defective fuel. The testing and replenishment process at the project's onset was poorly documented and lacked a standard procedure. The lack of documentation was a concern for the airport manager due to the safety concerns and the potential for random FAA audits. To gauge the extent of the process issues, the project team conducted measurements of time, motion, and defects.

The airport's refueling process is lengthy and conducted infrequently. The airport would intermittently order 8,500 gallons of either Jet-A or 100LL fuel throughout the year to replenish their storage tanks. The airport's manager identified this process as a weak point for the airport and expressed interest in improving it. The manager requested that the team focus on shortening the process, adjusting for more accessible, more consistent procedures, and recording FAA fuel test results. In addition to the airport, other customers, as noted in Figure 25.1, include fuel suppliers, recreational pilots flying in and out of the airport, and business aviation departments operating out of the airport.

The project team and process owner (airport manager) developed a project charter. The following are the details of the project charter.

Project Name: Fuel order testing

Project Overview: The airport is a national airport located in the Midwest of the United States. The airport has a lengthy and challenging fueling process whenever they order new fuel. These fuel orders include 8500 gallons of Jet A or 110LL fuel totaling upward of $20,000 for each purchase. The team must shorten and simplify the process and recording of FAA fuel test results.

Problem Statement: The airport manager reported a lengthy process to order new fuel. The process involves numerous tests and takes 30 minutes to an hour to complete. As such, the manager requested that the team shorten the process to make conducting and recording test results easier.

Customers/Stakeholders: Airport staff, local community, FAA, suppliers, and pilots.

* Contributing Authors: Mitchell Umano, Kendall Fitzpatrick, and Elizabeth Cudney.

DOI: 10.1201/9780429506192-25

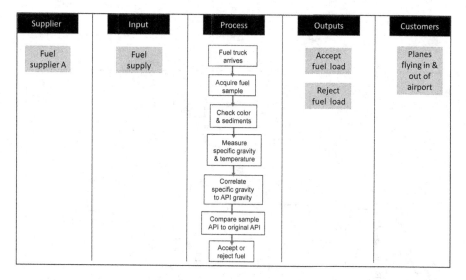

FIGURE 25.1   SIPOC diagram.

Goal of the Project: The main objective is to reduce the time required to complete the fuel ordering process while maintaining accuracy. The project will save labor and identify possible defects in the fuel order.

Scope: Airport operations regarding fueling are varied and quite broad. The project focuses entirely on the fuel order and testing before entering the airport's underground tanks. All other aspects of fueling will be outside the scope of this project.

Projected Financial Benefit(s): The airport will primarily save time on labor for the worker in charge of the testing process. However, should the process adjustments detect a fuel order outside the specifications, cost avoidance should be significant.

As noted in the charter, this project's scope is limited to ordering fuel and testing before any fuel enters the underground storage tanks at the airport. The manager and team agreed on the scope due to the tests and replenishment times. The process often takes between 30 minutes and an hour. In addition, results outside the specification limits require a re-test and possible fuel rejection. Should the project team venture outside of this scope, there are further regulations and issues to consider. As such, the team decided to work on establishing a streamlined and standard process. At the project's onset, the goals were to standardize the testing process by December, reduce process time by 15%, and continuously improve by rejecting all defective fuel and reducing wasted motion.

PROCESS FLOW AND BASELINE DATA

To accurately determine the current state of the process, the project team established a set of metrics as a focus throughout to gauge progress. The metrics focus on the cycle time, number of defects (quality assurance), and potential costs. One of the first tasks in dealing with the process was identifying the flow, as shown in Figures 25.2 and 25.3. Each fuel type follows roughly the same testing procedures; however,

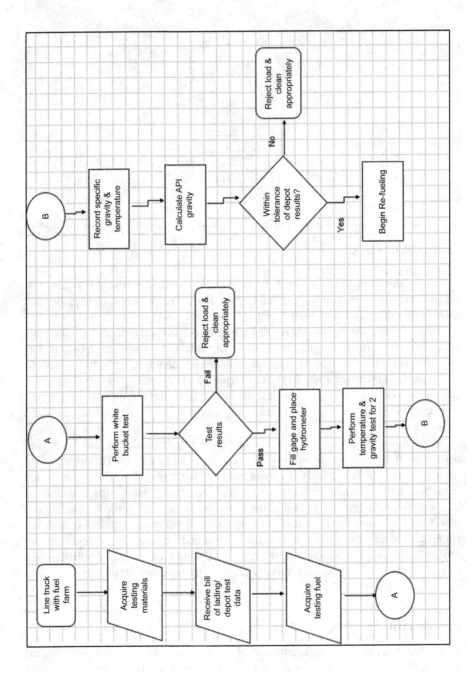

FIGURE 25.2 Process flow diagram for 100LL fuel.

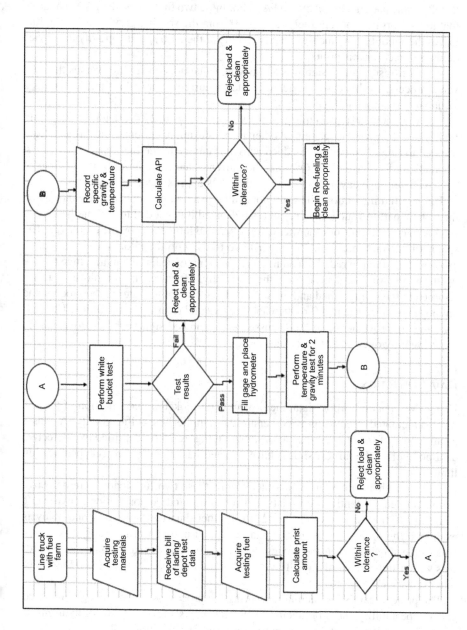

FIGURE 25.3   Process flow diagram for Jet-A fuel.

there is the added step of calculating the Prist amount when testing the Jet-A fuel compared to testing the 100LL fuel.

Each fuel load that arrives at the airport must undergo testing to ensure it is within the allowable parameters set by the FAA. For these two fuel types, the FAA mandates that the airport only accept fuel that is ±1.0 from the specific gravity when the fuel leaves the supplier. Any measurements outside of the ±1.0 specific gravity difference define a defect for this project.

A vital measure phase step was identifying value-added activities versus the non-value process. In this case, the team created a current state value stream map as a visual aid, as shown in Figure 25.4.

The value-added steps in this process, as seen in Figure 25.4, are universal to both fuel types. To properly gauge whether there are improvements, the project team decided to exclude other value-added activities unique to the fuel type, such as Prist calculations for Jet-A fuel. Overall, the current state map showed a lead time of approximately one day, while the cycle time was approximately 51 minutes.

Upon initial inspection, the team noted a large amount of unnecessary motion on the tester's part. As such, the project team deemed it beneficial to look at the wasted motion to collect tools or other items forgotten and left behind by the employee. The spaghetti diagram in Figure 25.5 details two trials, with the initial measurements in green and the final in red. As seen in green, the employee left the main office to pick up the work truck and headed to the fuel farm. However, the employee quickly returned to the storage shed and main office to collect tools. Later in the process, the employee realized she had forgotten another tool and returned to the office. The final trail after improvements, to be discussed later, showed significant improvement in requiring only one trip to the storage shed.

DATA COLLECTION

Using two years of airport data, the project team looked at the variation of the airport's calculated specific gravity versus the supplier's specific gravity. A closer examination of the historical data, as shown in Figure 25.6, identified two defective data points that the airport should have rejected based on the project specification limits.

The team then looked into possible reasons these two fuel loads were defective and attempted to identify a correlation. The team found no correlation between ΔT and ΔSG or the miles traveled vs. ΔSG. Further data measurements and analysis examined the process capability, sigma level, and non-conformance (Figure 25.7). Due to the small data set, the process had a relatively low-quality, un-centered process with a sigma level of 1.68. The overall non-conformance was 52,900 DPMO or roughly 5.29%.

The project team's last step in measuring the process was conducting a modified gauge repeatability and reproducibility (R&R) analysis for each type of hydrometer where the specific gravity of the control fuel was 41.2 (Figure 25.8).

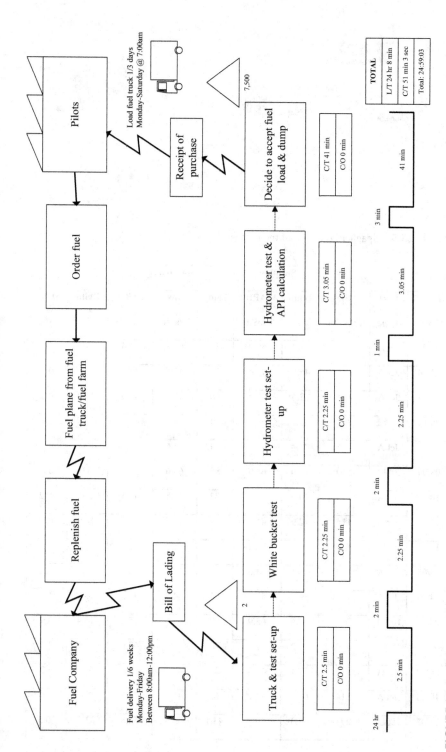

FIGURE 25.4 Current state value stream map.

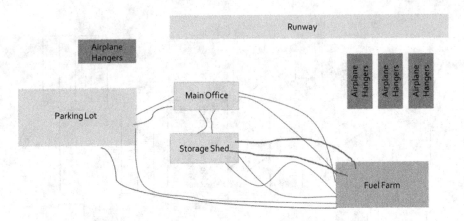

FIGURE 25.5   Spaghetti diagram of the process.

| Date of Order | Fuel Type | Miles Traveled | Supplier | | Airport | | | Delta T | Delta SG |
			Temp	API Gravity	Temp	Obs. Gravity	API Gravity		
02/29	Jet A	210	-	66.0	38	63.3	66.4	-	-0.4
03/04	Jet A	114	45.8	43.3	44	41.8	43.2	1.8	0.1
04/14	Jet A	114	53.6	42.2	66	42.4	41.9	-12.4	0.3
05/13	100LL	210	63.1	64.8	74	65.6	63.6	-10.9	1.2
07/06	Jet A	114	73.4	42.8	84	44.6	42.5	-10.6	0.3
08/04	100LL	210	82.0	65.0	88	68.0	64.2	-6.0	0.8
10/06	Jet A	114	70.0	42.3	72	43.5	42.5	-2.0	-0.2
12/15	Jet A	114	42.9	41.9	34	39.7	41.8	8.9	0.1
12/21	100LL	569	-	71.4	49	69.5	71.1	-	0.3
03/08	Jet A	114	53.1	43.0	54	42.3	42.9	-0.9	0.1
04/13	Jet A	114	59.5	43.2	75	44.8	43.5	-15.5	-0.3
05/15	100LL	210	68.6	65.9	82	67.6	65.0	-13.4	0.9
08/09	100LL	569	92.2	71.3	78	70.1	67.6	14.2	3.7
08/17	Jet A	114	77.1	42.2	74	43.2	42.0	3.1	0.2
10/18	Jet A	114	64.2	41.2	62	41.3	41.2	2.2	0.0
11/07	100LL	295	65.3	66.3	43.1	64.5	66.8	22.2	-0.5

FIGURE 25.6   Historical process data.

Standard Deviation	0.4788
Mean	0.1933
Z_U	1.6849
Z_L	2.4923
C_p	0.6962
C_{pk}	0.5616
Sigma Level	1.6849
% Non-Conforming	5.29%
DPMO	52,900

FIGURE 25.7 Data analysis.

Jet A	Gauge 1			Gauge 2		
Trial	1	2	$\bar{X}$	1	2	X
1	42.4	42.3	42.35	41.2	41.2	41.2
2	42.2	42.2	42.2	41.2	41.3	41.25
			$\bar{X}$=42.28			$\bar{X}$=41.225

FIGURE 25.8 Hydrometer gauge R&R analysis.

Due to mixing different fuel shipments with different specific gravities, the staff could only test the hydrometer gauges when receiving a new fuel delivery. This restriction led to a limited number of times staff could test each hydrometer within the time frame of this project. The modified gauge R&R allowed the project team to identify several issues with the airport's hydrometers. One of the hydrometers used to test Jet-A fuel was cracked and taking on fuel into the hydrometers center chamber. Therefore, the hydrometer could no longer accurately measure the fuel's specific gravity. The second Jet-A hydrometer's measurements matched perfectly with the control data.

Similarly, the team examined the 100LL hydrometers. One of these hydrometers had a broken thermometer with the mercury permanently stuck at 72°F. This observation determined that this hydrometer was no longer acceptable. Subsequently, the team disposed of this hydrometer. This thermometer issue may have been enough to adjust the American Petroleum Institute (API) gravity measurements to create the appearance of an out-of-specification result such as the one on August 9th. However, a more experienced fuel handler provided insight into the proper use of 100LL hydrometers. The fuel handler explained that separate hydrometers are needed to test 100LL fuel in cold and hot weather.

The project team concluded that the defect seen on August 9th was most likely the combination of a broken thermometer and the use of a cold weather hydrometer in August. The cause of the defect on May 13th is still unexplainable, but a closer look at the recorded data on that day led the team to believe the defect was nothing more than a clerical error. Should the airport's recorded temperature be switched with the calculated specific gravity, the result would be a ΔSG of only 0.5 instead of 1.2. The data was handwritten, messy, and difficult to follow, which may have caused this error.

OPPORTUNITIES FOR IMPROVEMENT

In the final stages of analysis, the team created a future state value stream map, as shown in Figure 25.9, to identify the specific steps that necessitated improvement per the project goals.

The team compared the two value stream maps and found a noticeable difference in the cycle times of each testing stage and an anticipated cut in several lead times. The time reduction in the future value stream will reduce cycle time by approximately five minutes and lead time by two minutes.

The poor data recording and several other factors led the project team to identify potential solutions to reduce errors and make the process smoother. As with the initial measurements, the team determined the major areas of waste stemmed from defects and wasted motion. Defects were the more critical of these two issues, so the first improvements the project team introduced aimed to combat the problems that arose with the infrequency of the process. A defect is a waste that has triple bottom line (TBL) implications: the defect results in an economic impact of the cost of poor quality, social implications for employees that deal with the working environment, and, lastly, environmental implications due to excess consumption of raw materials (Belhadi et al., 2018).

IMPLEMENTATION

The project team implemented work instructions and a check sheet for the airport employees to follow. The check sheet provided the employees with a general overview of the process steps in sequential order and boxes they could check off to ensure they completed each step, as shown in Figure 25.10.

The team provided the employees with work instructions, as shown in Figure 25.11. These work instructions gave detailed descriptions and instructions for each step in the process. The work instructions also provided pictures and warnings to help ensure staff performed each step correctly to minimize any error that could result in either a rejection of good fuel or an acceptance of out-of-specification fuel.

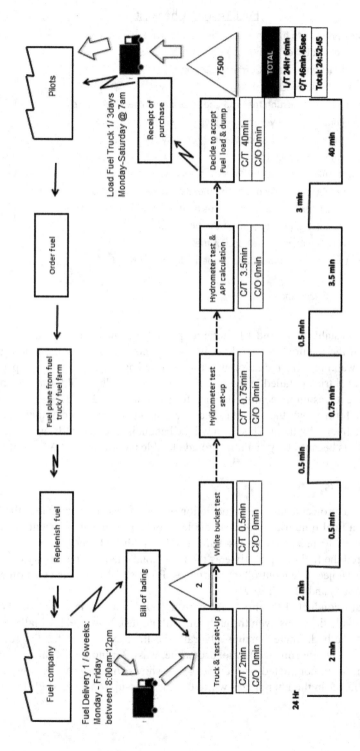

FIGURE 25.9 Future state value stream map.

Fuel Testing Checklist

1. Gather the appropriate hydrometer, forms and other equipment ☐
2. Receive and check bill of Lading ☐
    a. Record fuel type, date of order, tester, etc.
    b. If fuel is Jet A, check Prist %
3. Fill white bucket with testing fuel and check for particulates/ moisture ☐
4. Fill the fuel container for hydrometer (stop just shy of the top) ☐
5. Slowly lower the hydrometer into the fuel & gently spin ☐
    a. Set a timer for 2 minutes
6. After the hydrometer has set for 2minutes record gravity ☐
7. Pull the hydrometer partially out of the fuel determine and record temperature ☐
8. Using the whizz wheel (ensure you are using the proper fuel section) find gravity ☐
9. Check your calculated gravity against the bill of lading ☐
    a. If gravity is within +/- 1.0 accept fuel
10. Clean up tools and equipment and properly dispose of test fuel ☐

FIGURE 25.10 Check sheet.

The team established standard operating procedures and a check sheet to remind the tester of the required items. These improvements resulted in a reduction in the amount of walking. This reduction was proven true based on the previous spaghetti diagram's final trial, detailed in red (see Figure 25.5). The last tool for improvement for this project was implementing the data form (Figure 25.12).

The data form allows the airport to keep a clean, organized record of their calculations for each fuel shipment. This form will be beneficial for the yearly audits that the FAA conducts because they can now provide legible records to the FAA.

PROJECT RESULTS

Following the project team's implementation of these tools and documents, the team conducted a final time trial to discern the level of improvement. As mentioned, the timed sections focused only on tasks universal to both fuel types. In this case, the team ignored the fuel dumping time as the team conducted this by gravity drop and therefore is subject to uncontrollable variables. Figure 25.13 lists the cycle times for the first (Test 1) and final (Test 2).

The team conducted the first trial with a 100LL tanker delivered on August 17th. The cycle time was even throughout, with no task being substantially different except the hydrometer testing. Overall, the final cycle time for the sections measured, again ignoring actual fuel drop time, was 13 minutes and three seconds. The second trial, conducted on October 18th, shows that several tasks were significantly faster in the later stages while the early set-up time was slightly longer.

Hydrometer Set-up

1. Fill the container to 1" below top with fuel from the white bucket, be careful not to overfill.

2. Place the hydrometer into the gage slowly (as shown to the right) and gently spin. Start a timer for 2 minutes.

Gravity & Temperature Readings

1. To properly determine gravity read the number across the fuel surface (note red line on picture to the right).

2. Lift the hydrometer partially out of the fuel until the thermometer reading is visible.

3. Record the temperature without completely removing the hydrometer from the fuel.

The red line above is the flat portion where gravity should be read. Be careful not to read gravity at the raised portions.

API Gravity Calculations

1. Take your whizz wheel and ensure you are using the right side. Jet A should be on Jet A, 100LL should be on AVGAS/MOGAS.

2. Line up the temperature and gravity with your findings to determine API gravity by reading across the black line.

    a. In the example to the right, the temp (yellow) is 65 while gravity (red) was 42.6 making API = 42.2.

3. Accept fuel load if calculated gravity (API) is within 1.0 of gravity on the bill of lading.

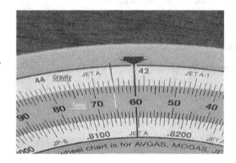

Calculate Prist% (Jet A Only)

1. Using the bill of lading check the gallons of Prist and overall gross gallons (circled in red).

2. Calculate the amount of Prist by dividing the gallons of Prist by the overall gallons.

    a. Prist should be at least 0.00125 or 0.125%

FIGURE 25.11 Work instruction examples.

Fuel Farm Testing Data Form

Tester Name:

Date & Origin of Order:

Fuel Type (circle one):   Jet A   100LL

%Prist

(Gal Prist / Overall Gal) = _____ x100 = _____ %

Prist =0.125%?   Y   N

White Bucket Test

Name (circle one):   Clear   Slight Particulate   Particulate   Dirty

Name (circle one):   Bright   Hazy   Cloudy   Wet   Surfactant

Hydrometer Tests

Tester Observed Gravity: _____

Tester Temperature: _____

Supplier Temperature: _____

Tester API Gravity: _____

Supplier API Gravity: _____

Gravity Difference: _____

Gravity within +/- 1.0?   Y   N

FIGURE 25.12   Data recording form.

This difference was due, in part, to acquiring materials earlier and the fact that the tester was a new hire. For conducting the process for the first time with little supervision, the overall time was three minutes faster. Between these two trials, the overall cycle reduction was 21%, about 6% better than the project team's original goal of 15%.

Test 1	Cycle Time (hr:min:sec)	Test 2	Cycle Time (hr:min:sec)
Truck arrival/line up with fuel farm	0:02:30	Truck arrival/line up with fuel farm	0:02:21
White bucket test set-up	0:02:15	White bucket test set-up	0:03:14
Gauge set-up	0:02:15	Gage set-up	0:01:04
Hydrometer test	0:03:35	Hydrometer test	0:02:54
API gravity calculations	0:02:28	API gravity calculations	0:00:45
Process sub-total	0:13:03	Process sub-total	0:10:18
Cycle Time Reduction = (13:03 - 10:18)/13:03 = 21.07%			

FIGURE 25.13   Time analysis.

The most important part of the project is ensuring the airport maintains the improvements after the project's conclusion. For this project stage, the team conducted informal meetings with employees and the airport manager to discuss the work completed. As a result of these meetings, the team created a control plan. In addition, the team shared all the electronic files they developed with the airport manager.

The control plan detailed the purpose of each tool used and implemented by the project team and its applicability to the airport staff. The control plan used the data collection forms and work instructions designed for this process. Several physical copies of the work instructions were created and left in areas of importance. The team secured waterproof copies of the instructions in a cabinet near the fuel farm and the main office with testing supplies. The work instructions serve as a visual reminder for current employees and a training tool for new employees. Using the work instructions allows for training new hires without wasting fuel with separate hands-on training. A new employee recently used the work instructions, and they expressed their appreciation for them. This employee found the pictures for each step and the warning for common mistakes especially valuable.

The most critical section of the control plan involved data recording forms. The team created these forms to provide an orderly method to show data regarding the fuel test results to the FAA or any other compliance authority. In the event of an audit, the forms will contain all pertinent information related to that fuel order. The data forms will include the order date, fuel origin, the tester, and all previously discussed test data. The information in the form will allow for easier tracking of testers if a question arises. The control plan focuses on increasing data accuracy and tracking and maintaining the organization created during the project.

FINANCIAL IMPACT

Aviation is one of the most expensive industries. The aviation industry is known for lawsuits ranging from several hundred thousand to hundreds of millions of dollars. As a result, this project was instrumental in mitigating the potential cost of liabilities for the airport. Should a defect in the fuel make it into circulation, there is the possibility of incidents that may lead to human injury or death. Using the data in Figure 25.14, the team estimated the costs associated with the worst-case scenario to be about $40 million.

The table breaks down the costs into low, medium, and high estimates based on several factors: the loss of fuel sales and the price of the defective fuel. Fuel sales are the primary income for the airport, and the loss of an entire fuel tank is a severe issue for the airport's bottom line. The low-end cost for loss of sales and a tanker of fuel is around $19,000, but the high-end estimate is near $50,000. If airport staff accepts defective fuel, they must track down any aircraft that purchased it. This event pulls away from normal employee operations and potentially costs the airport between $240 and $720.

The defective fuel must be removed and properly disposed of per DNR regulations. After pumping and disposal, the airport must professionally clean the tank to eliminate contaminants and minimize environmental impacts, such as water and air pollution. Pumping and cleaning the tank run would cost the airport between $7,500 and $12,000. The cost depends on the distance traveled by the certified cleaners, proper disposal fees, and other factors. The added environmental costs could also be determined, such as reclamation costs. A more holistic assessment of defective fuel costs, such as TBL, could motivate the organization in a search for more environmentally sensitive substitutions, such as biofuels. Recent developments in bio-fuels

	Low	Medium	High
The expense of defective fuel	$18,750	$32,000	$42,500
Loss of fuel sales	$0	$1,800	$6,700
Labor ($10/hr)	$240	$480	$720
Fuel removal and disposal	$7,000	$9,000	$11,000
Fuel storage cleaning	$350	$700	$1,050
Plane/engine liability	$15,000	$150,000	$15,000,000
Medical and legal liability	$1,500,000	$3,000,000	$25,000,000
Totals	$1,522,590	$3,161,980	$40,019,470

FIGURE 25.14   Potential cost liability.

have generated significant interest as an alternative to decrease decreasing fossil-fuel emissions. The desire for energy independence, foreseen depletion of non-renewable fuel resources, fluctuating petroleum fuel costs, the necessity of stimulating an agriculture-based economy, and the reality of climate change have created an interest in the development of bio-fuels, though significant challenges remain technically, capital costs, and low fossil fuel prices (Gupta, et al., 2010; Wang et al., 2019).

The worst scenario the airport should consider is their liability for injury or loss of life to pilots and passengers due to a defective fuel load. In addition to personnel injury, potential damage could impact the aircraft or assets in the aircraft during an incident. The team estimated this liability based on a single-engine prop plane for the low estimate, a twin-engine prop for the middle estimate, and a low-grade jet for the high estimate. The costs for aircraft repair (engine only) are $15,000, $150,000, and $15,000,000, respectively. The most expensive part of any incident is dealing with lawsuits for medical bills and trauma. The level of compensation for any lawsuit depends entirely on jurors and settlements. As such, the estimates were difficult to determine properly, but a range of $1.5 million up to $15 million was determined to be reasonable.

After discussing the various stages associated with a defect in the process leading to an aviation incident, the overall costs range from $1.5 million to $40 million. The critical takeaway from this scenario is these costs are associated with only a single aircraft crash. The costs will multiply should multiple aircraft have an issue or other pilots and businesses jump into a lawsuit. In short, the potential liability for the airport is massive, and while the project team focused only on a small process, the impact is substantial.

CONCLUSIONS

Throughout this project, the project team looked at all aspects of the airport's fuel testing process to determine the best solutions to implement for the airport. Based on the requests from the airport manager and the factors they could control, the project team focused their efforts on ensuring that the fuel testing process was performed as consistently as possible by all employees and the elimination of accepting defective fuel loads. After conducting the process measurements and data analysis, the project team found that standardizing the process was the best way to meet these requirements. The project team created and implemented work instructions, check sheets, and data forms to aid this process. These tools will provide the airport with the consistency and accuracy it needs to operate successfully.

From these measurements and historical data, the team determined that clerical errors and poor/lack of training plagued the process. Based solely on the last two years of data, the airport accepted potentially defective fuel in the past due to poor documentation. In addition, the team determined through measurements that several pieces of testing equipment needed were broken or not the proper tool. As a result, the project team established a standardized testing procedure using visual work instructions and a checklist. The addition of these tools allowed a newly hired employee to complete the process faster than the seasoned employee from the original time study. The team provided these items in laminated copies at strategic locations on the airport grounds. Doing so reduced the time and the amount of excess motion.

The project team also addressed clerical issues by introducing a new recording system for data. This form provided locations for documenting fuel and tester details and the data from the testing. The project team's direct efforts resulted in a 21% reduction in processing time and a 50% reduction in motion. The team provided details on all information learned of this process and electronic copies of the improvements to the airport manager. The team conducted the Lean Sustainability project as a potential cost avoidance. The aviation industry is expensive, and any incidents resulting in damage to a person or property due to the airport may incur millions of dollars in liabilities. Bearing the high risks in mind, the manager and several staff members expressed their appreciation for the work performed on this project.

The team reflected on the project by creating an A3 summary. Figure 25.15 provides the summary details for each project stage using the DMAIC strategy. For example, background, current conditions, and goals fit into the define phase. The analysis relates to the analyze phase, while countermeasures and planning occur during the improve stage. Lastly, the follow-up looks at parts of the control plan and follow-ups for the project.

As a direct result of the project, the standard procedures established were understandable to even a new employee. In addition, the project shortened the measured process cycle time by 21%. In addition, for all refueling tests conducted since implementing these countermeasures, the airport supervisor provided positive feedback. The supervisor specifically complimented the addition of the data form and check sheets. The addition of the data form is the most significant improvement, according to the supervisor, as it makes it easier to locate past information in the event of incidents or FAA audits.

From a Sustainability perspective, this project is vital from the perspective of reducing defects in measurement and potentially either rejecting fuel when it should not have been or not rejecting it when it should have been rejected. In either case, these errors could harm the environment by having to reject fuel and get a new shipment or use defective fuel, which could cause a catastrophic event. This project illustrates the importance of assessing processes and identifying and applying simple yet powerful Lean tools to improve a necessary process that could impact the environment and lives. These tools included standard work instructions, value stream mapping, spaghetti diagrams, measurement system analysis, improvements, and control plans, which resulted in a 21% reduction in the process cycle time.

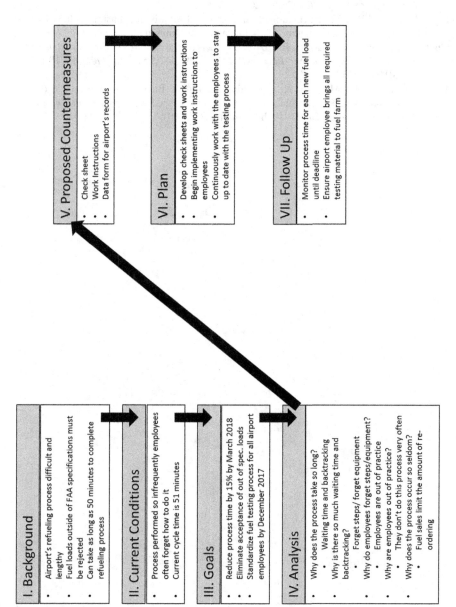

FIGURE 25.15   A3 summary.

REFERENCES

Belhadi, A., Touriki, F., & El Fezazi, S. (2018) Benefits of adopting lean production on green performance of SMEs: A case study. *Production Planning & Control*, 29(11), 873–894. https://doi.org/10.1080/09537287.2018.1490971

EPA. (1997). 62 FR 9872 - Regulation of Fuels and Fuel Additives: Adjustments to Individual Baselines for the Reformulated Gasoline and Anti-Dumping Programs.

Gupta, K., Rehman, A., & Sarviya, R. (2010). Bio-fuels for the gas turbine: A review. *Renewable and Sustainable Energy Reviews*, *14*(9), 2946–2955. https://doi.org/10.1016/j.rser.2010.07.025

Wang, M., Dewil, R., Maniatis, K., Wheeldon, J., Tan, T, Baeyens, J., & Fang, Y. (2019). Biomass-derived aviation fuels: Challenges and perspective. *Progress in Energy and Combustion Science*, *74*, 31–49. https://doi.org/10.1016/j.pecs.2019.04.004

26 Incorporating Lean Sustainability in Sterile Instrument Processing*

OVERVIEW

This chapter provides a case study for incorporating Lean Sustainability improvement in a hospital's sterile instrument processing within the surgical services value stream. The team used the plan-do-check-act (PDCA) improvement method, Lean and Sustainability principles, and tools to identify process improvements. The project aimed to reduce the costs of replacing lost surgical instruments and ensure that appropriate instruments are sterile and available for surgeries. A student team performed this project by partnering with the local hospital as part of their Lean Six Sigma course.

PROJECT METHOD

The healthcare organization includes value streams for emergency, inpatient, outpatient, surgical, and women's services. The team developed a value stream map for surgical services, as shown in Figure 26.1. The value activities consist of the following:

- Schedule surgeries
- Plan equipment, materials, instruments, devices, and supplies
- Prep equipment, materials, instruments, devices, and supplies
- Prepare patient
- Perform surgery
- Perform postoperative of patient

The Chief Operating Officer identified an opportunity to reduce surgical instrument loss and streamline the sterile processing of the instruments. The hospital lost instruments from the operating room to the sterile processing department and back to the surgical suite. The team defined the project overview, problem statement, and project goals.

Project Overview: Investigate and evaluate the primary contributing factors that lead to missing instruments in the sterile processing department (SPD) and operating room (OR), as well as make recommendations to prevent instrument loss.

* Contributing Authors: Sandra Furterer, Sandesh Sridhar, Naman Sharma, Pranoti Kamble, Sohith Sri Ammineedu.

DOI: 10.1201/9780429506192-26

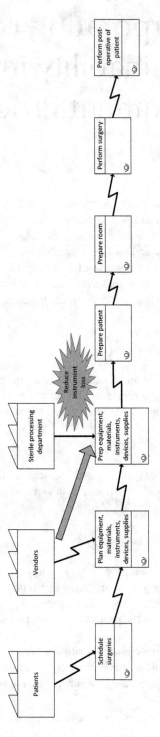

FIGURE 26.1 Value stream map for surgical services.

Problem Statement: Several tools in the hospital's SPD went missing following each surgery. The number of missing instruments and their locations were unknown to the SPD.

Goal(s): The project's primary purpose was to decrease and find lost instruments, enhancing productivity and reducing the expense of replacing missing tools.

STAKEHOLDER ANALYSIS

The team developed a stakeholder analysis to identify the process owners and other stakeholders with a stake in the instrument sterilization and preparation process. The stakeholder analysis also identified their role in the process, the impact on the stakeholder, and their receptivity to the process now and when they need to implement the improvements. Figure 26.2 illustrates the stakeholder analysis. The primary stakeholders directly impacted by the process or who "touch" the process were the

Stakeholder Analysis

Identify the internal and external customer roles and concerns to ensure their expectations are addressed. Define roles, impacts, concerns, and receptivity.

Stakeholder	Type	Primary Role	Potential Impacts/ Concerns	Initial Receptivity	Future Receptivity
VP of Operations	Secondary	Evaluate and coordinate improvements to the hospital's overall health care.	Help in developing new policies and training for process improvement.	Strongly Support	Moderate Support
SPD Manager	Primary	In charge of the sterilization of surgical instruments.	Help implement policies and changes for process improvement.	Strongly Support	Strongly Support
Decon Team	Primary	Proper cleaning of surgical instruments after surgery.	Adhere to the new policies and training methods for process improvement.	Moderate Against	Moderate Support
Assembly Team	Primary	Assembld cleaned instruments into the tray and identify the missing instrument.	Adhere to the new policies and training methods for process improvement.	Moderate Support	Strongly Support
Sterile Team	Primary	Sterilizd instruments and proper storage of instruments.	Adhere to the new policies and training methods for process improvement.	Neutral	Neutral
OR Nurse	Secondary	Help the doctors during surgery and makd sure that the instruments are properly returned back to SPD.	Adhere to the new policies and training methods for process improvement.	Strongly Against	Moderate Support
OR Doctor	Secondary	Request instruments for surgery from SPD and using instruments for surgery.	Adhere to the new policies and training methods for process improvement.	Strongly Against	Moderate Against

FIGURE 26.2   Stakeholder analysis.

Project risk analysis

Brainstorm the potential risks to a successful project, identify the likelihood that each will occur, the potential impact, and develop a mitigation strategy.

Potential risk to successful project	Occurrence of risk	Impact of risk	Risk mitigation strategy
Lack of proper support from management	Moderate	Very high	Showing progress and the potential benefits of the project in a long run.
Resistance from OR staff to new policies	High	Very high	Making them understand the benefits of change and introducing strict rules.
Resistance from SPD staff to new policies	Low	Very high	Making them understand the benefits of change and introducing strict rules.
Doctors refusing to undergo change	Very high	Very high	Upper management should introduce strict rules and actions.
Conflict within the project team	Low	High	Better communication and respecting each other's ideas.

FIGURE 26.3   Project risk analysis.

SPD manager, Decon (Decontamination) team, assembly team, and sterile team. The secondary stakeholders who did not perform the process but had a stake were the VP of operations, OR nurses, and OR doctors.

PROJECT RISK ANALYSIS

The team also performed a project risk analysis to assess any potential risk to satisfactorily completing the project. The purpose is to identify risks early in the project so the team can implement mitigation strategies and reduce the impact or probability that these risks will occur. Figure 26.3 provides the project risk analysis.

SUPPLIER-INPUT-PROCESS-OUTPUT-CUSTOMER

The supplier-input-process-output-customer (SIPOC) diagram is a tool used to scope the high-level activities that are part of the scope of the process to be improved. It details the prep equipment, materials, instruments, devices, and supplies activities from the value stream map. The SIPOC provides a check and balance for the stakeholder analysis by ensuring that the stakeholder analysis includes all suppliers and customers from the SIPOC. Figure 26.4 illustrates the SIPOC.

CRITICAL TO SATISFACTION CRITERIA

The critical-to-satisfaction (CTS) criteria capture the voice of the customer (VoC) requirements important to the customer for the sterile instrument processing department. The hospital wanted a reduction in the percentage of missing instruments, which could reduce the cost and re-purchase of additional instruments due to lost instruments. Reducing the lost instruments could also reduce the delays in delivering the sterilized instruments back to the OR for surgeries. The time it takes to look for missing or misplaced instruments and replace them if needed increases the waste, cost, and delays in the process. There is a desire to reduce the time to clean and

SIPOC

Explain the Customer / Supplier relationship in the process. Identify where the process begins and where it ends, and the activities included within the scope of the process to be improved.

Suppliers	Inputs	Process	Outputs	Customers
Doctor	Patient needs operation	Doctor request instrument for surgery	Recipe sheet sent to supply department	Doctor
SPD	Recipe sheet sent to supply department	Case cart prep	Surgical instrument sent to OR for surgery	Doctor
SPD	Surgical instrument sent to OR for surgery	Instrument used in surgery	Instrument sent to cleaning after surgery	OR Nurse
OR Nurse	Instrument sent to cleaning after surgery	Cleaning of instruments (Decon)	Decontamination and cleaning of surgical instrument after surgery	Decon Technician
Decon Technician	Decontamination and cleaning of surgical instrument after surgery	Assembly of instruments	Assembly of cleaned instrument	Assembly Technician
Assembly Technician	Assembly of cleaned instrument	Sterilization of instruments	Instruments stored for future surgery	SPD Nurse

FIGURE 26.4   SIPOC.

Critical to Satisfaction (CTS)

CTS' are basic elements that can be used in driving process measurement, improvement, and control. They are elements of a process that significantly affect the output of the process. What are the characteristics of the process are critical as perceived by the customer?

	Title	Description
1	Reduction in the percentage of missing instruments	After each surgery, the number of missing instruments should be reduced and make sure no instruments get lost in Decon.
2	Reduce downtime	Reduce the waiting time of carts from OR to Decon.
3	Faster cleaning and sterilization of instrument	Cleaning and sterilization consume most of the time in the whole process; hence, the time taken for both these processes should be reduced.
4	Quality control	Locating and replacement missing instruments, increase productivity at the workplace

FIGURE 26.5   Critical to satisfaction criteria.

sterilize the instruments through better organization and reduce lost instruments. The quality control step of searching for missing instruments also increases waste and delays in the process. Figure 26.5 provides the CTS criteria.

POTENTIAL BENEFITS

This project's potential benefits were identifying the root cause for missing surgical instruments, reducing the number of missing instruments after every surgery, creating new policies for process improvement, and creating a training program for OR and SPD staff on the new process and policies.

DATA COLLECTION PLAN

The data collection strategy outlines the processes and sequences the team must follow while obtaining data for a specific project. The team used the CTS to define the metrics and data to collect. This project's primary focus is reducing the percentage of missing instruments. The critical stage is the reduction of missing instruments, as mentioned in the CTS would be improved by collecting the data from the random cart and inspecting and reporting on missing instruments. Secondly, the team observed that reducing the downtime is more focused after the surgeries. Therefore, obtaining

Data Collection Plan

Identify metrics to measure and assess improvement that relate to the CTS' from the Define Phase.

Critical to Satisfaction (CTS)	Metric (short title)	Operational Definition (metric description)	Data Collection Source	Analysis Mechanism	Sampling Plan (size, frequency)	Process to Collect and Report
Reduction in the percentage of missing instruments	Counting	Reduce missing instruments after surgery and Decon.	Check Sheet	Statistics	Counting instruments form case carts every week	Selecting case cart randomly and counting instruments every week.
Reduce downtime	Average time	After each surgery case carts are made to wait outside OR and waiting time should be reduced.	Time study	Data collection	Collecting data on the process every week	Collecting data on the waiting time of the case cart in OR and Decon.
Faster cleaning and sterilization of instrument	Rate of cleaning	Cleaning and sterilization take a long time and the time required for this process should be reduced drastically.	Time study	Statistics	Collecting data on the process every week	Collecting data on the time required for cleaning and sterilization of each case cart.
Quality control	Feedback survey	Collecting feedback on the condition of the worker in the workplace.	Survey	Survey	Conducting interviews and collecting feedback every month	Interviewing people every month and collecting feedback from workers.

FIGURE 26.6 Data collection plan.

data on where and why the OR and Decon room consumed more time is necessary for further improvement. Due to less workload and downtime at Decon, the team collected data for cleaning each case. Additional training and communication would improve quality control. These are the important factors the team observed for the reduction of missing instruments and served as a focus of the data collection. Figure 26.6 provides the data collection plan.

VALUE STREAM MAP

The team developed a value stream map for instrument sterilization. The value stream map, shown in Figure 26.7, helped measure the time-consuming process and identify the steps to improve. Specifically, the value stream map indicated the OR, Decon, assembly, and sterilization should be goals for improvement in the future.

The value stream map provided several key observations. First, the Decon room has fewer employees, which creates more workload on the individual to complete the Decon process of all carts. Due to this, a queue of carts was pending to go through the Decon process. Therefore, further operations consume more time.

PROCESS MAP

The team developed a more detailed process map of the sterile instrument process, shown in Figure 26.8.

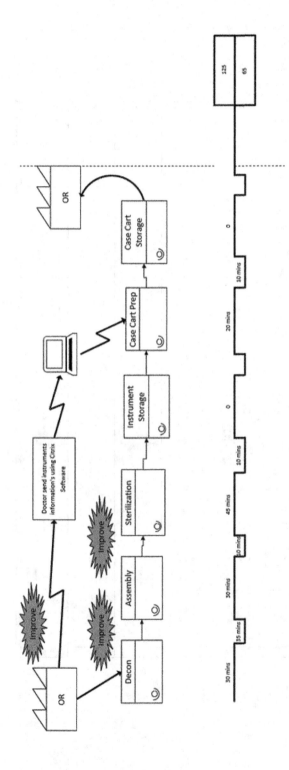

FIGURE 26.7   Sterile instrument processing value stream map.

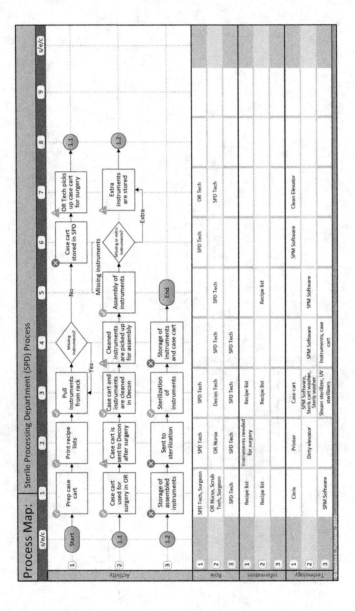

FIGURE 26.8 Sterile instrument process map.

No.	Case Cart No.	Location of Missing Instrument(s)	Missing Instruments Tally	Count
1	Case Cart - 172	Decon	////	4
2	Case Cart - 29	OR	////////	8
3	Case Cart - 120	Decon	/////	5
4	Case Cart - 90	Decon	///////	7
5	Case Cart - 12	Decon	///	3
6	Case Cart - 68	OR	//	2
7	Case Cart - 72	Decon	/	1
8	Case Cart - 197	OR	//	2
9	Case Cart - 145	Decon	/////////	9
10	Case Cart - 37	OR	///////	7

FIGURE 26.9 Check sheet for missing instruments.

CHECK SHEET

A check sheet ensures a team gathers data in the way it is requested or anticipated. The purpose of this check sheet is to keep track of the documents and note the missing instruments in each order throughout the day. The team took ten observations from ten different recipe sheets, followed by the number of case carts and the count of missing instruments observed in each case. Figure 26.9 provides the check sheet for this project.

AFFINITY DIAGRAM

An affinity diagram is a quality tool to gather and organize considerable language data (e.g., ideas, opinions, issues) and organizes them into groupings based on their natural relationships. The idea is to meld the perspectives, opinions, and insights of a group of people who are knowledgeable about the issues. Developing an affinity diagram works best when there are no more than five or six participants. Hence, the team had a mixture of six people from each department and had interviewed based on a set of questions. Figure 26.10 illustrates the affinity diagram.

HISTOGRAM

Graphs can aid in the visualization and communication of critical data discoveries. Histograms are visual representations of data that show the frequency distribution of the data. Visual feedback provides an instant advantage. The team can learn about the data distribution and whether it skews to one side and its general form by taking a quick look at a histogram. It can also provide information on likely outliers, central tendency, data compactness, and range. The histogram has a significant drawback because it requires variable data to be classified, leaving raw data out. The histogram

Voice of SPD Tech	Voice of OR Scrub Tech	Voice of Manager	Voice of OR Nurse	Key Problems
• Shortage of people • Decon is under staffed • Lack of teamwork • Problems created by OR Techs	• Lack of proper training for Decon Tech • Miscommunication between each department • Receiving missing instruments from SPD • Improper assembly of instruments	• Problems created 50% by SPD and 50% by OR • SPD should pay attention to details • SPD should change the water and filtration • Mistakes in OR are due to pressure	• Receiving missing instruments from SPD • No proper communication between SPD and OR • Receiving unsterilized instruments from SPD • Decon is under staffed	• High rate of missing instruments • Case carts waiting for a long period of time after surgery • Case cart waiting in Decon for a long period of time • High pressure while working in Decon • Slower cleaning and sterilization rate

FIGURE 26.10 Affinity diagram.

depicts the overall production time as well as an additional graph depicting the timings for each stage of production. Figure 26.11 provides the histogram of the total missing instruments.

DATA ANALYSIS

Data was collected based on how many instruments were missing in each case cart, and data were collected every day and collected using a check sheet. The team used Minitab to calculate statistics, as shown in Figure 26.12.

VALUE ANALYSIS

Using the Lean analysis tool, the team performed a value analysis on the SPD process and classified each activity as limited value-added, value-added, or non-value-added. The Lean analysis tool also assisted the team in identifying waste connected with a couple of operations. The percentage of value-added activities was 53.3%. Figure 26.13 shows the Lean analysis.

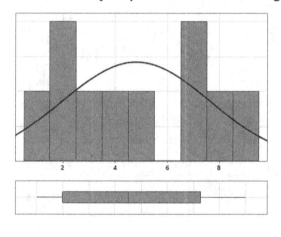

Summary Report for Total missing instruments

Anderson-Darling Normality Test

A-Squared	0.31
P-Value	0.484
Mean	4.8000
StDev	2.8206
Variance	7.9556
Skewness	0.14261
Kurtosis	-1.56250
N	10
Minimum	1.0000
1st Quartile	2.0000
Median	4.5000
3rd Quartile	7.2500
Maximum	9.0000

95% Confidence Interval for Mean
2.7823   6.8177
95% Confidence Interval for Median
2.0000   7.3423
95% Confidence Interval for StDev
1.9401   5.1492

95% Confidence Intervals

Mean
Median

FIGURE 26.11   Histogram of total missing instruments.

Variable	N	N*	Mean	Standard Error of the Mean	Standard Deviation	Minimum	Q1	Median	Q3	Maximum
Total missing instruments	10	1	4.800	0.982	2.821	1.000	2.000	4.500	7.250	9.000

FIGURE 26.12   Descriptive statistics for the total number of missing instruments.

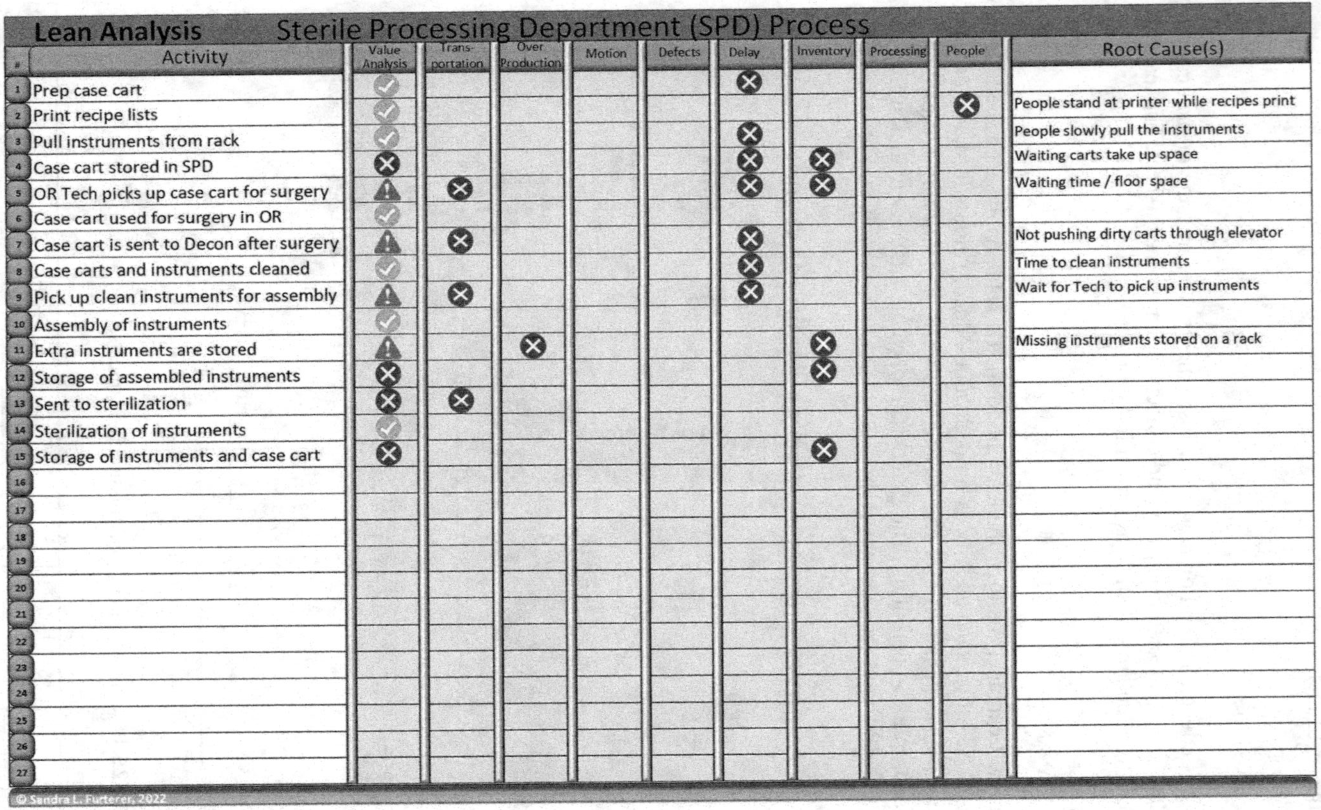

Lean Analysis — Sterile Processing Department (SPD) Process

#	Activity	Value Analysis	Transportation	Over Production	Motion	Defects	Delay	Inventory	Processing	People	Root Cause(s)
1	Prep case cart	⊗					⊗				People stand at printer while recipes print
2	Print recipe lists	⊗								⊗	People slowly pull the instruments
3	Pull instruments from rack	⊗									Waiting carts take up space
4	Case cart stored in SPD	⊗	⊗					⊗			Waiting time / floor space
5	OR Tech picks up case cart for surgery	⊗					⊗	⊗			
6	Case cart used for surgery in OR	⊗	⊗				⊗				Not pushing dirty carts through elevator
7	Case cart is sent to Decon after surgery	⊗					⊗				Time to clean instruments
8	Case carts and instruments cleaned	⊗	⊗				⊗				Wait for Tech to pick up instruments
9	Pick up clean instruments for assembly	⊗					⊗				
10	Assembly of instruments	⊗		⊗							Missing instruments stored on a rack
11	Extra instruments are stored	⊗						⊗			
12	Storage of assembled instruments	⊗	⊗					⊗			
13	Sent to sterilization	⊗									
14	Sterilization of instruments							⊗			
15	Storage of instruments and case cart	⊗									

FIGURE 26.13 Lean analysis for the SPD process.

© Sandra L. Furterer, 2022

PROCESS ANALYSIS

The process analysis method assisted the team in identifying several inefficiencies in various stages of the SPD process. The team identified and validated wastefulness, and its leading cause in the process's few steps/activities by examining the given inquiry criteria. The study aided the team in identifying tasks with potential time delays that may be decreased or eliminated. The team validated the current process map by asking simple questions about tracking and the requirement of all inputs and outputs. When the team focused on the bottom of the table, they realized that integrating chores such as replenishing the Decon with cleaning the workstation may fill in a considerable time gap, enhancing the overall efficiency of the process.

WASTE ANALYSIS

Waste generally refers to actions and resources that do not add value from the customer's perspective. Waste includes, but is not limited to, activities and resources that go beyond the customer's requirements and expectations. A waste analysis identifies, quantifies, eliminates, and prevents waste in production, service, and office environments. According to Lean Six Sigma, waste comprises eight categories: transportation, overproduction, motion, defects, delay, inventory, processing, and people skills. The team could boost the entire production process by efficiently eliminating these wastes. Figure 26.14 provides the waste analysis.

WHY-WHY DIAGRAM

The goal of the Why-Why diagram is to generate potential solutions. It is a method of brainstorming that a team may use to determine the root cause. The group posed the questions asked in the following figures, and the other group members analyzed the solutions to arrive at a final solution to the questions posed. Figure 26.15 illustrates the Why-Why diagram.

5S

The team used the 5S system to improve the system by making minor yet required and productive modifications related to the organization and cleanliness of the work environment, aiding in Lean and Sustainability aspects. The procedure begins with the separation of vital from non-essential goods. A team can assign multiple tags to it to keep it sorted. The 5S organization has already progressed to level 3 of the 5S system, as evidenced by the audit sheet shown in Figure 26.16.

RECOMMENDATIONS FOR IMPROVEMENT

The team discovered several opportunities to minimize the number of missing instruments and enhance the working experience in Decon. Figure 26.17 highlights the improvements that might remove or lessen the fundamental causes of inefficiency in all four CTSs. The team prioritized the opportunities by emphasizing enhancing the CTS of optimizing production time as the primary goal.

8 Wastes Check Sheet

Process Area: SPD

	Waste	Definition	Activity	High/Medium/Low	Root Cause
D	Defects	Information, products, and services that are incomplete or inaccurate	N/A	Low	N/A
O	Overproduction	Making more of somethin or making it earlier or faster than it is needed	Extra instrument storage	Medium	Missing instruments are stored in a rack without being used
W	Waiting	Waiting for information, equipment, materials, parts, or people	Case cart prep, pulling instruments Case cart kept aside, OR Tech picking up the case cart Case cart sent to Decon, cleaning, and assembly	High	Waiting time, floor space
N	Non-utilized talent	Not properly utilizing people's experience, skills, knowledge, or creativity	Printing recipe list	Medium	People standing in front of the printer until it prints all recipe sheets
T	Transportation	Unnecessary movement of materials, information, or equipment	OR Tech picks up the case cart for surgery Case cart sent to Decon Case cart picked up for assembly	High	Takes time to clean instruments
I	Inventory	Accumulation of parts, information, applications, and other items beyond what is required by the customer	Case cart kept aside OR Tech picks up the case Storage of instruments, extra instrument storage	High	Carts are waiting for a long time and taking up space
M	Motion	Any movement by people that does not add value to the product or service	N/A	Low	N/A
E	Extra-processing	Any steps that do not add value in the eyes of the customer	N/A	Low	N/A

FIGURE 26.14 Waste analysis.

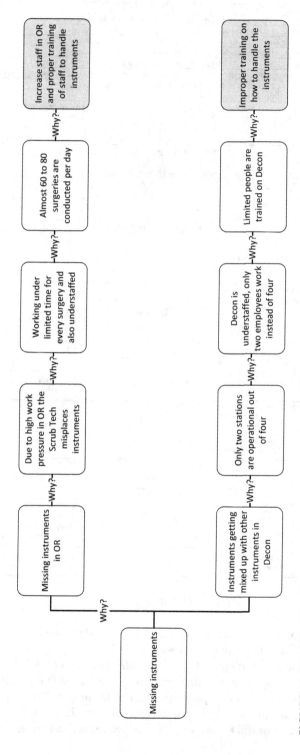

FIGURE 26.15 Why–Why diagram.

Category	Item
Sort	**Distinguish between what is needed and not needed**
	Sorting of miscellaneous, unnecessary tools and supplies in Decon
	Sorting and removing waste items from the workstations in Decon
	Sorting of miscellaneous, unnecessary tools and supplies in Assembly
Set in Order	**A place for everything and everything in its place**
	If there are missing instruments, the technician should restock at the end or beginning of the shift
	All the excess tools in the assembly area should be put in excess toolbox
	Some of the tools required for cleaning should be kept in proper location
Shine	**Cleaning and looking for ways to keep the workplace clean/organized**
	All the workstations should be properly organized after end of every shift
	All the technicians should clean their workstations in assembly at the end of every shift
	All the technicians should clean their workstations in Decon at the end of every shift
Standardize	**Maintain and monitor the first three categories**
	Decon workstations should be organized and standardized
	Create a standardized procedure to receive instruments from OR
	Creating a check list to locate missing instruments
Sustain	**Stick to the rules**
	Manager should conduct weekly 5S review and collect feedback
	Everyone should adhere to the 5S policies
	Random inspections and measurement of 5S performance

FIGURE 26.16   5S audit sheet.

Recommendations for Improvement
Identify Improvements that eliminate root causes, wastes, limited and non-value added activities. Use your Lean Analysis, FMEA, Why-Whys, current state process maps, value stream maps.

Improvement Ideas	Improvement Description	Root Causes	CTS	Priority
Increase number of employees in Decon	Increasing the number of employee in Decon will reduce the stress	Reduced staffing	Faster cleaning and sterilization of instrument	2
Improve training process for staff	Create a structured training process to improve the quality of work	Insufficient training	Faster cleaning and sterilization of instrument	3
Improve communication	Improve communication between SPD and OR to enable them to work and work together as a team	Miscommunication between SPD and OR	Quality control	7
Improve time management	Push the cart in elevator a minimum 5-10 minutes after operation	Miscommunication between SPD and OR	Reduce downtime	8
Improve in storage area	Improve instrument alignment for easy access and to reduce misplacement	Unorganized work environment	Reduce the percentage of missing instruments	4
Highlight changes in recipe sheet	Highlight the replacement of missing instrument to keep track of each instrument	Miscounts in recipe sheet (repeatability in printing the same recipe sheet)	Quality control	5
Introduce sorting section in Decon	Introduce a new process called sorting in Decon to sort instruments before cleaning	Unorganized work environment	Reduce the percentage of missing instruments	1
Create an action plan	Hold people accountable for their mistakes	Insufficient training	Reduce the percentage of missing instruments	6

FIGURE 26.17   Recommendations for improvement.

The Decon process becomes a bottleneck due to a need for more trained Decon personnel. The recommendation is to cross-train and increase the number of Decon resources. Overall better training of the SPD staff would also help the inexperienced employees. Improving communication between the OR and SPD will help to improve the work environment, eliminate pointing fingers or blaming the other department for lost instruments, and improve the overall process. Pushing the instrument cart into the elevator to move it to SPD more quickly will reduce the delays in sterilizing the instruments. The recipe sheets needed to be updated to minimize miscounts due to the wrong number of instruments listed on the recipe sheets for the surgical procedures. Introducing a new sorting process can reduce lost or missing instruments by sorting before Decon.

QUALITY FUNCTION DEPLOYMENT

Quality Function Deployment uses the House of Quality to link customer and process needs. In this project, the team wants to reduce the time and percentage of missing instruments. The enhancements are classified and aligned with the customer's needs and the determined CTSs. The project's requirements determine the relevance of each CTS. Improvements connected to each CTS have diverse impacts that make up the improvement category. For the project, the team specified influences as high (9), medium (3), and low (1). Figure 26.18 shows the QFD for this project. The team assigned a relative weight according to the absolute weight of the preceding improvement category.

Quality Functional Deployment (QFD) or House of Quality

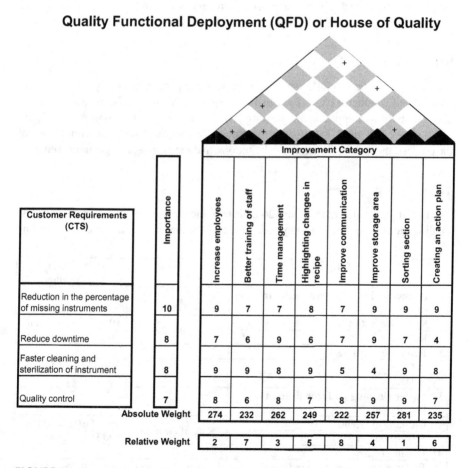

Customer Requirements (CTS)	Importance	Increase employees	Better training of staff	Time management	Highlighting changes in recipe	Improve communication	Improve storage area	Sorting section	Creating an action plan
Reduction in the percentage of missing instruments	10	9	7	7	8	7	9	9	9
Reduce downtime	8	7	6	9	6	7	9	7	4
Faster cleaning and sterilization of instrument	8	9	9	8	9	5	4	9	8
Quality control	7	8	6	8	7	8	9	9	7
Absolute Weight		274	232	262	249	222	257	281	235
Relative Weight		2	7	3	5	8	4	1	6

FIGURE 26.18   Quality function deployment house of quality.

It is critical to design an improvement plan for how the client or team will execute and sequence the changes to convey the required improvements. The team assigned each main area of improvement to a project, which included descriptions of the changes and the tasks that effectively executed each improvement category. The resource requirements, stakeholders of the implementation activity, and due dates for each activity are all included in the activity descriptions. The stakeholders are the SPD manager and VP of operations, as the organization will not be able to follow up with the project's improved execution. The due dates are "to be established" by the Lean team, giving scheduling flexibility in these unpredictable times. However, the team supplied a sequence number under the due date column to express the order to complete each action.

DASHBOARD

The team used a dashboard/scorecard to set performance goals for the metrics determined during the measurement process. The team built the dashboard using the CTS characteristics to track the performance of the present process after implementation. The team aimed to reduce delays and optimize the process by improving the time metrics. The dashboard in Figure 26.19 links to the CTS and the process map, both needing upgrades.

VOICE OF PROCESS MATRIX

The voice of process (VOP) matrix defines what the process says to you, what it can control, and whether it can accomplish its purpose. In other words, the team used the VOP to study and appraise the existing process. The VOP Matrix shown in Figure 26.20 shows how the CTSs align to the process factors that impact the root causes of the process, the metrics, operational definitions, and the proposed target improvements.

TRAINING PLAN

The training plan shown in Figure 26.21 is how the team wants to roll out the process modifications to the project's key stakeholders. The target audience is employees and

CTS	Metrics	Target for Improvement
1) **Reduction in the percentage of missing instruments**		
Reduction in OR	Counting	10-15% reduction in missing instruments
Reduction in Decon		
2) **Reduce downtime**		
In OR	Time	10-15% reduction in downtime
In Decon		
3) **Faster cleaning and sterilization of instruments**		
Cleaning in Decon	Rate of cleaning	10% faster cleaning and sterilization
Sterilization in SPD		
4) **Quality control**		
Better working condition in Decon	Survey (in-person)	Monthly feedback

FIGURE 26.19 Dashboard.

VOP Matrix

Update the VOP Matrix targets now that the process is better understood.

CTS (Y)	Process Factors (X)	Metric	Operational Definition	Target (%)
Reduce the percentage of missing instruments	Accuracy	Counting	Reduce missing instruments after surgery and Decon.	10-15%
Reduce downtime	Optimization	Average time	After each surgery, case carts wait outside the OR. This waiting time should be reduced.	10-15%
Faster cleaning and sterilization of instrument	Optimization	Rate of cleaning	Cleaning and sterilization take a long time. The time required for this process should be drastically reduced.	10%
Quality control	Suggestions from employees	Feedback survey	Collect feedback on the condition of the employee in the workplace.	None

FIGURE 26.20 VOP matrix.

Training Plan

Develop a training plan of how the process changes will be rolled out to the stakeholders.

Training objectives and outcomes:	Train on process improvement changes
Training audience and resources:	SPD Staff and SPD Manager
Instructional Strategies	
Exercise and case studies:	None
Assessments and exams:	Creating an action plan to track employee performance
Homework assignments:	None
Team and individual work:	Both
Project work:	5S subprojects to clean and organize Decon
Presentations:	none
Training mode:	Quarterly training of employees on new methods & new policies, in-person training, group activities, and Individually assigned training for employees
Training schedule and syllabus:	Creating new policies and new methodologies at the workplace
Training location:	SPD

FIGURE 26.21   Training plan.

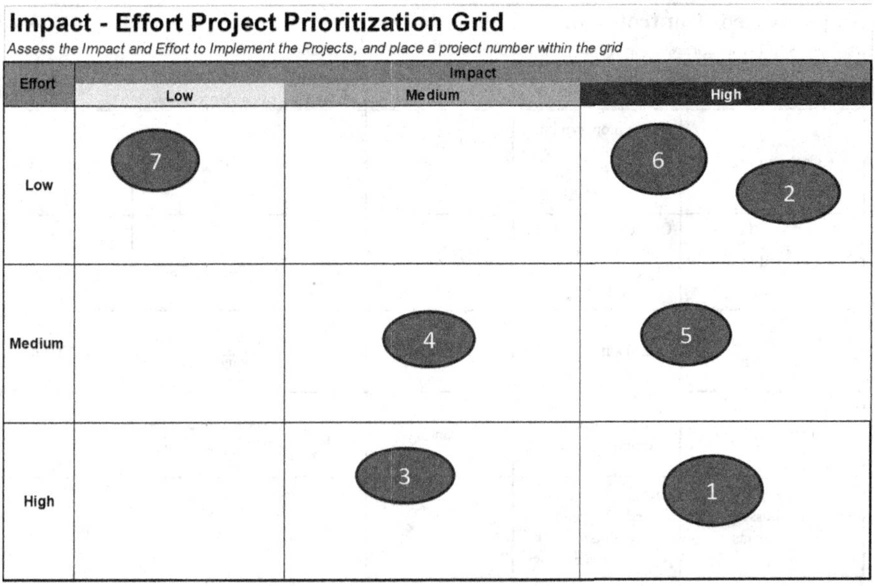

Impact - Effort Project Prioritization Grid

Assess the Impact and Effort to Implement the Projects, and place a project number within the grid

Effort	Impact		
	Low	Medium	High
Low	7		6 2
Medium		4	5
High		3	1

FIGURE 26.22   Impact–effort project prioritization grid.

managers, and the training focuses on teaching them how to make process improvements to obtain the needed results. The team defined the necessary training and the tasks while training was in progress. The main objective of the training process is to ensure that the employees get trained on the operations in SPD.

IMPACT-EFFORT MATRIX

The improvement suggestions offered in the recommendations of Figure 26.22 provide the improvement table used to structure the impact-effort matrix for prioritization. The improvement ideas included (1) increasing the number of employees in Decon, (2) training staff, (3) improving communication, (4) improving time management, (5) improving the storage area, (6) highlighting changes in the recipe sheet, and (7) introduce a sorting process in Decon. The grid shows which activities the teams should prioritize based on their impact and effect. The team prioritized other activities based on the amount of work required and the influence on the entire process.

IMPROVEMENT CONTROL PLAN

Improvement control plans identify control mechanisms to control the process and what actions to take if problems occur. Figure 26.23 provides the improvement control plan.

STANDARD WORK SHEETS

Figure 26.24 summarizes the detailed instructions for performing all activities. The team developed a standard work instruction sheet for the process. Standard work

Improvement Control Plan

The control plan is a detailed assessment and guide for maintaining all of the positive changes that you have implemented.

Process Steps	Control Mechanism	Measure/Metric	Criticality (H/M/L)	Action Taken if Problems Occur	Owner
Case cart prep	Create proper training and hold people accountable for mistakes	Feedback	M	Warning	SPD Manager
Case cart used in surgery	Create proper training and hold people accountable for mistakes	Counting	H	Make a note of the missing instrument	SPD & OR Manager
Instruments are cleaned in Decon	5S and kaizen projects	Counting	H	Make a note of the missing instrument	SPD Tech
Assembly of instrument	Create a structured training program	Counting	H	Make a note of the missing instrument	SPD Tech
Storage of assembled instruments	Create proper training and hold people accountable for mistakes	Feedback	M	Warning	SPD Tech

FIGURE 26.23   Improvement control plan.

Standard Work Instruction Sheet

Describes the detailed instructions for performing the work (process).

Activity	Time	Notes
Note the missing instrument in Decon and OR by technicians	1-3 mins	Inform the SPD manager or the OR team if any missing instruments are identified.
Sort all the instruments in the sorting section by Decon tech	4-5 mins	Inform the SPD manager or the OR team if any missing instruments are identified.
Mark/highlight the replacement of instruments	2-3 mins	Notify SPD manager to note the missing instrument(s).
OR inform SPD of misplaced instruments	1-2 mins	Mark missing instrument(s) on the check sheet.
Organizing instruments in proper order for case cart preparation	4-5 mins	-

FIGURE 26.24   Standard work instruction sheet.

helps to maintain the process, and ensure personnel are well trained and understand and can perform the process. Process audits ensure that the staff can consistently complete the work.

CONCLUSIONS

The sterile processing improvement project incorporated Lean and Sustainability aspects to identify inefficiencies, wastes, and improvement recommendations. The hospital planned to implement the improvements and assess the impact of reducing the number of lost instruments.

Index

Pages in *italics* refer to figures.

E

Economic pillar, 137, 141, 171
Effluent discharge, 20, 21
Emissions, 12, 14, 15, 17, 20, 22, 38, 70, 74, 131,
    137, 187, 188, 196, 199, 202, 216, 218,
    262, 279
Employee involvement, 34, 144, 188, 193, 208
Employee satisfaction, 22, 39, 52, 53, 55–56, 119
Energy consumption, 22, 23, 38–39, 74, 92, 112,
    131, 132, 141, 150, 187, 202
Energy efficiency, 1, 109, 112, 133, 149, 218–219
Engineered system, 24
Enterprise management system, 33
Enterprise system, 25
Environmental management systems, 39
Environmental perspective, 39
Environmental pillar, 1, 17, 20, 109, 130, 137,
    141, 172
Environmental Protection Agency (EPA), 20, 33, 38
Extended value stream map, 79
External setup, 128, 132, 135, 136–139
Extra processing, see Overprocessing

F

Financial performance, 118–119
Financial services, 25, 128–129
Fixed-value method, 157
Ford, Henry, 174
Ford Motor Company, 18
Ford Production System, 3
Fluorinated gases, 20
Fossil fuel, 14, 16, 20, 21, 279
Function check, 137
Functional clamp, 139
Functional decomposition diagram, 59, 86
Functional standardization, 138
Future state value stream map, 68, 272–273

G

Gemba, 6, 30, 32, 37, 76, 148–149
Gemba walk, 40–41, 70, 222
Genchi Genbutsu, 6
General Electric, 211
GlaxoSmithKline, 196
Global warming, 12, 17, 20
Global warming potential (GWP), 20
Good Agricultural Practices (GAP), 252–255,
    257, 262
Green culture, 28, 35, 40–41, 42, 222
Greenhouse gas (GHG), 20, 82, 92
Greenhouse gas emissions, 12, 14, 17, 22, 187,
    199, 202, 262
Green supply chain management, 9, 187, 189
Greenwashing, 132, 137

H

Hansei, 6
Hazardous waste, 22, 23, 37, 82, 110, 141
Health, 1, 15–17, 21, 22, 25, 109, 113, 130, 131,
    141, 148, 150, 229, 262
Healthcare, 1, 3, 25, 84, 111, 126, 128–129, 283
Heijunka, 6, 8, 73, 173, 175
Histogram, 124, 237, 239, 291, 293
Hoshin action plan, 196, 197, 203–205, 206
Hoshin implementation plan, 196, 197, 204–205
Hoshin implementation review, 196, 197, 205–206
Hoshin Kanri, 1, 9, 40, 41, 47, 126, 189, 192–209,
    222
Hoshin strategic plan summary, 196–200, 202,
    204–205
House of quality, 48, 55, 57, 57, 64, 246, 247, 299

I

Iceberg Model of Culture, 34
Iceberg theory, see Iceberg Model of Culture
Idling, 150, 151
Impact-effort matrix, 49, 62, 247–249, 303
Informative inspection, 154
Internal setup, 128, 131, 132, 135–139
International Organization for Standards (ISO),
    33–34
Inventory level, 38, 76, 108, 175, 188, 261
ISO 9001, 38
ISO 14000, 188
ISO 14001, 33–34, 40, 222
ISO 14006, 40, 41, 222
ISO 14044, 40, 41, 222
ISO 14046, 40, 41, 222
ISO 14067, 40, 41, 222
ISO 20400, 40, 41, 222

J

Japanese Institute of Plant Engineers (JIPE), 144
Jidoka, 5–6, 8–9
Jishu hozen, see Autonomous maintenance
Judgment inspection, 154
Just-in-time (JIT), 1, 3, 5, 77, 102, 108, 110, 173,
    175, 185, 188

K

Kaizen, 1, 5, 6, 9–10, 22, 31, 42–44, 68, 71, 74,
    88, 141, 148–149, 160, 165, 175, 185,
    199, 201, 205
Kanban, 1, 9, 40, 41, 73, 172, 175, 181, 184, 193, 222
Kanban cards, 183, 184–185
Kanban containers, 184–185
Kanban post, 73
Kanban signal, 6